D0849627

Proverbs

Proverbs
A Commentary on an Ancient Book of Timeless Advice

Robert L. Alden

Foreword by
Haddon W. Robinson

Baker Book House
Grand Rapids, Michigan 49506

Copyright 1983 by
Baker Book House Company

ISBN: 0-8010-0194-3

Library of Congress Catalog Card
Number: 83-72321

Printed in the United States of America

These abbreviations were used in Scripture references:

ASV	American Standard Version
JB	Jerusalem Bible
JPS	Jewish Publication Society
KJV	King James Version
LB	Living Bible
NAB	New American Bible
NASB	New American Standard Bible
NEB	New English Bible
NIV	New International Version
NKJV	New King James Version
RSV	Revised Standard Version
TEV	Today's English Version

Contents

Foreword

In our society wise men are easily confused with wise guys. We give high marks to knowledge, but low marks to wisdom.

If knowledge could save us, we would have more than we could handle. Since 1955 knowledge has doubled every five years; libraries groan with the weight of new books. New systems must be devised to store what old systems no longer have room for. In fact, our generation possesses more data about the universe and human personality than all previous generations put together. High school graduates today have been exposed to more information about the world than Plato, Aristotle, Spinoza or Benjamin Franklin. In terms of facts alone, neither Moses nor Paul could pass a college entrance exam today.

Yet by everyone's standards, even with all our knowledge, the world is a mess. Brilliant scientific thinking has produced machines and weapons that threaten to blow us off the planet.

With all our knowledge, society today is peopled with a bumper crop of brilliant failures. We probably do not have more fools than other nations, but as Jane Addams once said, "In America fools are better organized." Men and women educated to earn a living often don't know anything about handling life itself. Alumni from noted universities have mastered information about a narrow slice of life but couldn't make it out of the first grade when it comes to living successfully with family and friends.

Let's face it. Knowledge is not enough to meet life's problems. We need wisdom, the ability to handle life with skill. On the dust jacket of this commentary on the Book of Proverbs the publisher promises us "insight and skill to live a well-adjusted and prosperous life." That has a strong appeal.

Still Dr. Robert Alden has written a commentary that doesn't, in any way, take the place of Proverbs. He simply unwraps its maxims for us in such a way that we can partake of their sweetness. If you wish to be wise, try to read a chapter of Proverbs each day of the month (there are thirty-one chapters, one for each day). Read with your Bible open in one hand and this commentary in the other. The result can make you healthy, wealthy, and above all, wise.

Haddon W. Robinson

Introduction

The Book of Proverbs is like medicine. You cannot live on medicine alone, but few of us go through life without some medicine now and then. At least we take a vitamin. Likewise, a spiritual diet of Proverbs alone would be most unbalanced, but how sick a person might be that didn't occasionally ingest some of these potions and antidotes for the sake of his mental, spiritual, and even financial well-being. The Book of Proverbs is the kind of Biblical fare you should indulge in often, but not in large doses. The "stuff" of Proverbs has already been distilled so that its advice comes to us in highly concentrated form. These sage tidbits have been boiled down, trimmed, honed, polished, and sharpened to where a little goes a long way.

This commentary seeks to expand the proverbs in order to add flesh to their bones, and thus to reconstitute the highly concentrated medicine that they are. It seeks to offer suggestions on the many-faceted applications they have to everyday living. As with certain basic physical rules that never change, so there are basic unchanging principles here to guide us into acceptable and successful behavior. Proverbs addresses, by and large, "non-spiritual" dimensions of life. In some respects it, along with Ecclesiastes, is the most "secular" book of the canon because it is a guide to social and economic questions rather than theological ones.

First some introductory matters:

Outline

Part One-In praise of wisdom *1:1–9:18*
1 Prologue *1:1–7*
2 Warning against joining thieves *1:8–19*
3 The call of wisdom 1:20–33
4 The rewards of wisdom *2:1–4:27*

5 Warning against adultery *5:1 –23*
6 Warnings against cosigning, laziness, and deceit *6:1 – 19*
7 Warning against adultery continued *6:20 – 7:27*
8 In praise of wisdom *8:1 –36*
9 The two choices: wisdom or folly *9:1 –18*
*Part Two-*The proverbs of Solomon *10:1 –22:16*
10 Contrasting proverbs *10:1 – 15:33*
11 Synonymous proverbs *16:1 –22:16*
*Part Three-*The sayings of the wise *22:17 –24:34*
12 Thirty wise sayings *22:17 –24:22*
13 Further sayings of the wise *24:23 –34*
*Part Four-*More proverbs of Solomon copied by Hezekiah's men *25:1 –29:27*
*Part Five-*The words of Agur *30:1 –33*
*Part Six-*The words of Lemuel *31:1 –9*
*Part Seven-*The noble woman *31:10 –31*

Parts Two, Three, and Four have no discernible outline as far as content is concerned. There is no unifying theme or logical arrangement. About all we can do is note here and there small clusters of verses which seem to go together. The first nine chapters are difficult to outline too because there are extended sections warning against adultery as well as scattered pericopes on wisdom's invitations and rewards.

Proverbs is truly a collection of sayings with no arrangement, outline, order, or progression. When you think about it, however, life is like that. We try to bring order to life, but opportunities, crises, and unexpected intrusions come. Sometimes life is boring while other times its many activities almost overwhelm us. We seek order and coherence, but often are driven to despair because our efforts fail. Perhaps that is why Proverbs comes to us in the form it does.

Authorship and Date

Solomon's name appears in the opening verse of Proverbs as well as in 10:1 and 25:1, but to say that he authored the book is an oversimplification. First and most obviously other authors are mentioned in the book; Agur in 30:1, Lemuel (or his mother) in 31:1, and the wise men in 22:17. We are also told in 25:1 that section at least was copied or compiled by a man in the court of King Hezekiah who reigned about two hundred and fifty years after Solomon. In 1 Kings 4:32 we read that Solomon spoke 3,000 proverbs and more than 1,000 songs. The entire Book of Proverbs has 915 verses with only 375 proverbs in chapters 10–15. Chapters 25–29 contain another 128 proverbs, so no matter how we look at it 2000 to 2500 of those 3000 proverbs are lost. As far as the 1,000 plus songs are concerned, only Psalms 72 and 127 include Solomon's name in the title; almost all have been lost.

We know Solomon both collected and composed proverbs. He ruled during a relatively peaceful time. His father David had consolidated the kingdom and Solomon inherited a realm that allowed him the necessary free time and wealth to encourage the arts. We also know that wisdom literature was known, used, and collected from the Nile to the Euphrates. Anthropologists tell us primitive tribes as well as lettered people all over the world at this time distilled their experiences into pithy little sayings which we call proverbs. In Egypt and to a lesser extent Mesopotamia, whole collections of proverbs and wisdom literature have surfaced. From the Bible (1 Kings 10:14f., 28f.) we learn of Solomon's international trade relations. No doubt along with horses and gold there was also the exchange of languages and proverbs.

The truth about the origin of Proverbs lies somewhere between these two extremes: (1) All of the proverbs are unique to Israel, or (2) everything was copied from somewhere else. Wisdom cannot be copyrighted, so it is quite certain that different cultures can produce similar proverbs even though there is no contact between them. The living out of life teaches lessons which are transculturally true whether about thrift, industry, honesty, or patience.

At one time most Bible scholars thought wisdom literature was a later development; the tendency was to put all wisdom books (Job, Proverbs, Ecclesiastes, and Song of Solomon) late after the return of the Jews from the Babylonian exile and even into the Greek period. With the discovery of ancient essays on wisdom literature from Israel's neighbors, however, that has changed. Today nearly all scholars agree that the collecting of proverbs might very well have been going on in the time of Solomon more than 900 years B.C.

Purpose

We might say the Book of Proverbs is for anyone who is wise enough to listen. Quite obviously wise people will listen to instruction while fools will not. None of us, however, is either totally wise or totally foolish, but more or less wise or foolish depending on the situation. Sometimes wise people do foolish things, and fools do what is wise (17:28). The purpose of Proverbs is to make us less often foolish and more often wise, or to improve our overall performance in life.

Chapters 1-9 address "my son" a number of times (1:8, 10, 15; 2:1; 3:1, 11, 21; 4:10, 20; 5:1, 20; 6:1, 3, 20; and 7:1). Sometimes the plural, "sons" or "children" (4:1; 5:7; 7:24; 8:32) is used, while in 8:4 it is "mankind" or literally "sons of men." Even though "my son" does not appear so frequently in the rest of the book (cf. 19:27; 23:15, 19, 26; 24:13, 21; 27:11), the tone of a father instructing his son is heard throughout.

We might ask why only sons? Why not daughters? Much as we would hope that women had a higher position in the ancient world, it is simply a fact that they did not. Most decisions were made by men: the father, brothers, or grown sons of women. It was sons who were tempted by prostitutes and men who borrowed, lent, earned, and spent money. The men sat at the gate to adjudicate legal matters. On the other hand, consider the magnificent tribute to the noble woman at the end of Proverbs, and throughout the book note the direct (11:16, 22) as well as oblique (12:4) suggestions for women. Today there is every reason for women as well as men to read this book. Instead of avoiding the adulteress girls must be on guard against those who would use their bodies. Also, since today so many women control and spend money, how important it is for them also to heed proverbs which deal with frugality and wise investing.

Every reader should consider himself the target of Proverbs. Its pithy wisdom applies to all of us, regardless of age, sex, wealth, or learning. Proverbs offers spicy truth for us all.

Theology

We can think about this book two ways in terms of theology. Either the book is basically untheological because it does not speak directly about things such as laws, sacrifices, covenants, or cults; or else it is *very* theological because it teaches about wisdom, and the very foundation of wisdom is "the fear of the Lord" (1:7; 2:5; 9:10; 15:33, 19:23). It is our own definition of theology that will decide the matter.

Undoubtedly the book was written or compiled by people who feared the Lord, and since it is a part of the Bible, was written for God-fearers such as taxpayers in Solomon's kingdom, exiles in Babylonia, first-century Christian churches made up of many races from different geographical and religious backgrounds, or today's believers. Inherent in this book is the assumption that the reader is already a theist or a follower of the Yahweh of Israel, that he is a part of God's family, and that no matter how old or wise he is, the quality of his life can be improved.

Some scholars separate the book into sections on the basis of theology, putting all verses with the name of God or religious language into the category of later writings. Yet these verses are so mixed in with the rest that such a distinction seems artificial. It seems much more appropriate to believe that the collecter of these proverbs integrated theology into daily life. "The Lord" appears in verses that are otherwise quite secular; verses dealing with honesty in the marketplace (11:1), almsgiving (19:17), or civil justice (15:25).

What is implicit in Proverbs is that God is active and concerned with all the affairs of his people. He will not tolerate arrogance any more than he will accept insincere sacrifice. He will not accept gossip any more than hatred. He demands good behavior from his people not just in the temple or on holy days, but all through the week in the market, field, or home.

Canon

For a time Jewish scholars questioned the canonicity of Proverbs, partly because of the apparent contradiction of 26:4 and 5, and partly due to the explicitness of anti-adultery passages.

About twenty quotations or allusions from Proverbs appear in the New Testament, however (e.g. 3:11–12 in Heb. 12:5–6; 3:12 in Rev. 3:19; 3:27 in Rom. 13:7; and 3:34 in James 4:6 and in 1 Pet. 5:5), and James 4:6 quotes from Proverbs so directly that it supports the book's position in the canon.

In the Hebrew Bible, Proverbs comes after Psalms and Job, right before the five little scrolls (Ruth, Song of Songs, Ecclesiastes, Lamentations, and Esther), in the last third of the Bible known as the writings. The books of the prophets come earlier. Job probably was put before Psalms because for a long time its author was believed to have been Moses.

Text

Poetry is always more difficult to read than prose. It uses a larger vocabulary, scrambles word order for subtle effects, and implies rather than explicitly states its meaning. In addition to being poetry, the epigrammatic nature of the proverbs makes it more difficult to understand. Regrettably, some scholars thus assume the book's text is in poor condition, when really it is their limited knowledge of Hebrew that is at fault. If we do not understand everything in Proverbs, there is some comfort in knowing that others have had difficulty too. The Greek translation is one example; sometimes it expands on the text in a kind of amplified translation, sometimes it paraphrases the Hebrew, and sometimes it plainly misreads it.

Proverbs contains a number of words which appear only once in the Bible and it is these words which usually cause problems in translation, especially if the word is integral to the meaning of the text. On the other hand, we are helped by the widely used semitic device of parallelism in Proverbs. When two halves of a verse are parallel (either synonymous or antithetical), we can usually guess the meaning of an unknown word by its counterpart which is known.

Background

We have already noted two extreme positions on this question of background. One is that Israel developed in a vacuum, neither taking from nor giving to her neighbors. The nation was so isolated that it produced a sacred book that had nothing in common with anything before or after it.

The second position says Israel produced nothing unique; everything was copied, borrowed, or bought. The nation which provided our spiritual heritage was just one of many small kingdoms on the eastern end of the Mediterranean Sea. Only a quirk of history ensured the survival of its religion in its two basic forms of Judaism and Christianity.

The truth lies between these extremes. The question is, did Solomon or other sages compose these proverbs or are they borrowed, most notably from Egypt? Parallels to and in some cases nearly identical proverbs with the "Wisdom of Amen-em-ope" are hard to ignore, but the exact nature of proverbs' dependence on these collections is the point in question. Did Solomon's liaisons with Egypt (1 Kings 9:16; 10:28f.) in areas of commerce and diplomacy provide the interchange of ideas as well?

The wisdom of Amen-em-ope is the advice of a father to his son in the form of thirty sayings. A word in Proverbs 22:20 rendered "excellent things" in the King James version and translated "former things" in others, can also mean "thirty sayings" (NAB, TEV, and NIV). Some texts have 22:22–24:21 divided into thirty sections which occasionally correspond with the sayings of the Egyptian document (cf. J.B., NAB, NASB, TEV, and NIV). Did God in his providence deem this material worthy of inclusion into the Bible, and so prompted Solomon and wise men to incorporate the parts which were most suitable? Possibly, but others might suggest the borrowing went the other way; the Egyptians copied from the Hebrews. Still others might say these proverbs were common to both nations, but that the actual writing of them was done independent of each other.

Proverbs is written from the context of an ancient semitic society. Most people lived off the land as farmers and shepherds, thus the many references to sheep and cattle (e.g. 27:23ff.), rain (28:3), plowing (20:4), barns (3:10), and property markers (22:28). The Book also includes a number of references to urban life such as market places (20:14), city gates (1:21; 8:3), courts (8:15), and royalty (25:6). Most of the proverbs are domestic, dealing with choices people make every day between hard work and laziness, honesty and dishonesty, thrift and prodigality, lending and borrowing, patience and anger, quietness and talkativeness, riches and poverty. They speak of family relationships, business ethics, moral choices, and inner motivation. Generally they are context-less, universal in their appeal and application.

Whether we are children under the discipline of parents or parents seeking to correct the misbehavior of children, buyers or sellers of property, students or teachers, proverbs wonderfully adapt themselves to our situation. How often we feel tension between overwork and industry, laziness and relaxation, discipline and encouragment, spending and saving, or even generosity versus waste. Yet these are the very tensions of life itself. The way of wisdom teaches us how to achieve perspective and balance in that tension.

Bibliography

Wisdom Literature in General

James Crenshaw, ed. *Studies in Ancient Israelite Wisdom,* New York: Ktav, 1976

O. S. Rankin, *Israel's Wisdom Literature,* Edinburgh: T&T Clark, 1936

Patrick W. Skehan, *Studies in Israelite Poetry and Wisdom,* Washington, D.C.: C.B.A., 1971

John Mark Thompson, *The Form and Function of Proverbs in Ancient Israel,* The Hague: Mouton, 1974

Gerhard Von Rad, *Wisdom in Israel,* London: S.C.M., 1972

Commentaries

Franz Delitzsch, *Proverbs of Solomon,* 2 vols, Edinburgh: T& T Clark, 1884

Julius H. Greenstone, *Proverbs,* Philadelphia: J.P.S., 1950

R. F. Horton, *Proverbs* (The Expositor's Bible), London: Hodder & Stoughton, 1890

Edgar Jones, *Proverbs and Ecclesiastes,* London: S.C.M., 1961

Derek Kidner, *Proverbs,* London: Tyndale, 1964

William McKane, *Proverbs* (Old Testament Library), London: S.C.M., 1970

W. O. E. Oesterley, *The Book of Proverbs,* London: Methuen, 1929

R. B. Y. Scott, *Proverbs and Ecclesiastes* (The Anchor Bible) Garden City, N.Y.: Doubleday, 1965

Crawford H. Toy, *The Book of Proverbs* (International Critical Commentary), Edinburgh: T&T Clark, 1904

R. N. Whybray, *Wisdom and Proverbs,* London: S.C.M., 1965

PART ONE

In Praise of Wisdom

Proverbs 1–9

1

Prologue
Proverbs 1:1-7

The first verse of Proverbs is a title for the entire book. 1:1
We know from other titles in the book that the collection
includes more than the proverbs of Solomon; 22:17 introduces the "sayings of the wise men," 30:1 "The words of
Agur," and 31:1 "The . . . words which King Lemuel's mother
said to him" (TEV). Furthermore we learn from 25:1 that more
editorial work was done hundreds of years after Solomon.

Solomon is, however, a famous patron of wisdom. Just as
we associate the law with Moses and David with the Psalms,
so we put wisdom and Solomon together. During his reign
wisdom flourished. As heir to David's throne Solomon had
all the advantages of peace and prosperity to bring such a
collection together.

The Hebrew word for "proverbs" loosely applies to what
is in this book. The word means "rule" or perhaps "comparison" and those definitions fit best with the little tidbits of
wisdom found in chapters 10-29, but hardly apply to the
extended warning against adultery, the wisdom poem, numerical proverbs, and the acrostic on the noble woman. Perhaps the word really means any poem, advice, saying, or
extended essay on wisdom.

Verse 2 begins a list of terms for wisdom which is un- 1:2
matched anywhere else in the Bible. All six Hebrew words in
this verse are synonyms for wisdom: "recognize," "wisdom,"
"discipline," "understand," "sayings," and "insight." We see
them here all in one sentence but it would be beneficial to
study each word on its own.

The verb "recognize" or "know" which appears in a slightly

different form in verse 4 means basically what its noun form means elsewhere in the book. As a verb it is used almost a thousand times in the Old Testament. It also appears in the motto verse of the book, 1:7.

The second word is "wisdom," our English word meaning exactly what the Hebrew does. It also appears often, in Job, Psalms, and Ecclesiastes.

The term "discipline" is also typical of Proverbs. Its etymological meaning suggests correction or even chastisement in verses such as 3:11, 13:24, or 22:15.

The next words "understand" and "insight," are from the same Hebrew root as the preposition between. One who sees "between" things or reads "between the lines" is wise. By studying the Book of Proverbs you can become such a person.

1:3   Another cluster of synonyms for wisdom appears in verse 3. "Discipline" is repeated from verse 2, but to this the sage adds "intelligence," "honesty," "justice," and "fairness." The blending of moral qualities with intellectual ones came very naturally to the writer, since in his eyes the truly wise man was also righteous and the intelligent one was also godly. The wicked man who used his intellect for evil purposes would be described therefore as crafty, shrewd, or wily rather than wise or intelligent.

The word for "honest" is the most widely used and comprehensive word in this list, a word that suggests far more than what we think it means. The full meaning of this word would require a veritable thesaurus of terms, but if we must expand its meaning, then the words "right" and "good" might fill in some of the gaps.

1:4   Just as Proverbs uses many synonyms for wise, so the book offers many words for fools. The one used in verse 4 translated "inexperienced" or "simple" is the most pardonable type of fool because his foolishness results from lack of experience. He is not motivated by arrogance or pride, but simply fails to act wisely because of his limited exposure to the world. This kind of person has much to learn from Proverbs.

The word for "prudent" or "clever" here is a rare one, appearing only two times in Proverbs (8:5, 12), once in Exodus (21:14), and once in Job (9:4). "Clever" has a somewhat pejorative tone as if to suggest these proverbs will help us avoid crafty and devious people. The "prudent" of verse 3 is positive while the "prudence" of verse 4 seems more negative.

The contrast in verses 4 and 5 is the inexperienced young
versus the wise and educated adult. Proverbs helps all people
regardless of their age or level of wisdom. Most of the key
words in this verse have already been used except for "guidance" which now appears the first of five times in Proverbs
(only Job 37:12 has it outside this book). It may be related to
the word for "rope" and suggests the meaning of reins or
possibly bonds. As a crooked tree is forced to grow straight
with ropes, so this "guidance" will improve even the
"discerning."

This verse also contains the verb "hear." The ancient Hebrews recognized no difference between "hear" and "obey."
To disobey was to ignore or be deaf to instruction. Even wise
men must continue to "listen" to the words of this book if
they are to live successfully.

Two synonyms for "proverbs" are used in verse 6, but they
don't offer much more to our definition of a proverb. The first
of these used as either an adjective or a noun occurs elsewhere
only in Habakkuk 2:6 where the context is the same and
therefore not of much help. The "problems" or "riddles" wise
men raise are used many times in reference to Samson, yet
Samson's riddles are not as serious as what is referred to
here. Instead, this riddle is like the riddle of life itself. Finding
solutions to the series of problems it presents can demand
more wisdom than we have. Proverbs was written for all
people who face these problems.

So ends this introduction with its grand array of terms to
describe what Proverbs is all about. Its point is that everyone
can improve. We are taught to desire good behavior and
warned to avoid bad behavior. No matter how young or old,
how educated or illiterate, exposure to this ancient collection
of wisdom cannot help but improve our quality of life.

The question arises: where do we begin? How do we get
started? Where do we sign up for this course of study? Read
on. The answer starts with the next verse!

The Motto of the Book

Some outlines make verse 7 the conclusion of the introduction. Some make it the beginning of the next section containing advice to young men. Still others let it stand by itself.
I choose the last option.

Verse 7a is the same as Psalm 111:10 except that their word groups are reversed. It is also similar to Job 28:28 and very much like Proverbs 9:10 except for the word "first" or "beginning." The seventh verse is a kind of motto for the book. While some might suggest this motto is a later addition to the text as an effort to put more of God into the book, the verse is really not out of place here. Furthermore, the so-called religious verses or proverbs are so integral to the book it is hard to believe they were not part and parcel of the earliest editions. By and large these ancient people were more God-conscious than we are; no dimension of life was outside his domain. They did not leave him in the temple as we leave him in church, nor was he relegated to one day of the week or certain times of the day. They were much more aware of God's supervision and activity in their day by day routine.

The point of verse 7 is quite obvious. The first step of knowledge, the most important and intelligent thing we can do, is reverence the Lord. The translation "fear," negative most of the time, basically is a positive attitude we must have toward God. If we have done wrong and displeased God, then of course the usual emphasis of fear is proper, but if we are on good terms with God a better word might be "reverence." To acknowledge God's sovereignty in every realm is to take the first step toward successful living. The Bible's assessment of a smart person without God is "fool" (1 Cor. 1:20), and the humblest, least literate, untutored, but pious person is, in God's eyes, truly wise. How reversed we usually have it!

Verse 7 is the kind of antithetic proverb we find mainly in chapters 10–16. Such antitheses are separated in the Bible by "but" between two halves of a proverb. Verse 7 contrasts reverence and refusal as well as knowledge and stupidity.

A second kind of fool is introduced here (cf. v. 4). Of the twenty-six uses of this term in the Old Testament, nineteen are in Proverbs. The context of each teaches this kind of fool is unpardonable. This fool is arrogant (12:15), short-tempered (12:16), boastful (14:3), conscience-less (14:9), disobedient (15:5), argumentative (20:3), and incorrigible (27:22). In other words he is the opposite of a wise man who has reverence for the LORD.

2

Warning Against
Joining Thieves
Proverbs 1:8–19

Verse 8 has the first "my son" passage in Proverbs (cf. 1:8
1:10, 15; 2:1; 3:1, 11, 21; 4:10, 20; 5:1; 6:1, 3, 20; 7:1; 19:27;
23:15, 19, 26; 24:13, 21; 27:11). Most of these passages are
in the opening chapters and the "thirty sayings" part of the
book. While daughters are not mentioned specifically they
could be included especially today because now they have as
much freedom to make decisions as do sons.

It is interesting to note that both parents are included here.
It is the "advice" (v. 2) of the father and the "teaching" or
"law" (Hebrew *torah*) of the mother that the child should
heed. We might conclude from this verse that not only must
children honor both parents but also that both parents are
responsible for teaching and training their children. Neither
wisdom nor spiritual things are the exclusive responsibility
of one parent.

We probably should not read too much into the connection
of "law" with mothers, although godly mothers did play an
important role from Bible times right to the present (e.g. Han-
nah, Manoah's wife, Lemuel's mother, Lois, and Eunice).

We are not sure what kind of hat or necklace verse 9 refers 1:9
to, but it really doesn't matter since the point of the verse
which is a motive clause ("in order that . . ."), is that obedience is rewarding. What young man wouldn't want a "garland
to grace his head" or what young lady wouldn't want a necklace to improve her appearance? In order to have them this
proverb simply advises taking the seasoned advice and godly
counsel of one's dad and mom.

1:10   Verses 10–14 with 19 form a unit on the dangers of col-
laborating with violent people. The introductory verse is
clipped, one of the shortest in the book. Its key word is "tempt"
or "entice," warning against the deceitful nature of an invitation to join in wrongdoing. Often there is something very
alluring about doing wrong. Get-rich-quick schemes seem to
demand little accommodation of one's conscience yet may in-
volve, as this one does, some rather overt violence. No doubt
the invitation includes ridicule of traditional ethics and the
implication that to sin is to be free and enlightened.

1:11   Now however, verse 11 reveals the details of the heartless
plan. It is the most violent, cruel, and unprincipled sort of
plot ever. For a fleeting moment of pleasure wicked men are
prepared to take a life or pounce upon a fellow human being
to inflict lifelong hardship. Such crimes seem pointless, senseless, and unprovoked, yet they happen all the time. Check
your local newspaper for illustrations.

1:12   In verse 12 the rather foreign nature of the figure of speech,
"grave," in Hebrew requires some explanation. Here is a simple rendering of the original: "Let us swallow them like $sh^{e'}ol$
alive; and completely, like those who descend to the pit." The
ruthlessness of wicked men is incredible. We might discuss
in detail what $sh^{e'}ol$ is but basically it is the place of the dead,
the "pit" so often parallel to it in other sections of poetry. Its
use here reminds us of three Old Testament victims who were
thrown into pits: Joseph (Gen. 37:20ff.), Jeremiah (Jer. 38:6ff.),
and Daniel (Dan. 6:16–17). Also compare Psalms 40:2 and
88:4, 6.

1:13   In addition to the fun they get out of doing evil, the goal
of common criminals is to get rich. Thievery may take the
form of overpricing, selling shoddy merchandise, underpay-
ment of taxes, evasion of tolls, petty theft, shoplifting, bur-
glary, or even what we see described here, highway robbery.
The robbers use "we" in hopes of enlisting the hapless youth,
not telling him what they expect of him but doubtlessly an-
ticipating his role as dangerous enough to ensure he will be
the most likely one to be caught and blamed for the crime.

1:14   With verse 14 comes the climax of the invitation from sinners who urge the young man to cast his lot in with them in
order to share in the stolen booty. Never have they stated the
negative consequences of their crime; rather they have only

offered its rewards and potential benefits. That is the way it is with sin's allure. The devil puts his best foot forward to show his better side, and leaves the darker side and its ugliness to be discovered after it is too late.

Verses 10 to 15 are an extended protasis, a hypothetical situation beginning with "when" or "if" in verse 10 and ending at verse 14 with the apodosis, either an outcome or imperative based on what has preceded. Notice the words "my son" in both verses 10 and 15.

1:15

In contrast to the "come" of verse 11 is the "don't go" of verse 15, or "don't come"; the word is the same in Hebrew. The wise father now addresses his son who might some day be propositioned. To a righteous man it is better to be the victim of such a plot than to be the perpetrator of it. Two kinds of paths or ways are hinted at in this verse, reminding us of Psalm 1 with its two ways of life: the way of the righteous which the LORD knows and loves, and the way of the wicked which leads to doom.

The two sentences of verse 16 are the wise man's assessment of violent people whose company he's urging his son to avoid. His words imply haste; both verbs have the ring of urgency, suggesting the natural haste of evil men to get involved in sin. Isaiah 59:7 uses similar terms in describing sinners as does Paul in Romans 3:15.

1:16

Verse 17 has provoked some difference of opinion. Do birds avoid a trap they have seen set? Or is the author trying to say that a bird, because it has little sense, will fall into a trap even though it has seen the trap set? The latter explanation seems to fit better with the following verse which makes the point that robbers will be caught in their own traps (cf. D. Winton Thomas, "Textual and Philological Notes on some passages in the book of Proverbs," *VTS* iii pp. 280–292, who follows Rashi and Ibn Ezra as well as Ehrlich). Though criminals know crime doesn't pay and are aware of sin's consequences, yet they will proceed on with it to their inevitable doom.

1:17

This verse seems to suggest that birds will avoid such a trap, but another way to understand this verse is to propose that the innocent youth is the bird, and the father is describing how the trap is set for him. Since he has been warned about the trap he will surely avoid it.

1:18   There is little dispute about the meaning of verse 18. Evil people will reap what they sow. Trappers will themselves be trapped. Ambushers will be ambushed. Wicked plans will backfire; bad news for a criminal, but good news for one who has resisted such overtures.

1:19   Verse 19 expands on the preceding verse using the poetic device of repetition in Hebrew words. Literally the verse reads: "This is the end of all greedy with greed."

The Greek (Septuagint) reading is "end" rather than "path." Different as this sounds, it is just the reversal of two letters in Hebrew that makes the change. The vocabulary here makes little difference; the point is that a life of crime leads to ruin. The word "end" seems a bit more fitting here only because we are at the end of the opening pericope of the Book of Proverbs.

3

The Call of Wisdom
Proverbs 1:20–33

Wisdom calls out in verse 20 in the first of three verses 1:20–21 (the others are 8:1 and 9:3). Here and in 9:3 wisdom is plural, either an unusual form of the singular, or a plural of excellence. The verb however is feminine singular, "she is calling." The theme of Dame Wisdom and Lady Folly each seeking followers appears throughout the opening chapters, but in general wisdom makes her overture public "in the streets and market places," while folly and evil tend to be covert, secretive, and on the sly. For example, note the enticement of 1:10 and following; one cannot imagine this invitation being made out in the open. By contrast truth and purity have nothing to hide; the invitation to join them can be made publicly.

Three questions addressed to foolish people make up 1:22 verse 22. Foolish people and simple ones mentioned here come from the same root word that we saw in verse 4 which means naivete, inexperience, or ignorance. "Scorners" or "mockers," the second kind of fool, have a more serious malady because it takes willingness to be a scorner whereas one can be a fool without trying. In this verse we also find a third word for fool (one of the most common), which is used about fifty times in the book. This kind of fool is much like the one described in verse 2. He is arrogant, foul-mouthed, troublesome, deceitful, disrespectful, untrustworthy, and unpardonable; the kind of person also illustrated in the conundrum of 26:4 and 5. To illustrate its similarity to the earlier variety (cf. v. 7), check verses such as 14:24, 15:2, 14, and 17:12. Use them synonymously.

The questions asked in verse 22 are rhetorical, of course,

those every reader must answer himself. He must also ask, Should I put the Book of Proverbs down now because it insults me or should I read on because this is the kind of mental and spiritual medicine I need?

1:23   The wisdom teacher in verse 23 promises three things to those who abandon foolishness. Just as three questions in verse 22 call attention to three sick attitudes, so three antidotes are proposed here to improve those faults. They are "my rebuke," "my heart," and "my thought" (NIV). Note how typical these words are of Proverbs. The first occurs seventeen times in this book, eight more outside. The second and third are very general words usually appearing as "spirit" and "words," whose special meanings in this verse are determined by "rebuke," indicating reprimand, reproof, advice, or counsel.

Criticism is hard to take; few respond to it with ease. It is ego-damaging, yet accepting it and changing in response to it is the only way to succeed. Soil must be plowed, harrowed, and broken before it can be used. Clay must be kneaded and pounded before it can be shaped into a useful or beautiful vessel. People too must sometimes be broken in order to have bad habits and attitudes replaced with good ones. Blessed are those who take this sage's advice and listen to criticism.

1:24   Wisdom as a personified concept or else an itinerate wise man traveling through ancient Israel, has received no response. The complaint is clear in verse 24, extending into 25, and repeated in so many words in verses 29 and 30. It's an old story; we take the medicine too late because we are the last ones to realize there is something wrong with ourselves. When so few follow wisdom's way, why should we make fools of ourselves by joining such an unpopular minority?

1:25   "Rebuke" in the second half of verse 25 is the same word we saw in verse 23. The synonym "advice" or "counsel" in the first half is a new word, but a frequent one throughout Proverbs. It is one thing not to know one's faults; it is another thing to know them and choose not to correct them. It is people with this problem that this section addresses.

1:26–27   Four verses paired into two groups in this section predict the rewards of stupidity: verses 26–27 and 31–32. Structurally verses 26–27 are interesting because "disaster" and "calamity" occur in each verse but in reverse order. Verse 27 actually has a third grammatical member, "pain and misery" or "distress and troubles" which are increased because disaster and calamity have overtaken the fool like a "storm" or "whirlwind." We all know people who because of their own foolishness have led stormy lives. Each calm spell in their life is shattered by news of the next disaster.

We should note at this time that Proverbs deals with generalities and universalisms, not with particulars or exceptions to the rules. Such generalities include: God will make the righteous rich and the evil poor, poor people are good but rich people are bad, or crime doesn't pay but upright behavior does. Be prepared for such statements and don't spend time thinking of exceptions to the general rule stated in verses 26–27 that sudden terror will befall all fools.

In verse 28, instead of wisdom calling for fools, fools cry out for wisdom. The invitation has been withdrawn however, the opportunity is past. The chance to change is gone. The fool who has spurned wisdom when it was available has reached the point of no return. He is now irreversibly heading for destruction. It is a sad picture but altogether too familiar. **1:28**

Christ may have knocked on the door of a young and tender heart but postponement and putting off the offer of salvation has made the Savior's overtures less frequent, until finally the hope of salvation is virtually gone. Proverbs 29:1 is an unhappy reminder of the results of foolish behavior.

These two verses, 29 and 30, say essentially the same thing; since fools have rejected wisdom they must now pay the penalty. The "advice" and "rebuke" of verse 30 are the precise antidotes for foolishness that wisdom offered in verses 23 and 25 and the "knowledge" of verse 29 is the same word used in verse 22. **1:29–30**

The fool reaps what he has sown, say verses 31 and 32. Having refused the good seed wisdom offered, he now harvests brambles, the natural fruit of his kind of living. The Hebrew idiom in verse 31 suggests eating and being stuffed. It's not that folly doesn't reap a harvest, for that it surely does. The produce is unwholesome however, nothing but noxious weeds. **1:31–32**

The traditional translation of "prosperity" ("lack of concern" in TEV and "complacency" in NIV) is slightly inaccurate. Prosperity, peace, and freedom from worry are positive benefits of good living, but the kind of prosperity described here is willful carelessness. Freedom from care and living carefree are not the same. The fool indulges in the benefits of hard work, but that very indulgence will be his undoing. While young men may covet possessions of the old, lazy ones envy the industrious, or poor ones eye the rich; all fail to remember that such wealth or ease is the result of years of self-denial, hard work, and careful planning.

1:33   In verse 33 wisdom's rewards are security, safety, and freedom from fear. Security is big business today; night watchmen, guard dogs, alarm systems, and sophisticated locks are on everything from bank vaults to hub caps. How much better it would be if we trusted the Lord to guarantee our security and rid our lives of things and people that would harm us.

To enjoy peace and freedom from anxiety we must listen to wisdom. So far she has only taught us specifically to avoid violent companions (1:10–19), but essentially that is what Proverbs is all about. The more than 500 proverbs in chapters 10–29 only isolate certain situations in life. Would that we had the 3000 proverbs mentioned in 1 Kings 4:32! The sample that we do have, however, will teach us much about turning away from evil toward what is right. Ultimately it is not a matter of knowing what is wise anyway, but willing to do it. In the end we must still repeat the words Jesus taught us, "Lead us not into temptation but deliver us from evil" (Matt. 6:13).

4

The Rewards of Wisdom
Proverbs 2–4

Chapter 1 ended with the teaching that wisdom grants her rewards to those who follow her. The next three chapters are an expansion of that truth. Here and there the author digresses to give a warning against an immoral woman (2:16ff.) or an excursus on creation (3:19–20), but basically the theme is the one so well expressed in 4:18: "The path of the righteous is like the first gleam of dawn, shining ever brighter and brighter until the full light of day" (NIV).

We return to the father-son format with the words "my son" in 2:1, followed by the conjunction "if." This word, repeated in verses 3 and 4, is followed by the protases or conditions which will result in the happy events of verses 5ff. The expression "my commands" is like the "law" of 1:8, reminding us of the many synonyms for the Bible in Psalm 19:7–9 and Psalm 119. This doesn't mean a son was taught the whole Bible because much of it was not even complete at this time. On the other hand, what advice his parents gave him was undoubtedly in full accord with all the precepts of holy Scripture. So we could use this and similar verses to support the teaching of the Bible in the home.

2:1

The two parts of the body which receive and store wisdom are the ears and the heart. The two wisdom words, "wisdom" and "understanding" are very common ones used in the straightforward command from father to son.

2:2

Again in verse 3 the father encourages his son to do whatever is necessary to learn discernment. This time both wisdom words are from the same root word meaning "between." It is also one of the words in verse 2 which appears again in

2:3

verses 5, 6, 9, and 11. The Hebrew idioms in the preceding verse, "ears" and "heart," become "voice" in this verse.

2:4   The search for understanding is comparable to the search for silver or hidden treasure. In 1:9 the rewards of wisdom were a garland to grace the head and a chain to adorn the neck; here, as in Job 28:1–19, they are like precious minerals or jewels. We could expand on this comparison; note how scarce these treasures are. Also notice how much effort is necessary to find and excavate these jewels; and how these jewels can be used; like wisdom, these treasures are not usually discovered by a casual observer or chance passerby. They are excavated and enjoyed instead by the diligent, devoted, and determined.

2:5   Verse 5 is the apodosis, the "then" or the result clause. Understanding can be found, and the finding of it is like fear or reverence for the LORD (1:7). This is another way of stating the motto of the whole book which is that the first step in becoming wise is to know God and hold him in awe.

2:6   God is the fountain of all knowledge; intelligent people are, at best, channels through which God's wisdom flows. The words pile up in verse 6 three deep: "wisdom," "knowledge," and "understanding"! Tucked away in the Hebrew of this verse is the anthropomorphism, "mouth of the LORD." Wisdom comes, as it were, from his mouth to our ears (v. 2).

2:7   Verse 7 expands on the theme that wisdom comes from God, using a new, rarer word for wisdom translated "help" in the TEV and "victory" in the NIV. The word "shield" is also used in Genesis 15:1 and many verses in the Psalms (3:3; 18:2, 30; 35:2 et al.). Health, whether physical, mental, or spiritual, involves two things: taking in what is good and right, and avoiding what is not.

2:8   Verse 8 complements verse 7 as the second part of a pair, extending the theme of God's protection. The verse contains two rich words traditionally rendered as "judgment" and "saints." Both of these are misunderstood today; "judgment" means protecting what is right and true, not merely condemning what is false or wrong. "Saints" means covenant keepers, not just perfect Christians; those who fulfill their duty to God and thence also to fellow human beings.

2:9   Verse 9 in a new paragraph begins the same way verse 5 did, continuing the apodosis started in verse 1. All paragraphs are integrally connected by the repetition of key words or concepts; verse 9 uses "justice" and adds another synonym for "road," and "fair" is the same word as "righteous" in verse 7. The list of synonyms for "wisdom" and "righteousness" seems inexhaustible in this book.

From God's mouth to our ear and into our heart wisdom   2:10
comes, resulting in our becoming wise. Such a result is expected, yet another result is a pleasant surprise; knowledge will also give us pleasure. We are reminded here of a line from the catechism: "The chief end of man is to glorify God and to enjoy him forever." Glorify, yes. Fear, yes. Serve, yes. But enjoy? Yes! Nearness to God is a rewarding, fulfilling, and happy experience. Ignorance is bliss is not a Biblical proverb for though it may be true sometimes, this verse surely states the opposite; knowledge is bliss.

In verse 8 God protected his child, but in verse 11 "your   2:11
discretion" or "understanding" does it. What you have gotten from God is a part of him, doing for you what he does. The second term for wisdom here is the common one used often in these paragraphs.

Verse 12 flows directly out of verse 11, beginning with a   2:12
Hebrew verb in the purpose form, "will save." The use of "ways" links this verse to preceding verses such as 8 and 9. The second half of this verse also echoes the theme of 1:7 – 19 which is avoiding bad company. The term "perverse" is a translation of a word which occurs only ten times in the Old Testament, nine times in Proverbs and once in Deuteronomy 32:20. It is a word often connected with speaking (cf. 8:13; 10:31, 32; 23:33), and is probably related to the verb "overthrow." Such speech has as its goal the overthrow of what is orderly and right.

The theme of roads, righteousness, and the way of evil is   2:13
repeated in verses 13 through 15. All give further information about the kinds of people wisdom will protect us from. For instance, verse 13 says wicked men have abandoned the straight road and light of day to pursue a devious course under cover of darkness. Throughout the Bible darkness is associated with chaos (Gen. 1:2), cursing (Exod. 10:21 – 22; Job 3:4 – 6), and folly (Eccles. 2:13 – 14).

The next variety of evil people are those who enjoy evil,   2:14
says verse 14. Remember the murderer of 1:11 who stole

and killed for the fun of it? While the godly find pleasure in wisdom, the cursed ones find pleasure in committing senseless crimes (cf. 10:23).

2:15   The last kind of evil men in this list are those who are off the right road and who lead others astray. In the typical two-phrase structure of Semitic poetry we read the double charge, "unreliable" / "untrustworthy," or "devious" / "crooked." How different these men are from the Lord whose ways are right and true!

2:16   A new paragraph continues the theme of avoiding evil. In verses 12–15 we noted different kinds of evil men; now we are told of the immoral woman who lures one into sin. The criminals of 1:11–19 appealed to the vice of greed; this woman uses lust.

This is the first of several passages on the theme of avoiding the immoral woman (5; 6:20–7:27), giving us the distinct impression that things were not any different in ancient times than they are today. If warnings such as these reflect the society out of which they came, then apparently the cities of Israel had their seamy sides too. Opportunities to commit fornication and adultery seemed not too hard to come by.

At first the woman uses smooth, seductive words to lure the young man. We do not know what she says in this pericope, but much of it can be gleaned from more expanded sections such as 7:14–20.

2:17   Verse 17 poses two interesting questions. Who is this woman's partner, and secondly, what is the covenant she made before God? The word "partner" has many translations, but judging from its other uses in Proverbs (16:28 and 17:9), what it means here is probably "friend," or even "husband." Husbands and wives should be friends, partners in the true sense of the word, so "covenant" here is most likely marriage vows sworn in the presence of God. The Old Testament made no provision for a woman to divorce her husband, so her only alternative to a bad marriage was either to bear with it or else to engage in illicit sex.

2:18   Although both wisdom and folly are characterized as women in Proverbs, we do not get the impression in verse 18 that we are dealing with an allegory. The images are too concrete, the warnings too explicit. Fornication with this woman is to be avoided at all costs.

"Roads" or "paths" appear here again (cf. vv. 8, 9, 12, and 15); to walk this one with the adulteress will bring one straight to hell. The two terms "death" and "shades" both refer to that place of no return, the point being that you will reach life's end faster if you take the route through this woman's house.

That road is one way only according to verse 19. To what extent the author of this passage understood spiritual death, the second death, or life after death is unknown, but by and large people didn't ask such questions. Their great concern was simply to postpone death as long as possible. The point here is that adultery or fornication will put you in the grave much faster, heading down a road with no stopping place to turn around. 2:19

With verse 20 comes the positive perspective, the opposite course of action to its preceding verses. "Walking in the ways of good men" and keeping to their paths echoes the "road" theme of Psalm 1's two ways of life and the destinies of each. 2:20

People of integrity and goodness will enjoy the land of the living while sinners will by their own behavior be cut off from it. Remember the kind of generalization in Proverbs we spoke of before; without a single reference to the afterlife the author simply says good men will live and bad ones will die. 2:21

The last verse of chapter 2 sounds like the summary verse of Psalm 1. Wicked people may be men or women (in the immediate context we have a woman), but eventually the land will be purged by God of such offenders. Two verbs echo the agrarian context of the proverb; "cut off" and "rooted up." The significance of the word "land" is not easy to pinpoint; it may mean the land of Israel, the land of the living, or simply the earth. 2:22

More Advice to Young Men
Proverbs 3

The two themes central to chapters 1–7 are advice to young men and the rewards of wisdom. Although chapter 3 is titled with one of those themes, the other is present too (cf. vv. 13 – 18). "My son" occurs three times (vv. 1, 11, 21) in this chapter as well as in chapters 1, 4, and 6. Absent from this chapter, however, are any specific sins linked to murderers, thieves (chap. 1), or prostitutes (chap. 2). The advice is rather in general terms with much overlapping and repetition.

3:1   Verse 3 is a simple synonymous couplet introduced by "my son." The verbs in this pair are positive and negative; "don't forget" and "remember." The two words for a father's instruction are traditional "law" and "commands," although the Hebrew *torah* usually understood as "law," is really much broader in meaning than what the word implies. Apparently *torah* is from a verb meaning "throw" which came to mean "distribute," and eventually "teach." Since teaching in the Pentateuch is mostly legal the noun has come to mean law, but if we remember that law is only one facet of the word *torah*, we should appreciate its fuller meaning whenever we read "the law of the LORD" in the Bible.

We cannot imagine that the only thing the father gave his son was rules; much of his communication must have been in the form of illustration, anecdote, advice, and history. For such a range of techniques "teaching," not "law," is perhaps the better term.

3:2   Obedience to a father's advice will have two desirable benefits, says verse 2, long life and prosperity. Here again we find a common Hebrew word limited by its translation into English. The Hebrew word *shalom* in English is "peace," yet peace is just one dimension of *shalom*.[1] The word includes harmonious relationships within the family, payment of all debts, and the collection of all loans. It means rewards or wages, ultimately even a right relationship with God which comes through Jesus Christ, our peace. Prosperity is but one, though central meaning of *shalom*.

3:3   Verse 3 has two terms which also deserve more discussion. "Love" or "loyalty" (Hebrew *ḥesed*) and "faithfulness" (Hebrew *'emet*) overlap somewhat, but *ḥesed* has been the subject of at least two complete books.[2] It is also the word re-

[1]See Douglas J. Harris, *Shalom! The Biblical Concept of Peace.* Grand Rapids: Baker Book House, 1970.

[2]*Die Entwicklung des Begriffes Hasid im Alten Testament*, Lazar Gulkowitsch, Tartu, 1934, and *Das Wort Hesed*, Nelson Glueck, Topelmann: Berlin 1961.

peated in all 26 verses of Psalm 136. If we gave the word a long definition it would be "faithfulness to covenant promise," but if we choose one word for it it could be one of these: faithfulness, loyalty, love, lovingkindness, mercy, or fidelity. The other term '*emet,* is like our word "amen," implying such attributes as reliability, accuracy, dependability, truth, and faithfulness, its most common translation.

These noble attributes should grace the neck of the young man and be inscribed on his heart,[3] but because of the non-legal nature of Proverbs these laws are probably not a reference to phylacteries (little leather boxes containing copies of Deuteronomy 6:4 and the Ten Commandments which pious Jews tied to their arms and foreheads in literal obedience to Deuteronomy 6:8).

Obedience in these matters will bring acceptance from both God and men says verse 4. There is so much we can do to prompt the praise of men, but how hard it is to win approval from both God and man. True piety must express itself both horizontally to those we live and work with, and vertically to the God we serve. Neither way is optional; it is God who requires us to love both him and our neighbors.   **3:4**

Verses 5 and 6 are well known, unmarred by grammatical or linguistic subtleties which might alter its straightforward advice. The only thing to note here is that in this verse is a chiasmus where verbs in Hebrew are on the outside while prepositions are inside. Hence in Hebrew order the verse reads: **3:5**

> Trust
>> in the LORD with all your heart
>> on your own understanding
> Do not lean.

The meaning of the twofold command is obvious, warning against self-deception or the exaltation of one's own learning. It also might be seen as a warning against "trusting your heart," a common abuse among Christians. Trusting the Lord means becoming well acquainted with him through his Word, spending time in his presence in prayer, and seeking the counsel of others in the faith.

[3]The LXX omits the last phrase of this verse which some say was possibly borrowed from 7:3.

3:6   Two synonyms for "way" appear in verse 6, the same ones used in 2:8–20. Most chapters except for 18, 24, 25, and 27 make extensive use of these words. A modern application of this advice might be to consult a road map constantly while driving through a foreign city. The more you study the map the less likely you are to lose your way. Thus the more you study the Bible, the less chance you will find yourself going astray.

Included in the expression "right way" is the idea of the straight, level, or easy way. Doing things God's way is not difficult or burdensome because it is really the easiest, least complicated, and most direct path to happiness.

3:7   The few words of verse 7 include three commands which, if obeyed, would effect a mighty transformation in anyone: (1) Don't think you are wise, (2) revere God, and (3) refuse to do wrong. Most times our God is too small while our heads are too big. That perspective must be corrected if we are to succeed in the business of living. Paul also repeated this advice in Romans 12:16.

3:8   Fortunately most modern translators paraphrase the Hebrew idioms in verse 8. "Healed navels" and "moist bones" which are the literal translation of the Hebrew don't make much sense to us; the expressions are not only foreign but distasteful.

Yet more and more physicians today are realizing how important one's mental and spiritual health are to one's physical health. That relationship was well understood thousands of years ago. If you have a true assessment of yourself and if you really trust God, then you will be healthy and wise.

3:9–10   Verse 10 begins with a conjunction in Hebrew, "then," like almost every verse in the historical portion of the Old Testament. It ties both verse 9 and 10 together in a cause and effect relationship. If we give to God he will bless us. Again the context of this proverb is rural with words like "firstfruits," "barns," and "vats of new wine."

Some commentators say these verses are levitical and therefore out of place in a book like Proverbs. Yet note the other imperatives in this paragraph such as "trust," "remember," "obey," and "turn." Certainly "honor" is not out of context here, and is also not a very detailed cultic command. Nothing is said about what kind of an animal should be sacrificed, how many bushels of grain should be given, where they should be brought, or how they should be burned. The command is "honor the LORD"; the bringing of gifts is ancillary.

Grain and grape juice were basic ingredients of the ancient diet in bread and wine.

The structure of verse 10 is noteworthy because it is a perfect Hebraic chiasmus. In outline form it would look like this:

> They will be full
>   your barns
>   with grain
>   and with wine
>   your vats
> will overflow.

Another "my son" opens verse 11 beginning a new paragraph. The verse is a simple couplet with each half saying the same thing in different words. In Hebrew the verbs are negative, "do not resist" and "do not resent the LORD's correction and warning." The pianist, artist, or athlete who accepts and acts in response to criticism is the one who excels; it is never easy to be corrected, but to be mature enough to take it and do something about it is a mark of wisdom.   **3:11**

It is as difficult for the believer to accept discipline from the Lord as it is for a child to receive discipline from his father, says verse 12. A child who is being spanked usually doesn't believe the parent who says he is doing it because he loves him, but likewise it is hard to believe that God who loves us will also send hardship, testing, sickness or grief. But he does—because he loves us and wants us to grow in faith. Both verse 11 and 12 are quoted in Hebrews 12:5–6 (cf. Rev. 3:19).   **3:12**

The opening word, "happy" or "blessed" is typical of the poetic parts of the Bible. It appears in Psalm 1:1 and in twenty-five other places in the psalter. Here it serves to add one more reward to those who seek wisdom. Already in this chapter we have seen that such a person is accepted (v. 4), healthy (v. 8), prosperous (vv. 2, 10), and long-lived (v. 2). To these blessings verse 13 adds the promise of happiness.   **3:13**

The rewards of wisdom are silver, gold, and jewels, com-   **3:14–15** pleting the little saying, "healthy, wealthy and wise." Yet it is questionable as to what extent this saying should be taken literally. Undoubtedly Solomon thought wisdom and wealth went together, yet a lot of wise people don't strike it rich. That leads us to think these rewards may be figures of speech for other desirable things in life such as job security, satisfaction, or happy homes. Surely these things, like wisdom, cannot be bought with money.

3:16   The picture verse 16 presents is of a gracious lady offering gifts in both hands. She is wisdom who holds long life in one hand, and wealth and honor in the other. Her gifts are offered to anyone who will take them, but taking them involves marrying her or, in less graphic words, embracing or laying hold of wisdom. Who wouldn't wish that a spouse like this would provide one also with wealth and health?

An intricate connection between key words is the one between the noun "honor" in verse 16 and the imperative verb "honor" in verse 9. The connection is as simple as this: Honor the Lord and he will give you honor. The word "honor" is another word worthy of more extended treatment, but essentially here it means to be heavy, weighty or worthy.

3:17   Verse 17 in the KJV is a beautiful truth:

> Her ways are ways of pleasantness,
> and all her paths are peace.

Once more "way" is used as a term for "life" (see verse 2 for a brief discussion of *shalom*). It's a pity our language has no term as rich as the Hebrew to describe a happy state of being.

3:18   The paragraph closes with verse 18 which sums up the preceding verses. The reward of wisdom is longevity and happiness; to live long and to be happy are basic human goals. The trouble is most people almost kill themselves trying to live long, and push themselves so hard in an effort to have fun that they make themselves miserable. The problem is that man usually defines happiness in materialistic terms which are quite different from the Biblical definition. The unregenerate world's way of achieving it is poles apart from the prescription these ancient maxims offer.

3:19–20   Verses 19 and 20 differ from others in this chapter yet also develop the theme of wisdom. They are somewhat reminiscent of the theophany in Job 38–41 and the praise-of-wisdom chapter (chap. 8) in this book. Considerable scholarly discussion surrounds the question of the relationship between God and wisdom. Is wisdom here a part of the divine personality or a vestige of some female deity? Is it another member of the godhead? I think wisdom is either a part of God's personality or else a kind of surrogate for God himself. You might read verses 19 and 20 by simply eliminating "wisdom" and substituting "God." The point is that God is the creator of heaven and earth and under his sovereign direction all things endure. The water cycle is but one area he controls.

The lesson here is that if God used wisdom to make and run the world, how vital it is for us to have in order to occupy and subdue the earth.

Another "my son" begins verse 21 and introduces a new bit of advice. It is not enough to acquire wisdom; it must be retained and at all costs. It is very possible that even if you have found wisdom you might also lose it. Just as marriage must be worked at in order to be good, so the use and application of wisdom also requires constant effort.
3:21

Verse 22 adds little that is new. Wisdom's reward is long life (vv. 2 and 18), "an ornament to grace your neck." The long life theme also appears later in 4:10, 22; 8:35; 9:11; 10:11, 16, 17; 11:19, 30; 12:28; 13:14; 14:27; 15:4, 24; 16:22; 19:23; 21:21; and 22:4.
3:22

Wisdom is not like a good luck charm, talisman, or St. Christopher medal, but is more practical like a flashlight or climber's rope; wisdom will keep you from stumbling or falling. We feel much safer driving on a well-lit street or paved highway than on a dark, gravel road. Wisdom is like that safer road; it prepares you for the eventualities of the unknown journey that lies ahead.
3:23

Verses 24–26 expand on verse 23, speaking of the full-time vigil wisdom keeps over those who have it. A good night's sleep can be a desperate wish especially for those robbed of it by sickness, anxiety, fear, or noisy neighbors. How wonderful for them is the promise of wisdom's fearless "sweet sleep."
3:24

Two Psalms come to mind in connection with verse 25: 91:5–6 and 121:3–6. Because we have espoused wisdom, which means putting our faith in God (in New Testament
3:25

terms received Christ as our personal Savior) we need not be afraid of the future. All the phobias and fears of people today have no effect on us because we trust God and his power.

3:26   The linking of God with wisdom is even clearer in verse 26, the conclusion of this paragraph. The paragraph started with wisdom and insight and their benefits, but somewhere in the middle the author made a switch from wisdom to God. Exegetically we must not try to distinguish too carefully between God and his wisdom. Notice 1 Corinthians 1:30; God has made Christ to be our wisdom.

3:27   Verses 27–31 begin with "don't" in Hebrew. Verse 27 is difficult to interpret; the words are familiar enough but their usage is so unusual. A wooden rendering would go like this: "Don't withhold good from 'lords' when it is in the 'god' of your hand to do." This may be a play on the words ba'al — "lord" and 'el — "god," but both are paraphrased even in the most traditional versions to something like "to those it is due" and "power."

The second idiom has parallels elsewhere (Gen. 31:29; Deut. 28:32; Neh. 5:5; and Mic. 2:1), but the one about "lords" is unique here. Most scholars agree that this verse teaches either punctuality in paying bills or generosity to the poor. This may have been Paul's idea too when he wrote in Galatians 6:10: "As we have opportunity, let us do good to all people" (NIV). That is the force the verse has in most translations but we can't be positive it is accurate. In principle however, this interpretation is supported elsewhere.

3:28   Verse 28 is much less problematic and reinforces the interpretation that verse 27 is concerned with almsgiving and neighborly generosity rather than prompt bill paying. "Tomorrow" might have meant to ancient Israelites what mañana means to South Americans; we must not put off deeds of kindness but do them while we still have the chance. One of my favorite sayings goes, "If not now, when? If not here, where? If not I, who?" The answer to who is my neighbor is the same here as it is in Luke 10:29ff. where Jesus gives the parable of the good Samaritan.

3:29   Verse 29 continues the theme of doing good to our neighbor, illustrating another way we are obligated to him. An enemy might not trust us, but a neighbor should. To plot harm against him would be a double crime involving both the crime itself plus a breach of trust.

The fourth of five "don'ts" in this series is against unnec-   3:30
essary arguing. Certain people just love to argue. They either champion an unpopular cause or, for the sake of argument, take an opposite position. Such discussion may serve to clar-ify the sides of an issue, but rarely does it build friendships or strengthen community spirit. In Romans 12:18 Paul tells us to do everything possible to live at peace with each other. The Hebrew verb in 3:30 even includes a word which sug-gests something stronger than argument; this "accusing a man" has legal overtones. How much more must unjustified lawsuits displease the Lord!

The last warning in this series is against jealousy, imme-   3:31
diately bringing to mind the extended treatment of that sub-ject in Psalm 37:1–8. It is too bad that so many children's toys today encourage violence. The mass media is partly to blame for that, but so is our sinful nature which turns to violence rather than love. Only the power of new life in Christ can overcome the spirit of vengeance which seeks to solve all problems through the use of force.

In verses 27–31 we learned the rules. Now in verses 32–35   3:32
we learn reasons for those rules. Don't do any of these bad things because God will surely reward people with what they deserve. Curses for the wicked and blessings for the righteous are mentioned several times in this paragraph, many times in the book, and countless times in the whole Bible.

Typical of contrasts in this passage is "hatred" toward perverse men versus "confidence" in good ones. We would expect "love" or "blessing" toward the upright man, but "con-fidence" is an interesting term pointing to the intimacy God enjoys with those who serve him.

The typical contrast of "curse" and "blessing" is presented   3:33
in verse 33. Each half of this verse includes a word for "house," but probably not too much significance should be read into that. The sage is not necessarily referring to buildings, but neither is he speaking of families or dynasties.

Epithets for good and bad men are in verse 34: "conceited   3:34
mockers" and "humble men." Arrogance was as distasteful in ancient Israel as it is in our society, and God hates it just as much as anyone else. In fact he may hate it more because he

can see through people to their hearts. Both James (4:6) and Peter (1 Pet. 5:5) cite this verse when they urge Christians to be humble.

3:35   The list is complete: verse 32 with "evil" and "righteous"; verse 33 with "wicked" and "righteous" (a different Hebrew word from verse 32); verse 34 with "conceited" and "humble"; and verse 35 with "wise" and "foolish." A similar list might be made for the contrasting attitudes and actions of God:

> verse 32; hates-confides
>
> verse 33; curses-blesses
>
> verse 34; mocks-favors
>
> verse 35; honor-disgrace

The Benefits of Wisdom
Proverbs 4

The fourth chapter of Proverbs brings to a close the extended treatment of the rewards of wisdom, but it also contains additional advice from a father to his son (vv. 1, 10, 20).

4:1   Verse 1 is the only place where "son" is plural, yet it is doubtful this is significant because later in this chapter the author reverts to the singular.[4] Two things might be implied here. Either daughters are included (notice "mother" in v. 3), or else this is a classroom situation rather than a domestic one. As I said before gender is of little consequence today. Girls as well as boys should read the Book of Proverbs, and though the father is mentioned here, both parents are responsible for the teaching process (1:8; cf. 6:20; 23:22; 30:17 and 31:1).

4:2   Verse 2 includes a kind of double motive both following and preceding imperatives. Sons should listen (v. 1) because

---

[4]It is possible that this plural is a copyist's error. The additional letter that makes this word plural is also the first letter of the next word. If it is plural, then the possessive pronoun "my" should be absent.

"my teaching is sound" (2:9); and because it is good they should not forget it.

To be first-born was extremely important both in ancient times and in royal families today, yet being an only son was something to worry about since only one person could inherit and pass on the family name and property. Parents would be very protective of such a child (e.g. Isaac, Samuel, or Samson) and especially concerned about his spiritual upbringing. *4:3*

First Chronicles 3:5 says Bathsheba had four sons of whom Solomon is mentioned last. Since the Bible doesn't say any more about the other sons, it is very likely Solomon here is speaking to his son Rehoboam and referring to David and Bathsheba as his parents. Solomon might have been the only son of that union for a time although several half-brothers were older than he. The point here is that wisdom is passed down from parents to children, and the author is trying to impress the children with the continuing nature of this advice. Tradition, in this sense, is a good thing to pass on.

Chapter 3:1 and 4:4 are very similar; typical of the first part of Proverbs. The Hebrew words in this verse (unlike 3:1) contain only two positive verbs, "remember" and "do." *4:4*

After a four-verse introduction we come to the advice: two positive, identical verbs and two negative ones make up the simple command. Get wisdom, get insight, don't forget, and don't ignore. The perfect symmetry of these parallel lines is hard to match. *4:5*

Verse 6 includes another beautifully structured proverb. Each half has two clauses with a command and a promise. One command is negative ("don't forsake her") and one is positive ("love her"). In response to obeying her, wisdom will protect and watch over us. *4:6*

Verse 7 seems painfully redundant; the Greek translation omits it altogether. The author is trying to impress us with the importance of "getting" (which can also mean buying) wisdom. That verb is used three times in verse 7. *4:7*

The structure of verse 8 is almost identical to verse 6; do something for wisdom, and she will do something for you. The structure here is chiastic; commands are the first and fourth elements while promises are the second and third. In Hebrew the verse reads: "Love wisdom and she will exalt you; she will bring you honor because you embrace her." *4:8*

We are to respond to wisdom by both "esteeming" and "embracing" her, both rare Hebrew verbs for actions which do not really parallel each other.

4:9   The two lines of verse 9 can be condensed into one with little loss of meaning. The idea of wisdom as head covering or jewelry is mentioned elsewhere in the book, but this verse may also include a play on a Hebrew word which means both "head" and "first." If wisdom is "first" in our life (v. 7) then wisdom will in turn crown our "head" (v. 9).

4:10   "Listen" (the watchword of the Jewish faith *sh^ema'* in Deut. 6:4) and "my son" in verse 10 introduce a new paragraph. Once more we are told long life is the reward of wisdom (see list at 3:22).

4:11   Two words for "way" appear in verse 11, resulting in a kind of Hebrew pun suggested by this wooden English translation: "in the *direction* of wisdom I will guide you. I will *direct* you on straight *paths.*"

4:12   Palestine is a hilly land of rocks and stones. This topography is reflected many times in Scripture (e.g. Isa. 5:2 or 40:3–4). Anyone who has hiked off the beaten path or climbed away from a clearly marked route can appreciate these figures of speech.

4:13   Verse 13 gives three commands with one motive clause. "Hold on," "don't let go," and "guard" are three ways to ensure the safety of "your life."

Although the father in Proverbs speaks in general terms about wisdom, how much difference does education, another kind of wisdom, make in earning power today? This verse was not intended to be a plug for higher education, yet our modern system does provide a measurable way of illustrating the truth of this ancient statement.

4:14   Verse 14 is a straightforward prohibition against walking in the ways of evil men. In Hebrew the second sentence would place the object first and the verb second, but what may be beautiful Hebrew may not be appropriate English. Once again we learn that life is like a road which one must choose; the way of evil men or the path of the righteous (v. 18 *et al*).

4:15   Verse 14 used two verbs and two objects, but verse 15 has four verbs and one object, "it." This repetitive warning underscores the urgency of a father cautioning his son against evil.

In Psalm 36:4 and verse 16 of this chapter, we read about wicked people who lie awake at night thinking up ways to steal and kill. Sleep comes to them only when they have done their evil and left some victim by the roadside to die. How sick to find peace only at the price of another man's misfortune. 4:16

Wicked people thrive on violence. Someone once said we are what we eat. A steady diet of vice, crime, violence, sex, and perversion not only makes men insensitive to their horrors but actually encourages their appetite for them. Paul warned against this when he wrote in Philippians 4:8, "Fill your minds with those things that are good and that deserve praise: things that are true, noble, right, pure, lovely, and honorable" (TEV). 4:17

Verses 18 and 19 continue the "way" theme of the righteous and the wicked. For the first time (except maybe for 2:13) we read about the contrasting ways of light and darkness. Verse 18 compares the good way to the rising sun; at first it is an almost imperceptible glow in the eastern sky, then it appears in rays announcing the day, then finally it reigns over the sky in all its blazing glory. 4:18–19

The contrast to that bright morning is the utter blackness of night, realm of the wicked. Man is not a nocturnal creature by nature and therefore is apt to lose his way or get into trouble at night. The image of "stumbling in darkness" is the way of the wicked.

Verse 20 uses an idiom which suggests bending the ear to listen; "My son, pay attention to what I say." "My son" helps mark the beginning of a new paragraph. 4:20

The first half of 4:21 is like the last half of 3:21, reminiscent of other verses where "heart" appears (2:2, 10; 3:1, 3, 5; 4:4 and about eighty more times in Proverbs). It is possible this phrase also suggests "learn by heart" or memorize. We who read tend to have less retentive memories than those who do not read, but there are certain things much too worthy to write only on paper — they should also be written, as it were, on our hearts. The sound counsel of godly parents is one kind of advice that ought to be memorized. 4:21

Long life and good health are mentioned often as wisdom's rewards (e.g. 3:2, 8), usually thought of in terms of physical health and years of life. Yet we might also think of these 4:22

rewards in terms of mental health and spiritual life, even everlasting life in light of what we read in the New Testament.

4:23   The truth of verse 23 seems to lie behind what Jesus said in Matthew 12:34b–35: "For out of the overflow of the heart the mouth speaks" (NIV). This proverb cuts both ways, exalting those who speak of noble things, and condemning those who talk only of earthly things. Indirectly this verse tells us to fill the empty places of our minds with good things in order that our lives may be shaped by them.

4:24   The only thing worse than evil is evil that tries to look good. Lies, deceit, hypocrisy, and falsehood don't ever belong in the mouth of a wise man. The first adjective ("perverse") in Hebrew refers to crooked roads. The opposite of this is our idiom "straight talk." The other term ("corrupt talk") is used as a noun nowhere else in the Bible, but as a verb only once in Isaiah and five times in Proverbs. This term also refers to crooked paths.

4:25   Shifty eyes, furtive glances, and winking are all characteristics of deviousness. By contrast the sage in verse 25 recommends looking straight ahead, reminding us of Matthew 6:22 where Jesus said, "If your eyes are good, your whole body will be full of light" (NIV). The eyes, more than any other part of the body, betray ones thoughts. If the inner man is good his eyes will be honest.

4:26–27   Two words for path are used in verse 26, while the words "your feet" tie verses 26 and 27 together. The author of Hebrews used this passage in 12:13, saying people often get lost because of uncertain plans, faulty roadmaps, or unclear goals. Proverbs provides both a goal and route. The goal is successful living and the route is the way of wisdom.

The precepts of Proverbs are like signposts at critical junctions in life where we might stray from the road. Carefully mapping out our journey, marking intersections which might be confusing, and noting the dangers to be avoided along the way are the best ways to guarantee a safe trip. These are the metaphors of verses 26 and 27.

5

Warning Against Adultery
Proverbs 5

Chapters 5–7 are an extended warning against adultery with Proverbs 6:1–19 the only deviation from that theme. Illicit sex must have been readily available in ancient Israel or such an extended warning would not have been necessary. Either that, or the devastating effects of this sin must have prompted the author to give it such heavy treatment. Another possible reason for the serious warning might have been the author's own preoccupation with this vice; a kind of warning from experience. Solomon's problems all started by marrying women he shouldn't have. First Kings 11:1–11 chronicles the sad story of a king who married Pharaoh's daughter yet eventually lost his kingdom.

5:1–2   Chapter 5 begins much like 4:20; a father urging his son (who sounds like he's married in verses 15ff.) to heed his advice. Proper action and judicious speech are the foci; our words can be as grievous as our deeds. Salvation is a matter of doing as well as saying (Rom. 10:9–10).

5:3   In graphic terms the author begins painting a picture which will take him three chapters to complete. Some question whether "lips" and "mouth" in this verse mean words or kisses, but I prefer "mouth" or "speech" because of the imagery. "Honey" and "oil" are tasted and felt as are kisses. What is hard to accept is the abrupt way in which the adulteress greets her victim; kissing preceding even an exchange of words. On the other hand, chapter 7 describes a prostitute who makes her initial contact with an embrace and a kiss (7:13). Talking comes later. Perhaps that was how it was done back in Solomon's time.

5:4   In contrast to sweet, smooth honey and oil is the bitterness of gall and pain of a sword. Literally the second image reads "sharp as a sword with mouths." In Hebrew swords had two "lips" or "mouths" which "ate" their victims, affording the author here a play on words. The mouth of the adulteress which was so tasty will all too soon become an instrument of pain and death.

5:5   Death and the grave mark the road she travels; imagery we are by this time very familiar with. We are not certain this woman is another man's wife (vv. 3 and 20 don't necessarily say that) like the woman of 6:24ff, so it is possible she is the kind who will transmit some disease which will induce her partner's premature death.

5:6   The subject of verse 6 could be "she" or "you" (in Hebrew the forms are identical). The KJV offers an alternative to most recent translations, but if the feminine subject is correct, then not only will her partner find himself on the road to destruction but the woman also will be going down a hopeless one-way street.

5:7   The pericope in verses 7–14 describes in vivid detail the agonizing grief an adulterer brings on himself by yielding to lust. Verse 7 is typical of the opening verses of Proverbs. Note "sons" is once again plural as in 4:1. The structure of this verse is also typical, with one positive command and one prohibition; "listen" and "don't forget."

5:8   The woman of verse 8 is clearly the adulteress of verse 3. The best way to avoid her seductive embrace is to stay away from even the part of town where she lives. To put ourselves in the place of sin, then to ask God to deliver us from temptation is presumptuous as well as foolish. A regular diet of pornography will eventually lead anyone to indulge in illicit sex.

Jesus emphasized this teaching when he said that anyone who looks at a woman and wants to possess her is guilty of adultery in his heart (Matt. 5:28). If even a look leads to sin, don't get close enough to look. If this teaching was emphasized in ancient times when women were modest, how much more ought men to be on guard today when sex is exploited in almost all of advertising and entertainment.

5:9   Adultery results in loss of self-respect, disease, and possibly even death. The term "strength" or "respect" occurs just once in Proverbs; outside the book it is used as an accolade

for God. We're not certain here if the life of the adulterer is shortened by the revenge of an offended husband, the contacting of venereal disease, or just in general from leading such a sordid life.

Accumulated wealth will be sacrificed too by the man who falls prey to lust. This might refer to the cost of sin, or might suggest the actual expenses of adultery. First one must pay the harlot or mistress. If she is a married woman it might also mean paying off her husband, and if she happens to get pregnant, one might also be obligated to pay child support.

5:10

Verse 11 is explicit about one effect of adultery; illicit sexual activity brings on venereal disease which often proves excruciatingly fatal.

5:11

Eventually the man who succumbs to lust is reduced to poverty, disgrace, and disease. It is too late, however, for regrets. He can only utter a long litany of "if onlys": if only I had listened to my father; if only I hadn't gone my own way; if only I had taken others' advice; if only I could have known an hour of pleasure would result in a lifetime of regret.

5:12–13

The loss of health and wealth aren't all the sinner loses; he also faces the loss of respect in the community, one kind of disgrace which has led many to suicide. Just what this loss meant in Bible times is uncertain; in general Proverbs does not offer detailed Levitical precepts which might include a priestly ban on sexual offenders. Today, unfortunately, sexual offenders usually do not suffer embarrassment or disgrace. The church advises counseling sessions instead of any guilt-inducing discipline, thus encouraging rather than condemning immorality. Public confession and discipline are unfortunately almost unheard of.

5:14

Verses 15–19 describe the wholesome, pure alternative to sexual immorality. A word-for-word rendering of the Hebrew would say: "Drink water from your own cistern, that flows out of your own well." Or, in other words, be faithful to your own wife. Elsewhere the images of fountain and wife are connected as in verse 18 and Song of Solomon 4:12, 15. A drink from another well really isn't any sweeter than that from your own. Notice wife (cistern or well) is singular. Although God permitted some Old Testament heroes to have several wives, creation testifies to his original plan that each

5:15

man should have one wife, and each wife one husband. God created only Eve for Adam.

5:16   The motif of "water" and "springs" continues in verse 16. The semitic image here is someone who throws water from his wells into the street, a foolish and wasteful gesture. In the east water is so scarce that this picture of waste is even more meaningful, illustrating the activity of an oversexed male who fathers children all over town. When they are born he doesn't even acknowledge them; they in turn do not know him as father.

5:17   The children a man produces should grow up in his own home, help him farm the land, bring honor to his name with good behavior, and eventually inherit his wealth. Populating orphanages or taxing a woman not one's is no honor.

5:18   The fifth and last Hebrew synonym for "fountain" appears in verse 18, a kind of summary statement of verse 15.

5:19   In words similar to those used in Song of Solomon (2:9, 17; 4:5; and 7:3) the author compares a man's childhood sweetheart who is now his wife to a beautiful and graceful deer. Her breasts are forever satisfying and her love always captivating.

5:20   Two rhetorical questions are asked in verse 20: why should a son be captivated by an adulteress, and why should he embrace another man's wife? The answers are all too obvious; one should not become involved with any woman other than his wife.

An uncommon verb ("captivated") appears in 19c, 20a, and 23b. Its root meaning is to wander or stray, leading to the idea of being captured, captivated, or ravished. The latter meanings seem to fit our passage best; perhaps "captivate" would work in verses 19 and 20, but "capture" would go better in verse 23.

5:21   Verses 21–23 might just as easily appear in the miscellaneous section of chapters 10–29. They are a reminder that God is all-seeing and all-knowing; "nothing in all creation is hidden from God's sight. Everything is uncovered and laid bare before the eyes of him to whom we must give account" (Heb. 4:13, NIV).

5:22   Verse 22 is another "crime doesn't pay" verse (cf. 1:19, 31; 4:19 *et al.*). The trap which backfires on the wicked man found elsewhere in Pss. 7:15–16; 57:6 poses a subtle ques-

tion. Does God actively bring about this catastrophe or does
life simply rebel against those who don't cooperate with the
natural order? Think of Romans 8:28 in reverse.

Two key words in the Book of Proverbs appear in verse 23;   5:23
an unhappy end comes to the man who is unfaithful in marriage. The word "self-control" appears 42 times in this book
and "folly" 40 times. Those who do not have self-control are
those who live in folly; those who love folly lose self-control.
Yielding to immoral sex means losing control of one's life. It
is stupid and the way of a fool.

6

Warnings Against Cosigning, Laziness, and Deceit
Proverbs 6:1–19

The extended warning against adultery is interrupted in chapter 6 by warnings against three other sins: cosigning, (vv. 1–5), laziness (vv. 6–11), and deceit (vv. 12–19). Verses 16–19 are subordinate to the last section but might be considered separate because they are such a neatly definable unit.

"My son" appears twice in this chapter, once at the begin- 6:1
ning of this three-part warning and once where the anti-
adultery theme begins again (v. 20). Verse 1 is tricky,
prompting some alternative interpretations. The father warns
his son not to take responsibility for the debts of a stranger.
Cosigning a note for a relative or friend is kind and generous,
but cosigning for a stranger or enemy is just plain foolishness.
The verse is essentially a warning against foolish business
dealings, but may also hint at a general suspicion of commerce. The wise man is safer on the farm than he is at the
market. Proverbs 11:15, 17:18, and 22:26 address this same
subject.

Speaking up on a neighbor's behalf in financial matters is 6:2
just one more place where your mouth can get you into trouble, says verse 2. What may have seemed like a good deed
has turned out to be foolish. The cosigner has failed to count
the cost of his ready generosity.

This folly, however, is not so insidious as adultery, because 6:3
this foolishness offers some hope of escape. It may be painful
and humiliating to kneel at your creditor's feet to ask for

mercy, but that is far better than having to pay the debt you cosigned for. Perhaps the creditor is better able to sustain the loss than you, and maybe you could even ask to be responsible for only a part of the loan.

A rabbinic proverb says "When a fool goes to market the merchants rejoice!" Here is a fool who has signed papers without reading the fine print.

6:4–5   Verses 4 and 5 stress the urgency of acquitting oneself of financial obligation. Don't let another day pass, don't wait until after the siesta. Set the record right *now* and get out from under its obligation.

The author plays with the Hebrew word for "hand" in this section; verse 1 warned the son not to "shake hands" on a business matter, but verse 3's "hand" means something more like power. In verse 5 "hand" takes on still another meaning like "trap," or "snare." The animal who is caught in the grip of a hunter is engaged in a life-and-death struggle, but so, in a way, is the son who is trapped into an ill-advised contract by a hasty handshake.

6:6   Ants are mentioned in the Bible only in verse 6 and 30:25; both times they illustrate industriousness and diligence. Lazy people can learn a lesson from them by simply watching how hard they work, how heavy their loads are, and how they cooperate with each other. They seem never to rest, unlike the sluggard who wastes so much of his time.

6:7–8   Two other observations about ant life deserve mention here. First, they apparently have no obvious leaders, yet their community functions smoothly and efficiently (possibly a veiled criticism of bureaucracy that burdened Israel during its monarchy). Second, ants store up food for the future which is what anyone with any sense does. Only lazy people fail to do it.[1]

---

[1]The Greek version adds three verses here. The translation from the Jerusalem Bible reads:

Or go to the bee
  and see how diligent she is,
  and how considerable the work she does.
Kings and commoners take what she yields for their health.
  She is sought after and revered by all.
Her strength may be feeble,
  but because she does homage to wisdom she wins respect.

The sage sounds almost impatient in verse 9 as he asks   6:9
twice when the lazy man is going to get moving. The theme
of laziness and its counterpart, industry, is continued through
chapters 10–29. In fact, fourteen uses of the word "lazy" in
the Old Testament are in Proverbs (a verb form is in Judg.
18:9, a noun from the same root in Prov. 19:15; 31:27; and
Eccles. 10:18).

"A little sleep, a little slumber, a little folding of the hands   6:10
to rest" (NIV) is the response of the lazy man. Nothing is
wrong with sleeping in once in a while or even taking an
afternoon nap, but when naps begin to intrude on the best
hours of the working day something is drastically wrong.

Verse 11 does not say an actual robber victimizes the sleep-   6:11
ing man; his sleep itself robs him. In a sense he robs himself
by wasting away his time, talents, and earning power. Precious hours, important opportunities, and years of productivity are squandered because he lacks enthusiasm and initiative.

Throughout Proverbs pictures are boldly sketched in black
and white; there are few gray areas. Few men may be as lazy
as the fellow described here, yet few of us work as hard as
we should. Don't excuse yourself automatically when reading
this passage; nobody works as hard as an ant.

The third pericope in the first half of chapter 6 deals with   6:12
lying. Deceit, perversity, deviousness, and deception are all
dimensions of lying, and God hates them all. Wise people
don't lie because in the end it doesn't pay.

Body language is not new; the eyes, feet, and fingers of   6:13
verse 13 all indicate the deceit of the "scoundrel" and "vil-
lian." Of these three gestures we are most familiar with the
wink of the eye. The other movements of feet or fingers must
have been subtle rather than overt, yet clear signals that this
person was up to no good. Counterparts in our culture would
be any look that is put on, be it surprise, shock, or suspicion.

Gestures, tone of voice, and even facial expressions are   6:14
calculated methods of deception; behind a facade of sincerity
lurks a perverted mind and spirit of discord. "Discord" or
"dissention" is another familiar word in Proverbs; fifteen of
its eighteen uses in the Bible are in this book (15:18; 16:28;
17:14; 18:19; 21:9, 19; 22:10; 23:29; 25:24; 26:21; 27:15;
28:25; and 29:22).

As other sins eventually are exposed, so this one too will   6:15

be exposed. Two words for "sudden" in Hebrew emphasize the unexpected nature of the punishment liars will receive. Some evangelists use verse 15 to impress on sinners the urgency of making a decision for Christ, saying judgment on the wicked in the form of incurable disease may strike at any time.

6:16   Verses 16–19 are a succinct list of things the LORD hates, "six he hates, seven that are detestable to him" (NIV). This use of one number plus one is not unique to Proverbs.[2] Every combination from one plus one to seven plus one is used, with two large clusters of three plus one used in Amos 1 and 2, and Proverbs 30. Most modern translations set these verses up in such a way that the structure is obvious.

6:17–19   For the most part seven items in this list refer to deceit; and form a nice conclusion to the preceding paragraph. Verse 17 includes three items: haughty eyes, a lying tongue, and hands that murder. "Haughty eyes" links back to verse 13's "eyes that wink," and the "lying tongue" is an echo of verse 12's "corrupt mouth." "Hands that shed innocent blood" might even clarify the movements of fingers in verse 13 which betray the deceit of the liar.

Verse 18 describes two more parts of the body, "the heart that devises wicked schemes" is the same phrase used in verse 14 and the "feet that rush into evil" are like the feet of verse 13.

The sixth and seventh things God hates are not parts of the body, yet key words link them together such as "dissension" in the last half of verse 19 and verse 14. This word has a legal tone in it which suggests court cases. God does not tolerate men who drive wedges between friends, neighbors, and relatives. In religious circles such a person would be called "schismatic."

---

[2]See W. M. W. Roth, "The Numerical Sequence x/x plus 1 in the O.T." *VT,* 12:1962, pp. 300–311. He lists all examples plus some from the apocrypha, the N.T., and many from Sumerian, Akkadian, Babylonian, and Ugaritic literature.

7

Warning Against Adultery Continued

Proverbs 6:20–7:27

The warning from father to son against adultery continues in verse 20. After four verses of introduction verse 24 again introduces the immoral woman. As in 1:8 the son is advised to heed the instruction of both father and mother, in fact 1:8b and 6:20b are exactly the same.

6:20

Verse 21 echoes earlier verses; keep these teachings always in your heart and tie them around your neck.

6:21

Verse 22 is a nice three-part verse which describes the delightful companionship wisdom gives. When you travel it leads you, when you lie down it protects you, and when you wake up it advises you. Travel, of course, means more than physically going from one place to another; its fuller meaning is making your way through life (for comments on wisdom's night vigil see the remarks at 3:24). The verb "advise" or "speak" in this verse is only used once in Proverbs, but in other contexts such as Psalm 77 and Psalm 119 the word implies meditation. Wisdom, like a faithful mate, will constantly be by your side as a friend and a helper (compare 31:12).

6:22

Almost every word of verse 23 is characteristic of Proverbs. The list includes:

6:23

lamp	way
command	life
teaching	correction
light	instruction

In this list only "lamp" is new to our vocabulary; it will appear at least six times more in the book (cf. 4:18 for a comparison of wisdom to light).

6:24   In verse 24 we finally reach the primary teaching of chapter 6; a teaching which will be emphasized to the end of chapter 7. Wisdom is a woman who does not want to lose her man to another woman. The other woman is bad because she is willing to ruin her own marriage as well as any man's she becomes involved with. Wisdom's job is to warn against such a course of destruction in any way that she can.

6:25   The first warning against the adulteress says her beauty and particularly her "captivating eyes" are deceitful. Her love is not sincere. These eyes may attract by flirting (cf. 6:13), or by the artful use of eyeshadow to make them even more beautiful. Remember Jezebel's attempt to impress Jehu with cosmetics (2 Kings 9:30; cf. Jer. 4:30 and Ezek. 23:40).

6:26   The words of verse 26 are difficult to understand because they seem to suggest two different things. First the verse says a prostitute's services are as inexpensive as a loaf of bread, yet next it says adultery is so expensive that it might cost you your life. Is this a contrast between the harlot who is cheap and an adulteress who is expensive? Proverbs can hardly be recommending whoring while condemning adultery! The NIV translation seems to clear up the confusion somewhat; prostitution "reduces one to a loaf of bread," or strips a man of almost all that he has, just as the adulteress "preys upon one's very life" by reducing it to poverty, dishonor, and a shortened life.

6:27–28   Two rhetorical questions in verses 27 and 28 use similar figures of speech to illustrate the unavoidable pain that accompanies sex outside of marriage. The illustrations are quite obvious; if you play with fire you'll get burned. The images of fire and hot coals are probably used because each implies a second meaning; scooping fire into a man's lap illustrates holding another man's wife, and since elsewhere in Scripture "feet" is a euphemism for the male organ (cf. Isa. 6:2; 7:20; Gen. 49:10; Judg. 3:24; 1 Sam. 24:3; 2 Sam. 11:8), walking on the "hot coals" of illicit sex are certain to burn or harm one's manhood.

6:29   Verse 29 is the explicit application of previous illustrations.

Fire which warmed your lap momentarily might also destroy you. Coals which warmed your feet on a cold day might also burn you. Going to bed with your neighbor's wife is dangerous; the temporary satisfaction she provides might soon destroy you with consuming fire.

Verse 30 may be interpreted two ways; both make good sense. The first says some might excuse or tolerate a man who steals to satisfy his hunger yet be intolerant of the man who steals another man's wife to satisfy his lust. You won't perish if you deny yourself sex, therefore no one will tolerate your sinning to get it.   **6:30**

The other interpretation suggests something different which seems to fit in better with what follows. It says people *do* despise a thief regardless of his inner motivation, and if one who steals only food becomes an object of public scorn, how much more will an adulterer be shamed?

The price for stealing, according to verse 31 is repayment, seven times what was stolen. According to Exodus 22:1–8 the required sum was two, four, or five times what was taken, but the terms are even more severe here. It is possible seven may be used merely as a poetic round number for endless repayment.   **6:31**

If the first interpretation of verse 30 is correct, then the point is not public reaction to a crime such as theft or adultery, but the nature of punishment for each crime. Even if a thief must pay back sevenfold, it is less than the adulterer's punishment, who may have to pay back his "theft" with his life.

Verse 32 gives in no uncertain terms the main point of this section. The adulterer destroys himself. Here we see the first of only two uses of this particular term for adultery in Proverbs, although it is used elsewhere in the Bible. The Hebrew word meaning "lacks judgment" also occurs here for the first time, appearing a dozen more times in the book but never again in this same sense.   **6:32**

The offended husband is mentioned in verse 33; eventually he or his relatives exact vengeance on the adulterer by beating him up. Even the community joins in to heap scorn on the man who yielded to seduction. Notice the obvious silence here concerning the fate of the guilty woman; Leviticus 20:10 prescribes death for both.   **6:33**

6:34   Potiphar (Gen. 39) sided with his wife against Joseph even though she was obviously guilty. Perhaps a husband's ego is at stake here; it is easier to charge a man with raping your wife than it is to admit your wife wants someone else instead of you. It is a matter of pride then that causes the wronged husband to protect his wife even as he explodes in vengeful fury against the man who fell prey to her seduction. The double-crossing wife seems to get off the hook without penalty.

6:35   Bribery may work in some situations (17:8) but not in this one. The price the angry husband demands is non-negotiable. He will be satisfied with nothing less than the death of the man who violated his wife.

7:1   Verses 1 to 4 offer a brief interlude from the anti-adultery theme, a kind of introduction similar to the other "my son" passages (1:1–6; 5:1–2; 6:20–23).

7:2   The first phrase, "my commands," of 7:2 is identical to the last phrase of 4:4. Most English translations have the father instructing his son to keep his commands as "the apple of thine eye" (KJV). The Hebrew word for "apple" is diminuative for "man," "mini-man," or "man-kin." If you are close enough to look into someone's eyes, you may see yourself reflected in them. The advice here is for the son to keep his eye so closely fixed on his father's teachings that they are constantly reflected in his eyes. Deuteronomy 32:10 and Psalm 17:8 also use this expression.[1]

7:3   Verse 3 is almost identical to 3:3, except that in 3:3 the son was to tie the father's teachings around his neck while here he is to tie them around his fingers (again compare Deut. 6:8).

7:4   The personification of wisdom in verse 4 is interesting because it anticipates the extended allegory of chapters 8 and 9. In chapter 9 wisdom sets a table and invites her guests to enjoy the rich fare she provides. If "sister" means wife (Gen. 20:2, 12; 26:7; Song of Sol. 4:9, 10, 12; 5:1, 2) perhaps this noble woman of verse 4 is eligible to be wed unlike the immoral adulteress.

[1] Proverbs 7:9 and 20:20 have the Hebrew word in question but not with this meaning.

The happily married man who has a wife who meets all   7:5
his expectations usually has no interest in other women. If he
is married to Dame Wisdom he is protected from the folly of
adultery. Wisdom's words are excellent, right, and true
(8:6–8); the wayward wife speaks only in seductive words.
The Hebrew word for "seductive" here means "smooth" or
"slippery" like the olive oil kisses of 5:3.

From verse 6 to the end of chapter 7 we see an extended   7:6
description almost like a series of slides which show in vivid
color what happens to the "youth who lacks judgment."[2] The
pictures are described by some unidentified person who
watches what happens from a latticed window.

Many who pass by this window are foolish, yet only one   7:7
is particularly vulnerable. Among the young men is one youth
who "lacked judgment," a man already introduced in 6:32.

Whether this young man knows where this harlot lives, or   7:8
just happens to pass her house is unclear, yet it is probable
he is somewhat familiar with what could happen in this part
of town. His presence here and her obvious willingness to
take advantage of that proximity all contribute to the tragedy
that is sure to follow. If you want to avoid the devil, stay
away from his neighborhood. If you suspect you might be
vulnerable to a particular sin, take steps to avoid it.

Verse 9 includes five Hebrew words which mean darkness   7:9
as if to emphasize more than just the day's end. Darkness
itself settles over this scene; the prince of darkness is in control of two hearts that now have lost the light of understanding. We are reminded of two verses from John: "[people] loved
darkness rather than light, because their deeds were evil"
(3:19b); and "[Jesus] said, '. . . Whoever follows me will never
walk in darkness, but will have the light of life' " (8:12).

The woman dressed like a prostitute now approaches the   7:10
foolish young man. What her clothing was, specifically, is not
mentioned, but apparently it was a distinctive outfit (cf. Gen.
38:14–15). Even today the way a woman dresses makes a
statement about her availability.

[2]Note the pictures at the top of the pages in Proverbs in certain editions of the
TEV.

7:11   Verse 11 describes the woman as brazen and defiant, someone who is in the habit of defying the laws of God and man. She has a house, not a home. If she has a husband and children she is not committed to them (cf. v. 19). They mean nothing to her. She is, in today's terms, a streetwalker.

7:12   This kind of woman doesn't stay at home, but frequents public places where potential customers might be found. In today's world she would certainly appear in the lobbies or bars of big city hotels during business conventions. The verb in verse 12 suggests "ambush" or "attack by surprise," a tactic which gives her targets little time for reflection. Her objective now is to snare a young man in her net.

7:13   We have met both characters in this tale now; the foolish young man who is wandering aimlessly through the streets and another wanderer who has a definite plan in mind. The two meet, and before the lad realizes what is happening this voluptuous woman has thrown her arms around him and smothered him with kisses (the same kisses described in 5:3). Now this rather effusive woman, however, "hardens her face" (a literal translation no standard version gives), and with brazen conviction speaks to him.

7:14   Her words are strange; she has made her offerings and fulfilled her vows? A couple of interpretations are possible here; one is that this woman has fresh meat left over from a sacrifice which she will share in a little banquet with this young man. Leviticus 7:11ff., especially verse 15, supports this view, however it's a rather unusual way to invite someone to supper

Another interpretation of this verse is that the woman is ceremonially clean, thus her victim will not become defiled by consorting with her. This view seems weak too since such a high view of the ceremonial law in light of such immorality is grossly incongruous.

Another possible explanation may include a reference to Leviticus 15:19–30 which regulates sexual behavior during menstruation. This woman may, in effect, be saying that her period is over, and that the young man need not worry about having sex with her because she won't get pregnant. Whatever she is saying, however, is calculated to make him accept her offer.

Her sincerity is dubious. It is true she was out looking for someone, but did she really come looking just for this one special fellow? Only a fool — perhaps this one — would believe her. 7:15

Four of the six Hebrew words in verse 16 appear only once in the Bible (one is also in 31:22), so every translation uses some guesswork. The gist, however, is quite clear; the woman has prepared her bed in an exotic and attractive manner. The three spices she used in it (words borrowed from Hebrew although by uncertain routes) were myrrh (in Hebrew *mor*), aloes (*'ahal*), and cinnamon (*kinnamon*). They all smell wonderful, reminding us that making love involves all the senses. In fact, this passage refers to all five senses. The young man *sees* the way she is dressed (v. 10), *hears* her invitation and flattery (vv. 14–15), *feels* her embrace, and *tastes* her lips (v. 13, cf. 5:3). Now she appeals to his sense of smell by using fragrant spices. 7:16–17

If the proposition wasn't explicit before, it is by verse 18. This woman doesn't just want conversation with a dinner partner; she wants sex. That's what drives her out of her home, compels her to make such elaborate preparations, and engages her in this tireless search. "Let's enjoy ourselves with love!" (NIV) she says boldly. 7:18

Throughout the preceding chapters it is unclear whether the temptress is an unmarried prostitute or an unfaithful wife. Just when we are sure she's unmarried (as in vv. 10ff.), we are given reason to believe otherwise. Verse 19 now says specifically this woman has a husband. 7:19

Whether she is or isn't married isn't important though; Scripture teaches all sex outside of marriage is wrong whether it's adultery or fornication. Our little arguments about sex harming only those who engage in it fail in every way to measure up to God's demands for holiness and purity.

Obviously this woman is a two-timing wife who cheats on her husband without any hesitation. In fact, she brings her lovers into the very bed that she has shared with her husband. That husband may be a scoundrel who cheats on her in another city on a business trip, but Scripture condemns marital infidelity regardless of the circumstances. Sex outside of marriage is plainly, simply, sin. (cf. 2:17).

7:20　　The adulteress is quick to assure the young man that he is in no danger from her husband; he has "gone on a long journey" and won't be home "till full moon" (NIV). Most translations either read "new moon" or "full moon" (each are two weeks apart), the point being that the young man needn't fear spending the night with her.

7:21　　He's on the edge now; he has been seduced by her smooth words and is about to be led astray. The story is nearly over; though the lad isn't in her house yet, at this point he is no longer able to resist her invitation.

7:22　　The image of an ox going to slaughter in verse 22 is a graphic statement about the witless character of the man who yields to an adulteress.

7:23　　In addition to being an ox going to slaughter, the young man is likened to a "deer in a noose" or a "bird in a snare," images which focus on the naivete, oblivion, and blindness of each victim. Even if this young man had any conscience about engaging in sin, he certainly seems oblivious to the grave consequences of such action here. The woman may have appeared to be wealthy, respectable, and worthy of attention and courtesy despite her obvious overtures, but this young man should have done what Joseph did with Potiphar's wife; turned on his heel and walked away. But Scripture says, "He did not realize that it will cost him his life."

7:24　　The moral of the story begins with a reference to sons in verse 24, most like 5:7 in its wording. Enough detail has been given already; imagination can fill in the rest. Now the teacher asks for attention. He is about to make his point.

7:25　　The father's advice is simple; don't go near such a woman. If you avoid going near a potentially troublesome situation you reduce the chance of falling into danger.

7:26　　The author now speaks of something more than one woman; he talks now about the effects of all adultery. How many men have been ruined by this temptation to eat stolen bread (9:17)? This sin doesn't just cripple efforts or put one in second place; this sin ultimately results in the death of "a mighty throng."

7:27　　The route of adultery is a short cut to death, whether at the hand of an offended husband, the contraction of veneral disease, or just from the stress of living a double life. Mental, spiritual, and physical health is more likely enjoyed by those who remain faithful to marriage vows in a relationship of faith and mutual trust.

The choice is ultimately between life or death and, as always, the Bible urges us to choose life (Deut. 30:19).

8

In Praise of Wisdom

Proverbs 8

Chapter 8 is different from all others in Proverbs; here wisdom speaks as a person. Not a concerned father admonishing his son, a sage instructing his disciples, but wisdom herself makes her appeal to the world. Almost every verse includes "I," "my," or "me."

Wisdom is feminine. The Hebrew language has only two genders, masculine and feminine, so grammatically speaking there are no "its" in the language. As a rule concepts such as righteousness, wickedness, love, truth, and law are feminine. Wisdom fits into that category and appears as "she" in this chapter.

Wisdom is feminine also as the personification of a woman who is to be loved, honored, and wed. Proverbs includes a number of interesting comparisons between the adulteress, or Lady Folly, and Dame Wisdom. They both stand at the crossroads to persuade men to follow them. They both make promises and give rewards.

Some scholars have offered elaborate explanations about wisdom's personification and cosmic descriptions (especially vv. 22–31), but no theory is conclusive. Certainly it is wrong to suggest wisdom is a member of the godhead, a deity, or even the wife of God. Other religions may have had divine couples or families, but there is no hint of that anywhere in the Old Testament.

Some people have equated wisdom with Jesus Christ, pointing to verse 22ff. for support and comparing it to John 1:1ff., or comparing verse 30 to Hebrews 1:2. I personally think wisdom is just one of God's attributes which is personified here for the sake of illustration. Wisdom cannot be separated from God because it is a part of him. In such a way righteousness, holiness, justice, and love (for the last cf. 1 Corinthians 13) might be personified.

All of chapter 8 is a praise song of wisdom to tell us again and again how important she is and where to find her.

8:1   "My son" does not mark this new chapter or any paragraphs in it. The change of subject matter makes this a new
pericope, verse 1 like 1:20 has wisdom calling out to us. She
makes not a thin, secretive suggestion but a bold, firm an-
nouncement. Sometimes wisdom is hard to find (2:4), but
here she is hard to miss. We don't really have to search hard
for one whose presence is so obvious (Rom. 10:8).

8:2–3   Wisdom stations herself in public places such as hilltops,
intersections, and city gates. In that sense she is like the harlot
(7:12), but their objectives are miles apart. The harlot goes
to public places to meet men in order to destroy them. In
contrast to wisdom's "raised voice," the evil woman slinks
about waiting to ambush her victim and whisper flattery and
vain promises in his ear.

Roads and paths appear again in verses 2 and 3, "way"
meaning more than places people walk. More often than not
the word means way of life, course of action, or series of
actions (cf. e.g. Ps. 119:105). Crossroads represent places of
decision where you can take a new direction, follow another
signpost, or even get confused or lost. This is where wisdom
is needed most so here is where she takes her stand.

8:4   Wisdom's appeal is universal, a raised voice to all mankind. No one can live without her, and happily she offers
herself to all without reservation. In verse 4 wisdom begins
to speak. Her speech will continue to the end of the chapter.

8:5   Verse 5 is a well-balanced verse; the verb in both halves is
the same and in each segment are words for fool and words
for wisdom. Three of these four terms are used often, but the
term for wisdom, "prudence," in the first half is unusual. It
appears only in 1:4 and 8:12 (and Exod. 21:14 and Josh. 9:4).
Its limited use here seems to deal with applied wisdom; its
abuse taking the form of deceit, craft, or guile. Here the term
is positive as it is in its verb form (Prov. 15:5; 19:25).

8:6   Wisdom says her words are excellent and right. The first
adjective, "worthy," as a noun means some kind of leader.
The word is related to a preposition meaning "before" or "in
front of," so the leader is one who stands before his people.
Wisdom may be saying here that her words are right in front

of you, meaning they have no double or hidden meanings. The other adjective of this verse, "right," has the primary meaning of "straight" or "flat." Again wisdom denies any duplicity or devious words; how different from the promises of Satan and his servants!

A somewhat unusual word for mouth is used in verse 7, the same one as 5:3 which spoke of the oil-smooth kisses of the strange woman. Wisdom's mouth is not like that; what she speaks is true. Lies are hateful to her. **8:7**

Verse 8 emphasizes what wisdom has just said in 6 and 7 by saying it still another way. What she says is trustworthy; she will not lead anyone astray. You can trust her to put you on the right path. During World War II the towns on the east side of England prepared themselves for invasion by arranging that the citizens should turn all the road signs in the wrong direction to confuse the enemy. Wisdom would never do that to you. **8:8**

Some things seem terribly difficult to learn, yet these very things are simple to those who do know them. The Chinese language may seem impossible for us to learn, yet children of China learn it with ease. So it is with wisdom. Wise people do the right thing by nature, but those who are not wise view her path as strange and difficult. First Corinthians 1:18–25 is a commentary on this truth as it relates to understanding the Gospel. **8:9**

Wisdom's introductory statement ends with verse 10. She compares what she has to give with silver and gold and urges us to pass up worldly wealth in favor of that which cannot be bought. Two other verses make the same point (3:14 and 8:19), but Psalm 19:10 even more vividly links God's Word with the price of gold. **8:10**

Gold, silver, and wisdom are alike in so many ways; all are rare, not manmade, precious, beautiful, and functional. They are not easily gotten. They retain their value and are recognized worldwide. They cannot be destroyed. Yet wisdom urges us to choose her instruction and knowledge above any silver or gold.

The use of "rubies," another valuable jewel, links verse 11 with 10. When you think of all the hard work, long hours, and years of intrigue, risk, and even crime people engage in to acquire wealth, you begin to realize the price-tag wisdom puts on herself in these verses. **8:11**

8:12   Verse 12 brings us to the heart of the chapter. Wisdom speaks boldly, in the first person singular. Notice how many times she begins verses with "I." Four words for wisdom dominate this verse: "wisdom," "prudence," "knowledge," and "discretion." Not since the first six verses of Proverbs has there been such a list of terms.

8:13   Often positive and negative ideas are juxtaposed in Proverbs; things about good and bad people are placed in adjoining verses (e.g. vv. 6–7). In verse 13 wisdom offers a series of alternatives to what is right and true. The point about fearing the Lord and thus learning wisdom has already been made (1:7), so now we are told what wisdom is not. Yet the verb is stronger here than "is not"; wisdom actually *hates* evil, pride, and falsehood.

8:14   Both lines of verse 14 say essentially the same thing; wisdom not only knows what to do but has the resources to execute those plans. Knowing *what* to do is often not the problem for most of us. It is *doing* what is right that trips us up. We so often find ourselves in the same dilemma as Paul (Rom. 7:15–20). Wisdom assures us here, as God's surrogate, that he always has the power to help us accomplish his will for us and live a consecrated life. He gives both understanding as well as power.

8:15–16   Verses such as 15 and 16 which refer to kings and government support the view that much of Proverbs emanated from the Solomonic court. Although many proverbs deal with the laboring class, more of them are reflections on the wealth and power of the upper class. Urban life as opposed to rural life seems better represented too, especially in these early chapters.[1] Verses 15 and 16 give four terms for leaders: "kings," "rulers," "princes," and "nobles," the point being those who rule well do so because they are wise. Political acumen and international statesmanship depend on wisdom. Blessed are the people whose rulers are wise.

8:17   Jesus may have been quoting verse 17 in John 14:21. While God or wisdom loves those who love him, God loved us while we were yet enemies. Romans 5:11 puts it succinctly: "We

---

[1]Some Hebrew manuscripts read here "earth" (*'eretz*) while others read "righteous" (*tzedek*).

also rejoice in God through our Lord Jesus Christ, through whom we have now received reconciliation" (NIV).

The last half of this verse sounds as if it contradicts opening verses of this chapter. We were told there wisdom sought out every man; now men must seek her out. Still, it is amazing how some people fail to see what is so very obvious. Wisdom must be actively sought after; she is not hard to find but she can be missed if you constantly avoid her.

Verses 10–11 compared wisdom and wealth; now wisdom 8:18–19
tells us that when we find her we will also have riches, honor, prosperity, success, gold, and silver. The word for prosperity is another one typical of Proverbs; eighteen of twenty-six occurrences in the Old Testament are in this book. In this verse prosperity is more than wealth. It is ongoing or enduring wealth, something like an endowment or a self-regenerating reservoir of wealth that you can draw from.

Verse 20 is rather general with the familiar lesson that if 8:20
you are going to accompany wisdom you will have to walk where she walks in paths of righteousness and justice.

Verse 21 is an echo of 18 and 19, "those who love me" is 8:21
also found in verse 17. In verse 21 we must remember that Proverbs reflects Old Testament economy while speaking in generalizations. The Old Testament measured success by accumulated wealth such as herds, crops, clothing, or children. The generalization is that wise people are rich and fools are poor. Remember here the author does not bring up exceptions or examples which disprove his general rule. But don't necessarily think you are an exception to the rule either; if you aren't rich, maybe you're not wise either.

The section on wisdom's rewards ends, and a new theme 8:22–23
about wisdom's role in creation begins with verses 22 and 23.

In this section wisdom impresses us with her great antiquity. It is strange to think of God creating his own attributes, so we must take care not to interpret this highly poetic material too literally. What we learn here is that wisdom is eternal; God needed her to help him in the creation of the world, so he created her first. As in Genesis 1 the question is not how, why, where, or when (in terms of years) she came into being, but who made her. The answer is "the LORD."

The term "beginning" in verse 22 is the same one used in the opening verse of the Bible. The verb "installed" in verse 23 is an unusual use of a common verb; Psalm 2:6 is the only other parallel to it. The point is God put wisdom in her honored place long before anything else came into being.

8:24–26   Genesis 1 says before dry land appeared the globe was covered with water. Wisdom says her birth preceded even the water. Note the order of elements in these verses which parallels the creation account:

World (v. 23) and day one (Gen. 1:1–5)

Water (v. 24) and day two (Gen. 1:6–8)

Land (vv. 25–26) and day three (Gen. 1:9–13)

8:27–29   Wisdom's birth prior to oceans is repeated in verses 27–29. The term "deep" appears more than once here and is the same one Moses used in Genesis 1:2, 7:11, and 8:2. The structure of this passage seems to be chiastic; the ideas of verses 22–24 are repeated here in reverse order (earth, 23; oceans, 24; hills, 25–26; oceans, 27–29a; and earth, 29b.

8:30   The most important word in verse 30 is unfortunately unclear. Did wisdom aid God as a "craftsman" or "little child"? Considerable ink has been spilled on this question because the root word is so well known. The same letters in Hebrew spell several words which have little etymological relationship. I prefer to read the word as an adverb: "I was *faithfully* by his side."

Wisdom was present at creation then, but the other point of this verse is that the relationship between God and wisdom was a harmonious one, a poetic way of saying God was wise when he made the world.

8:31   The climax of creation was the sixth day when God created Adam and Eve; it is the climax of this pericope as well. The Garden of Eden was a place filled with happiness; subsequent events introduced discord, folly, and sin. The same words for happiness found in verse 30 are in this verse as well.

8:32   "Mankind," more literally "sons of Adam," were the closing words of verse 31. "Sons" also introduces verse 32, the point being that if people for whom the world was made would only embrace wisdom, they could return to primeval happiness with her. Verse 32 begins the conclusion to the chapter and says essentially what its opening verses said, "Listen."

Verse 33 includes three imperatives: "listen" (also in 32), "be wise" (scattered all through the book), and "do not neglect." The last verb is less common but was used in 4:15. We are told in no uncertain terms to heed the counsel of wisdom.

8:33

Verse 34 is fascinating because of how it incorporates ideas from preceding verses and works them into pictures. Key words here are "happy" or "blessed" (vv. 30, 31, 32), "listen" (vv. 32, 33), and "every day" (v. 30). One picture is of a young man sitting at the feet of wisdom, listening to her advice. He comes to the door of her house, sits on the steps, and listens to her talk about life and God.

8:34

One word for "door" in this verse is "doorposts" which reminds us of the command in Deuteronomy 6:9: "Write them (the commands of God) on the doorposts of your houses and on your gates." Some Christians hang Biblical slogans, Christian greetings, or even symbols of a fish on their doors. This may not be exactly what Deuteronomy or Proverbs had in mind, but at least it reminds us whose we are and why we're here.

The long life theme is repeated in verse 35 (see comments on 3:22 for more verses on this theme), and the idea of God's favor or pleasure occurs here for the first time (see also 11:1, 20, 27; 12:2, 22; 15:8; 18:22).

8:35

The Gospel of John echoes the point of this verse that life belongs to those who belong to God (3:15, 16, 36; 4:14, 36; 5:24, 40; 6:40; 47, 54; 8:12; 10:28; 12:25, 50; 17:2, 3; 20:31).

Either a man loves wisdom and life or avoids her and dies; the choice is simple. Chapter 8 ends with the grand theme of choosing between two ways: the way of life or the way of death; the way of piety or the way of sin.

8:36

9

The Two Choices:
Wisdom or Folly

Proverbs 9

Chapter 9 offers a kind of transition between the lofty heights of chapter 8 and the workaday world of chapters 10ff. It also eases the reader away from solid blocks of teaching in earlier chapters to the pithy and isolated proverbs of chapters 10–29. Wisdom still is personified here, but her role is reduced somewhat.

Students of Proverbs have struggled with "seven" in verse 1 in an effort to find some hidden meaning or outline to the chapters that follow, even suggesting it is an allusion to another ancient work on that theme.[1] I think seven is a number of perfection, meaning wisdom's house is both sturdy and complete (cf. Matt. 7:24–25).

9:1

Since wisdom has a house and a substantial one at that, we now read about the banquet she is planning. Her menu reflects the opulence of the house: meat, wine, and all the accompanying dishes. The whole illustration is very much like Jesus' parable of the feast in Matthew 22:1ff. and Luke 14:16ff.

9:2

Wisdom issues her invitation and sends out her servants to spread the news. They station themselves like their mis-

9:3

[1]See e.g. Patrick W. Skehan, "Wisdom's House" in *Catholic Biblical Quarterly,* 29 (1967) pp. 162–180 which appears revised and reprinted in *Studies in Israelite Poetry and Wisdom,* Washington, Catholic Biblical Association, 1971, pp. 27–45. It is a rather fantastic scheme to show the whole Book of Proverbs in 45 columns in three groups. The center group e.g. is 15 columns of 25 lines each. Thus all this is connected to the cubits in Solomon's temple!

tress in public places where they can call out to the largest number of people; a kind of Old Testament *kerygma* proclamation, or evangelistic appeal.

9:4–5   The message is for both the foolish and ignorant which includes most of the population. The message is simple; "Come and eat and drink." It includes no prerequisites, dress requirements, entrance fees, or R.S.V.P.'s. It is like the New Testament banquet; all who are hungry and thirsty may come.

Proverbs, too, is a book available to all. It is not meant just for one particular stratum of society; all who are needy are urged to partake of its rich fare.

9:6   Verse 6 once more urges us to "leave the simple ways" to follow wisdom. Other fools might discourage a man from taking this path of wisdom so it often takes courage to come to the LORD. The choice is worth it, however; with it comes the promise of life.

9:7   Verse 7 introduces the theme that it is futile to correct a fool but a wise man will appreciate suggestions. The advice is for those who correct or rebuke as much as for those that need correction.

It also stresses the danger of reprimanding evil people. Some automobile drivers, for instance, will retaliate if you just blow your horn when they commit a traffic offense. Is it worth the risk to try to correct such people?

The other question this verse prompts is how do we take rebuke? Are we willing to take suggestions? Do we retaliate or become defensive when someone reprimands us?

9:8   If you want to be hated by a violent person, just tell him he is violent. Wise men, on the other hand, appreciate criticism. Hebrews 12:7–11 echoes this point. Those that accept discipline will later be grateful for it.

9:9   Verse 7 dealt with evil men, verse 8 with both bad and good, and verse 9 with just the wise man. We now have three lines about bad people and three lines about good ones.

As people become older they tend to settle into the direction they went in youth. Ill-behaved children often end up as criminals while disciplined children become self-disciplined adults. Thus, says Proverbs, get in the habit of accepting criticism. It will make you gracious and wise now and forever (Rev. 22:11).

Verses 10–12 are typical wisdom injunctions. Verse 10 re-   9:10–11
peats the book's motto (cf 1:7 and Ps. 111:10), and "Holy
One" is a title for God that Isaiah loved to use (more than
thirty times in fact). It is found in Proverbs only here and
30:3.

Verse 12 is best understood by means of paraphrase since   9:12
the traditional translation is enigmatic. It is difficult to convey
the cryptic nature of the Hebrew idiom, but in simple terms
it is good for you to be wise and harmful to you to be wicked.[2]

The Hebrew idiom of verse 13 is unclear also; we recognize   9:13
words but inflecting them or putting them into a sentence is
difficult. Still this verse does fit in well with what follows. In
the paragraph we have the picture of Lady Folly who is not
necessarily the adulteress of chapters 5–7, yet provides marked
similarities especially in verses 17–18.

Lady Folly summons followers from the busy markets and   9:14
streets below her hill. She also sits at the door of her house
like wisdom (v. 1) and calls out to those passing by to dine
with her.

We see a picture of busy people going about their daily   9:15
chores. All are active except for this woman who sits on her
stoop trying to detain those who have other places to go.

[2]Both the Greek and Syriac versions have lengthy additions at this point and at
the end of the chapter. Here is how the first reads from George M. Lamsa, *Holy Bible
From Ancient Eastern Manuscripts* (Philadelphia: Holman, 1933):

> He who denies things falsely feeds on winds
>   and pursues fowl of the air;
> For he has forsaken the way to his vineyard
>   and the paths of his labor,
>   to journey in the wilderness without water;
> In the places that are trodden he travels thirsty
>   and gains nothing.

The second addition reads like this:

> Now rise up,
>   and do not abide in that place;
> Do not cast your eye at her;
> Thus pass by the waters of strangers;
>   cross over a strange river,
>   and turn away from the waters of strangers;
> You shall not drink of the waters of strangers.
>   For in doing so a multitude of days and years of life
>   shall be added to you.

While wisdom's audience seemed to consist mainly of fools, folly's audience consists mostly of those who seem to be doing worthwhile things.

9:16   Verse 16 is identical to verse 4 with folly offering the same invitation as wisdom's. She beckons the simple, "those who lack judgment," to come in. Her prospective clients are the same ones that wisdom appealed to.

9:17   Lady Folly says something in verse 17 that sounds like a bit of folk wisdom; something that has been passed along many times before. We will see many more of these starting in the next chapter.

Everyone can relate to the truth of her simple words; we may have eaten some delicacy forbidden by our deity (a literal translation of the verse), or we may have indulged privately in some sin which we wouldn't have done in public. She forgot, and so do we, that there is no escaping the eye of God.

Most people think folly's words are just one more reference to illicit sex. That may well be, especially in light of the disaster described in the next verse.

9:18   Lady Folly's house is not a home but a mausoleum. If you enter it you will not leave it alive. Choosing the way of folly is a one-way street away from good things wisdom might have given you. Why become a ghost (the literal meaning of the Hebrew) when you can have life?

PART TWO

The Proverbs of Solomon

Proverbs 10:1–22:16

10

Contrasting Proverbs
Proverbs 10:1–15:33

In some respects the Book of Proverbs begins with chapter 10. Some think the title, "Proverbs of Solomon," was moved forward when chapters 1–9 were added to the book by ancient scribes such as the men of Hezekiah (25:1). Whether the first nine chapters should come before or after the next section matters little; the New Testament quotes from both early and late chapters with the same authority.

With chapter 10 comes the listing of a series of 375 isolated maxims which better fit our traditional definition of proverbs. We will not return to the kind of extended poems, pictures, and pleas of earlier chapters. No break comes until 22:17 where there is another introduction type verse.

The first proverb in chapter 10 sounds like something we read before. Chapter 1:8 spoke of honoring the teaching of parents as does this one. What you do affects your parents, making them happy or sad. Do not assume from the verse that mothers aren't proud of wise children and fathers don't grieve over foolish ones. Of course they do. This is poetry with beautiful parallel lines not meant to be read separately. Note the similarities with 15:20 and 17:25.

10:1

Antithetic parallels characterize these chapters, meaning there is usually a "but" between two halves of a verse, or lacking that, a clear opposite in the second line of the verse. Verse 2 is a typical antithetic parallel.

10:2

For a time wealth gained by dishonest means may be satisfying, but in the long run it will be your undoing. Proverbs (the whole Old Testament for that matter) rarely speaks of the final judgment, rather it speaks in terms of judgment

before death or the punishment of premature death (21:6).
Most people who are rich admit happiness doesn't necessarily
come from an abundance of things. Rather it is honest living
that brings satisfaction and lets you sleep at night. A clear
conscience cannot be bought with money.

10:3   Verse 3 reminds us that Proverbs speaks in generalizations. As a general rule good people do not starve and wicked
people do not get what they want (see also Ps. 34:9–10 and
37:25). Good people work hard, do not waste money on alcohol, or gamble their possessions away. They are prudent
with their money, not investing it unwisely or buying things
with inflated prices. The wicked, on the other hand, want
happiness too. What they do not realize is that it doesn't come
from stealing property or taking another man's wife.

10:4   The word "poor" in verse 4 is another word which occurs
many times in Proverbs; 16 of 24 usages in the Bible are in
this book. The generalization here is that the industrious,
conscientious worker is eventually recognized by his superior
and promoted, while the man who constantly watches the
clock and puts forth as little effort as possible will stay in the
same job slot forever, if he manages to keep his job. Not only
physical work is implied here; studying, investing, talking, or
writing are all work which must be wisely and conscientiously
done in order to bring rewards.

10:5   A sense of timing in agriculture is a fine art. The wise
farmer studies his crop, weather, and calendar in order to
determine the best time for harvesting, while a foolish man
lets prime time pass. Sleep is so important to him that he
pays the price of a lost harvest. This principle applies not
only to farming but to the utilization of opportunities when
they arise; one must stay alert for precisely the best time to
speak or act.

10:6   Verse 6 is not an antithetic parallel; it is rather a synthetic
parallel. The wicked man is contrasted with the good in this
verse, but verbs and objects are not parallel with each other.
The first half of this verse reminds us of 2, 4, and 7, while
the second half matches the second half of verse 11. The
meaning of "blessings crown the head with righteousness" is
fairly obvious; the second half of this verse is more subtle. It
speaks of hypocrisy and deceit, explained in a NIV footnote
as "the mouth of the wicked conceals violence." You simply

can't trust what a wicked man says. Like the seductive woman his promises are lies. He says what is advantageous to him with no concern about its truth.

The verb "rot" is graphic in verse 7, but the best translation of a Hebrew word which describes the destiny of the wicked. Words like "wicked," "righteous," and "bless" link this verse with the preceding one.   **10:7**

The verse makes reference to the idea still present in Judaism that people live after death in the memories of the living. Unfortunately we remember both the wicked and righteous, but in God's memory the righteous occupy a special place.

Sensible people do more than accept good advice, verse 8 says. In addition to receiving suggestions they submit to authority, acknowledging the necessity of rules. The Hebrew word for commands hints at the ancillary laws of the Pentateuch, suggesting that sensible people are also well-behaved people.   **10:8**

The idiom "comes to ruin" in the second half of the proverb is rare, appearing only once more in Hosea 4:14 where the context is similar. The two lines of verse 8 are not exact antithetic parallels.

The security of the righteous in verse 9 is a seondary theme in Proverbs. We noticed it first in 3:23 and will see it later in 18:10 and 28:18. Perhaps the most extensive treatment of this theme is in Isaiah 33:15–16.   **10:9**

The use of "caught" or "found out" in some modern translations versus the "known" of the KJV is helpful here. That is exactly what verse 9 means. Elsewhere Scripture makes it clear that the wicked cannot hide forever; sooner or later all their deeds will come to light (1 Tim. 5:25).

"Winking" in the first part of verse 10 reminds us of 6:13–14, but this verse is not too different from the one preceding it. The idea of not telling the truth links them together.   **10:10**

In Hebrew the second half of this verse is identical to the second half of verse 8, possibly a scribal error caused by the close similarities of the last words in the first half of each verse (technically known as dittography caused by homoeoteleuton). The Greek version of this passage (made from the Hebrew 200 or so years before Christ) had as its second line "but he who bodily reproves makes peace" (RSV). That certainly makes better sense in this context.

Sometimes it takes courage to tell the truth. It may cost you friendship, money, or even personal safety to warn others of wrongdoing, but in God's sight you are named a peacemaker who Jesus said was blessed.

10:11   The second half of verse 11 is identical to 6b, but it fits better here.

The metaphor of the fountain of life reminds us of Jesus and the woman at the well (John 4:10ff.); "The water that I shall give him will become in him a spring of water welling up to eternal life" (v. 14; cf. John 7:38). Luke 6:45 also offers commentary on the same principle; "For the mouth speaks what the heart is full of" (TEV).

10:12   The first line of verse 12 hardly needs comment. We all know people who carry a chip on their shoulder or are thin-skinned because where hatred and distrust dominate, so also exists a constant fear of confrontation, conflict, and war.

The second line was apparently a favorite; both James (5:20) and Peter (1 Peter 4:8) quote it. The love chapter of 1 Corinthians 13 is also an extensive treatment on "love which covers all wrongs" (NIV).

The word "hide" or "overwhelms" of verse 11 is the same as the word for "overlook" or "covers" in this verse; perhaps the reason why these verses appear together. The wicked and righteous both hide or overlook sin but for different reasons. The wicked man hides his own sin; that's deceit. The righteous man overlooks another's sin; that's forgiveness. The most deceitful are often least forgiving while the most forgiving are least deceitful. The diligence you exhibit in exposing the shortcomings of others may be a barometer of your own faults.

10:13   Verse 13 is the first use of the theme of corporal punishment (others are 13:24, 18:6, 19:29, 22:15, 23:13–14, 26:3, and 29:15) known as the "rod" or "stripes" passages (on the theme of child discipline see comments on 13:24).

In general Mosaic legislation included fines and ostracism as forms of punishment, although death by stoning was also used as the extreme penalty. Perhaps the Hebrews' high view of life and prohibition of body mutilation tilted punishment in that direction; Philistines and Babylonians plucked out eyes

(Judg. 16:21; 2 Kings 25:7) and displayed dead bodies (1 Sam. 31:9–10). Canaanites cut off thumbs and toes (Judg. 1:7), and Ammonites ripped open the bellies of pregnant women (Amos 1:13). In contrast, Israel was taught to respect the human body, even the dead bodies of her enemies (Josh. 10:26–27; 2 Sam. 18:17).

Corporal punishment such as beating or spanking was practical as well as recommended. This form of punishment did not leave scars or cause mutilation. Unfortunately today we see a decided swing away from this advice on correction with regard to children in the home as well as hardened criminals.

The first line of verse 14 is a good proof text to quote for the furthering of education. Wise people know books help them to live and since life is limited, the wise man needs even more knowledge to help him choose the way that is best.

The second half of this verse introduces a word which again is frequent only in the Book of Proverbs. This kind of "ruin" or "destruction" is mentioned seven times in Proverbs (the next in the next verse) and four times elsewhere.

The proverb in verse 15 describes what *is* rather than what *should* be. A number of proverbs are like this, hardly to be taken as advice. Rather they are reports on the regrettable state of things as they are. Today's idiom for this verse is "the rich get richer, and the poor get poorer" or even "them that has gets." Proverbs 22:7 says it even more succinctly: "The rich rule over the poor" (NIV).

Verse 16 is a variation on the principle that people reap what they sow. Good people live longer as well as better with abundant life rather than mere existence. Sinners, however, only reap punishment; what a beggarly crop from all their efforts!

The theme of taking advice in verse 17 repeats what is said in 9:10–12; listening to correction will help you. Rejection of criticism will undo you. Reproof may be humiliating, ego-crushing, and hard to act on, but those who accept it will be able to "show the way of life" (NIV).

Resistance to correction in childhood results in an indomitable case of pride and arrogance in adulthood. Count critics as friends and remember what it says later in this book: "A friend means well, even when he hurts you. But when an

10:14

10:15

10:16

10:17

enemy puts his arm around your shoulder — watch out!" (27:6 in the TEV).

10:18   Neither person in verse 18 is commendable; the first one "who conceals hatred" is a liar and the second one "who spreads slander" is a fool. Little connection between these halves seems to exist except possibly to show both exhibit hateful feelings in wrong ways.

Note the first half of the verse does not recommend that hate *should* be demonstrated, especially by someone who has a problem with deceit. Both hatred and deceit are wrong; both should be avoided.

The anti-gossip theme appears a half-dozen times in Proverbs (16:28; 18:8; 20:19; 26:20, 22) though not always with the same Hebrew word. The only other time "slander" appears in Proverbs is 25:10. Gossip or slander might be defined as saying something about your neighbor he wouldn't say about himself. What you say may be true, but saying it might be unnecessary as well as cruel.

10:19   Verses 18 through 21 are loosely connected by the theme of right talk. While verse 18 cautions against deceit and gossip, this verse warns against verbosity and commends restraint. We all know people who are guilty of "many words" and can remember times we said things we shouldn't have said. James 3 is a lengthy treatise on the dangers of a loose tongue. If we can learn how to control it we will also learn how to control our lives.

10:20   Verse 20 is a fine example of a contrasting pair of lines. "Choice silver" and "valueless" are opposites as are "righteous" and "wicked." Synonyms in the pair are "words" (more literally "tongue") and "ideas" (literally "heart"). The good man's words are like silver; scarce, beautiful, and valuable.

10:21   The last of four verses on right talk offers another contrast; wise words of a good man benefit many people, but stupid words lead many to death. Think, for example, of the preaching of the Gospel. They may be called the words of good men "par excellence." Through them many find life. The contrasting parallel to believing the gospel is trusting in lies. The first lie recorded in the Bible is the one the serpent made to Eve. Because she believed what he said all her heirs would die.

10:22   The meaning of the first half of verse 22 is clear but the second half is a bit ambiguous. The Hebrew word in question can be translated "hard work" or "trouble" and can be either the subject or the object of the verb; the syntax does not clarify which. The traditional rendering has a ring of determinism implying that if God makes you wealthy no more efforts on your part can add to that wealth. Another translation of the second line which says "the LORD doesn't add sorrow to your wealth" implies God's gifts include happiness as well as wealth.

The verse is hard to explain because it seems to contradict so much of Proverbs that says wealth is the result of honesty, hard work, and wise investment. The best way to reconcile these differences might be to say the verse speaks about the man who is already wise and good. This man receives riches from God because God has ruled that wealth belongs to wise and good men.

Another explanation takes into account our sinful condition before God. At best we all deserve his wrath, certainly not wealth or blessing. Any good things we do receive from him are only because of his mercy.

The fool who "finds pleasure in evil conduct" is engaged **10:23** in the kind of immorality mentioned many times in Ezekiel as lewd behavior on the part of virgin Israel (chapters 16 and 23). Words like disgusting, obscene, and immoral apply here; the dozen other places where the word appears in the Old Testament are in contexts of sexual abuse. Judges 20:6 is the most striking illustration; illicit sex and perversion are pleasures of the fool. He keeps the pornography business going today and encourages programs of violence and sex on television and movie screens.

The good man delights in seemingly dull things by contrast, but that's because our definition of wisdom is too narrow. Wisdom means anything that edifies, is wholesome, or in Paul's words "things that are good and that deserve praise: things that are true, noble, right, pure, lovely, and honorable" (Phil. 4:8, TEV).

Job must have thought his friends were right and that he **10:24** was wrong because he confessed in 3:25 that everything he feared and dreaded came to him. We know Job was the grand exception to the rule. The rule is stated succinctly in verse 24. The righteous get what they want, but the wicked get everything they dread. Freedom from fear is such a great blessing; we simply don't appreciate it until it is taken away.

10:25   The second use of "storm" in Proverbs occurs here (cf. 1:27), apparently one which comes with suddenness and severity ("whirlwind" in the old translation). This reminds us of other verses which stress the sudden calamity that will strike the wicked (6:15; 24:22; 29:1). The contrast to this uncertain future is the enduring security of the righteous.

10:26   The three-part proverb of verse 26 is similar to the numerical proverbs of chapter 30. Two of three things are known while the third thing is stressed in the proverb. Smoke bothers the eyes, vinegar hurts the teeth, and a lazy employee is a pain to his employer. As you avoid the first two so should you be wary of the third.

10:27   Verse 27 is a straightforward contrast between two familiar themes: longevity which God grants to those who fear him, and the uncertain and brief life span of the wicked. This is another "fear of the LORD" passage; others are 1:7, 8:13, 9:10, 14:26–27, 15:33, 19:23, and 22:4.

10:28   Verse 28 is a simple contrast between the righteous and the wicked. The good man hopes for and finds joy while the wicked man's hopes for anything come to nothing (see also 11:7).

10:29   The Hebrew includes a mixed metaphor in verse 29; the "way" of the Lord is also a "stronghold." The meaning is clear, however; those who walk God's way follow a road that leads to safety. The wicked, by contrast, pursue a course that will bring them to destruction.

10:30   The future of a righteous man is secure, says verse 30, while wicked men "will not remain in the land" (NIV). As in 2:22, God will not tolerate evildoers forever; eventually he will uproot them and cast them out of the land of the living.

10:31   The two halves of verse 31 are not truly antithetical. "Lips of the righteous" and "mouth of the wicked" are opposite enough, but the verbs are not parallel unless the verse means righteous men will continue to speak wisdom while wicked ones will be stopped.

10:32   Verse 32 is the last verse in this series about right talk and the destiny of good and bad people. Good men generally use few words (vv. 19 and 20) which are appropriate as well as pleasing. Evil men, by contrast, talk too much; their speech which is basically worthless or deceitful often hurts others. So if you don't want to be hurt, don't listen to an evil man, and if you find yourself hurting others by what you say perhaps you should ask yourself if what you say reflects folly or wisdom.

Why chapter 11 begins here no one really knows; most of the verses in chapters 10–29 are disconnected with no clear break until after 29. On the other hand each chapter contains roughly the same number of verses, so whoever divided them into chapters used some kind of order. 11:1

Verse 1 begins the first of four passages in Proverbs which use weights and measures to speak about how the Lord demands honesty in commerce (cf. 16:11 and 20:10, 23). The teaching reflects the legislation of Leviticus 19:35–36 in poetic rather than legal terms. Apparently cheating in buying and selling is as old as the marketplace itself.

"Why not?" a seller might say. "If I buy with a heavy weight and sell with a light one I'll make more profit on every deal." Amos (8:5) denounced the merchants of Samaria for making the ephah (volume measure) small and the shekel (customer's cost) large. Each merchant had stone weights which supposedly matched some national standard, yet many had more than one set of stones; marked the same but with different weights. God hated such deception.

Today we have butchers with thumbs on scales or elaborate packaging techniques that deceive; both are as dishonest as the differing stone weights of ancient Israel.

Two items in verse 2 are noteworthy. The first four words in Hebrew might be translated woodenly as "pride comes, calamity follows," but actually the verbs are the same. A modern counterpart of this proverb might be, "easy come, easy go," or "work hard, play hard." If you want to avoid disgrace don't become proud. 11:2

The second half of this verse includes a word for modest which is only found here and Micah 6:8 ". . . walk humbly with your God. . . ." We are given a kind of equation here; modesty equals wisdom.

The Hebrew noun which translates as "dishonesty" or "duplicity" in verse 3 appears only here and 15:4. As a verb it appears four times in Proverbs (13:6; 19:3; 21:12; 22:12) and three times elsewhere in the Old Testament. This verse 11:3

says both honesty and dishonesty are rewarded, implying some dynamism in the natural order that destroys injustice and honors integrity.

This verse also teaches that if you are good, sooner or later you will be treated the same way. Conversely, if you are dishonest you will be cheated by others. Mutual trust is a wonderful thing but mutual distrust is awful.

11:4 Verse 4 is much like 10:2; in fact the last halves are identical. What Solomon believed about afterlife is not known, but it is unlikely he is thinking here in terms of eternal life. Rather he is saying what he has said before; the bad die young while the good are rewarded with long life.

Tension is building in the book. On the one hand wealth is the reward for hard, honest work, but on the other hand, wealth will do one little good at death. This same tension is also causing division between generosity and frugality, thrift and prodigality, and giving and saving.

Verse 4 reminds me of a rabbinic proverb which says "shrouds have no pockets."

11:5 Again and again the truth of verse 5 is stated, each time in a slightly different way. All the verses which make this point use basically the same vocabulary words such as honesty, righteous, wicked, or destroy. Sometimes these words are used as nouns, sometimes verbs, and sometimes adjectives. In one verse, for instance, we read of the good man's honesty, while in another we see the honest man's goodness.

The idiom of "straightening" or "leveling out the road" is a very apt picture in verse 5, especially when you think of how rocky and hilly Palestine is.

11:6 Verse 6 is like verse 3; both tell us eventually righteousness pays off. Their point is much like that of our saying, "honesty is the best policy." The rabbis said it still another way: "if you always tell the truth you don't have to remember what you said." Dishonesty will eventually expose itself.

11:7 Verse 4a and verse 7 are alike also, although verse 4 is an antithetic parallel while 7 is a synonymous one. The pairs include "hope" and "confidence," "wicked" and "riches," (or "power") and "dies" and "comes to nothing." The word for "confidence" or "expectation" is not too common, appearing only three times in Proverbs (10:28; 11:7; 13:12) and three times elsewhere in the Bible.

We might be tempted to read theology into this verse making it say our hope to regenerate a sinner dies at his death, but the verse really means the wicked man's hope for long life perishes in death.

Older translations of verse 8 which read "the wicked cometh in his stead" (KJV) in the second line didn't make much sense; fortunately more modern versions clear up any misunderstanding. The NIV, for instance, reads "The righteous man is rescued from trouble, and it comes on the wicked instead." The point is the obvious one of verses 3, 5, and 7; being good is good for you while being bad is bad for you. 11:8

Although most words in verse 9 are similar to those in preceding verses, another theme, right talk, is introduced now. What we say can destroy or restore. Chapter 10 said a lot about the use of the tongue (verses 6, 8, 11, 19, 20, 21, 31, 32); verse 9 is not specifically as much as generally like them. Idle chatter, a foul mouth, glib remarks, and ill-founded gossip destroy people, while the speech of a wise man is pure, well-thought out, considerate, and true. 11:9

The contrast in verse 10 is between the prosperity of the honest and the death of the wicked. City is personified here, given the ability to be happy. Generally wicked people don't like people like themselves; they can't trust each other. Thus even though many wicked people may live in a city, generally they prefer to be with righteous people rather than wicked. Even they rejoice when wicked people perish; the good fortune of the righteous which includes good business and a healthy economy is much more advantageous. 11:10

What verse 11 says about a city is also true of a family or nation. Good people must work to maintain and improve the institutions they belong to; their presence improves marriage, schools, the economy, and the world because God blesses their efforts. Without good men the world would deteriorate and die largely because of neglect, since everything wicked men say and do harms it. I am reminded here of an old saying: the only thing good people have to do in order for evil to take over is nothing (cf. 29:8). 11:11

The theme of right talk continues in verse 12; the pastime of complaining and talking behind people's backs must be ancient. The sage here warns against such devisive and un- 11:12

wholesome practice in words which remind us of the maxim "If you can't say something nice, don't say anything at all."

11:13   Verse 13 is the last verse on the subject of right talk. We all know people who can't be trusted with secrets. Some find the temptation to tell others irresistible and offer juicy tidbits to one person at a time. Others give broad hints or innuendoes which give away secrets to those keen enough to put clues together. Both kinds are to be warned against; only a wise man can be trusted to keep his mouth shut.

11:14   Verse 14 reminds us of the well-known and generally misunderstood verse which says "where there is no vision, the people perish" (29:18). There people perish because they lack vision, while here they are defeated because they lack guidance (see also 15:22, 20:18, and 24:6).

The contrast in verse 14 is between a nation that falls because of lack of counsel and one that has "sure victory" because of many advisers. We think first here of military counsel (what most other verses on this theme speak of), but more than that is implied here. People should get several opinions before they make important decisions in matters such as college, marriage, jobs, surgery, or new business ventures. If we rely only on feelings while rejecting good advice in making such decisions, we may live to regret it.

11:15   Chapter 6:1–5 gives an extended warning against cosigning for debts of someone you don't know. Verse 15 repeats this warning as do 17:18 and 22:26. The advice may sound cruel and heartless even though it is fiscally responsible, but we must remember that today we have elaborate systems of credit checks and collection procedures. In the days of Proverbs everyone in town knew each other; undoubtedly there was little hesitation to cosign for a neighbor. The stranger, however, the fly-by-night borrower, was a fast talker you should avoid. If you did sign for him, perhaps you should only cosign for money you would be prepared to lose.

11:16   The Greek translation gives a different reading of verse 16 than the Hebrew. Most translations from the Hebrew (such as the KJV, RSV, NASB, and NIV) read something like this:

> A gracious woman attains honor,
> And violent men attain riches. (NASB)

Translations from the Greek (JB, NEB, and TEV), however, look like this:

> A gracious woman brings honour to her husband,
>   she who has no love for justice is dishonour enthroned.
>
> The indolent lack resources,
>   men of enterprise grow rich. (JB)

Did the Greek translators have a better Hebrew text, misread what they had, or dislike the original pair of lines enough to expand each half?

Verse 16 is not a bad pair of lines, but scholars are uncertain whether they are antithetical, and, if so, what is the contrast. The long version suggests a contrast between the ease with which a gracious lady wins respect, and the hard effort men must put into producing wealth. It also distinguishes between the gracious lady and aggressive man; "aggressive" is for the most part a pejoritive term in Hebrew (just as it is in British English). Grace is obviously a contrast to lack of justice, and honor antithetical to dishonor.

The second pair of lines in the expanded translation has no more connection with the first two than any other proverb in chapters 10–29 is related to what precedes or follows. The contrast in the second half of the longer version seems to be between laziness and aggressiveness as well as between poverty and riches.

The shorter Hebrew version contrasts graciousness and violence. Both honor and riches are desirable but the means of attaining them are poles apart.

"Kind" in verse 17 is the many-faceted Hebrew word that we discussed in 3:3. Whoever is faithful, reliable, trustworthy, loving, and "kind" will eventually benefit himself; the one who keeps the faith and fulfills his obligations will reap rich dividends from others. 11:17

The contrast comes in the second half with a word for "cruel" which is not too common. It was used in 5:9 and again in 12:10 and 17:11. Otherwise it appears only four more times in the Bible. Cruelty, like kindness, will compensate itself with like treatment.

Verse 18 teaches again that honesty pays off and wicked- 11:18

ness betrays one in the end. The words for "vain gain," "deceptive wages," and "reward" sound similar in Hebrew; undoubtedly referring to a subtle play on words. This kind of pun (paranomasia) is common in Hebrew, but unlike our puns which are supposed to be funny, is serious in scripture. Unfortunately these puns are nearly impossible to translate.

11:19   The theme in verse 19 is also familiar; the righteous will live but wicked men will die. We ought not read too much into the word "pursues" which does not refer to those with an incurable urge to sin as much as all mankind outside of Christ.

11:20   Most words in verse 20 are typical of Proverbs. "Hate" appears twenty times in Proverbs, more than any other book except Ezekiel. Seven of eleven uses of the word for "evil" are in Proverbs. "Mind" appears almost ninety times. The word "love" appears fourteen times in the book, and the word "way" appears seventy-five times.

11:21   Like three verses which precede it, verse 21 says the righteous will survive while wicked men will perish. Included here is an almost untranslatable idiom in Hebrew which literally reads "hand for hand;" probably a reference to the law of retaliation (Exod. 21:24; Lev. 24:20; Deut. 19:21). God overlooks no trespass and pardons no unconfessed sin. He will eventually demand payment for every last offense.

11:22   The language of verse 22 is so colorful that the picture it describes by itself conveys the parable. Imagine a pig with a gold nose ring! Why put such a beautiful ornament on such an unworthy body? The comparison is to a beautiful woman who shows no discretion. There are so many people in the limelight today that fit that description. "You can't make a silk purse out of a sow's ear" is a kind of modern paraphrase of this parable.

11:23   Wicked men won't admit their goal is to anger people but that is exactly what happens. Righteous people, on the other hand, only want to achieve good things. Another possible interpretation of this verse is that the unfulfillment of his hope angers the wicked man. Verse 23 is not easy to understand; the Greek translators had problems with it too.

11:24   The rich get richer and the poor get poorer is the substance of verse 24. Generally you must have money to make money. In most countries of the world the poor are trapped in an endless syndrome of poverty from which they cannot free themselves. But just saving what you have isn't enough, either. Financial experts tell us we must invest our money in something that increases in value. Verse 24 does not tell us to invest in order to have a hedge on inflation but rather that God blesses the generous and ignores the niggardly. This idea leads into the next verse.

Verse 25 says it precisely; "Be generous." Second Corinthians 9:6 is an expanded version of the same principle; "Whoever sows sparingly will also reap sparingly, and whoever sows generously will also reap generously" (NIV). **11:25**

Verse 26 is practical, down-to-earth advice on how to handle wealth; frugal management of investments ought also to include the dimension of kindness. Most of us are simply trying to keep afloat financially, but others who seem to have more than they know what to do with also need to know how to remain open to the needs of others. **11:26**

The verse doesn't ask the rich man to give away his goods. Instead it denounces greed which never allows him to ignore growling stomachs and parched lips of people who are hungry and thirsty. The accumulation of wealth creates a spiritual problem which can only be cured by the application of the wisdom of God.

Verse 27 repeats the thoughts of 17, 23 and others; you reap what you sow and get back what you give. **11:27**

Verses 4 and 7 tell us wealth is not to be counted on forever; what matters is a generous attitude toward it. Wealth is like the greening of leaves in spring and falling of leaves in autumn; a picture of transitory satisfaction (see also Job 14:2; Pss. 1:3–4; 90:5–6; 103:15–16; Isa. 40:6–7; James 1:10–11; 1 Peter 1:24–25). Jesus spoke of this quality of wealth too in the parable of the rich fool (Luke 12:16–21). We ought to lay up treasures in heaven (Matt. 6:19–20), he said, rather than accumulate wealth which can only rot away or be taken from us. **11:28**

The two halves of verse 29 seem unrelated; the connection between them not obvious at all. The traditional rendering of the first half is "He that troubles his own house shall inherit the wind." If you stir up a little draft in your house the end result will be a disastrous storm. This is the principle of sowing and reaping again; what you sow in small measure you **11:29** will harvest in abundance. Sow a little trouble in your little corner and sooner or later a storm will break over your life. Woe to the man who makes trouble for the rest of his family (cf. 15:27).

The second half of this verse reminds us of 22:7 where the borrower becomes the slave of the lender.

11:30   The Hebrew idiom in the first half of verse 30 is a tree of life, an interesting metaphor in light of other trees in the Bible such as the tree of the knowledge of good and evil and the tree of life in the Garden of Eden, the good man who is like a tree in Psalm 1 and Jeremiah 17:8, and the tree of life in Revelation 2:7, 22:2, and 14.

The second half of this verse, "He that winneth souls is wise" in the KJV sounds totally different in the NAB which reads "violence takes lives away." How can such different translations represent only three Hebrew words?

The answer becomes clear when we realize the Hebrew word for "wise" is very similar to the word for "violence." Greek translators chose the word "violence" as do some modern translations, while other versions use "wise." "Wise," however, does not suggest personal evangelism in the "winning of souls" as we think of it. The verb here may be translated "win," but also as "receive," "take," or "take away." A free translation of the Greek in the second half of the verse might read "righteousness gives life and the wise receive it," the two parts of the verse becoming a synonymous parallel.

11:31   Peter might have quoted Proverbs 11:31 in 1 Peter 4:18. His words certainly sound like a paraphrase of the original. Phrases such as "you can be sure" or "how much more" are literary English for one two-letter participle in Hebrew usually translated "also" or "likewise."

Proverbs here does not speak in eschatological or cosmic terms, but addresses the here and now. Righteousness is generally rewarded in this life and sinners generally become miserable. Furthermore the New Testament tells us that what Proverbs tells us is generally true will be true without exception in the life to come (Mark 10:30; Luke 18:29–30).

12:1   The theme of accepting discipline versus hating correction appears again in 12:1. The wise man not only accepts criticism but actually welcomes it because he knows acting in response to it will make him a better person. For example, think of opinion polls that advertising firms consult to tell them how best to market their product. Think of athletes and artists who pay lots of money to coaches and critics who will suggest ways in which they can improve. Think of industries who hire efficiency experts to boost productivity and therefore profits by showing areas of waste. Think of yourself; do you welcome criticism?

Verse 2 refers directly to the Lord, the last verse to do so for quite a long time. Basically Proverbs deals with secular life; although God is in all of life he is not named as often here as in the worship passages of Psalms, for instance. Verse 2 repeats the truth that God rewards the righteous and condemns the wicked. The first half of this verse is nearly identical to the last half of 8:35. 12:2

The images suggested in verse 3 are two plants. One which represents the wicked man is planted in sandy or loose soil and will not withstand violent weather. The other which is the righteous man has a stout root which prevents it from being torn from its place. Verse 3 reminds us of the parable of the wise man who built his house on a rock (Luke 6:48–49). 12:3

Sometimes we say behind every successful man is a supportive wife. Verse 4 says this too, also including what happens to the man who has a non-supportive wife. The woman who brings shame on her husband also brings about his downfall. The ancient Hebrews may not have known much about bone cancer, but the "decay" or "rottenness" in this verse suggests actual physical disease. The suggestion is clear; a husband and wife who work together will reap success while those that work at odds with each other will only find trouble. A "disgraceful woman" may be anyone from an adulteress to a nag (cf. 19:13; 21:9, 19; 25:24; 27:15); both succeed in tearing down rather than building up their husbands. 12:4

A crazy notion exists today that says the man who does not lock up or nail down his things is offering to have them stolen. Implicit in this notion is the idea that crime isn't bad, getting caught is. If you can get away with it you deserve whatever you have stolen. Honest people don't believe that. They are honest even when no one is looking and wouldn't steal even if they had the chance. What is just rules their lives; they submit to this just as they expect others to submit to it. 12:5

The wicked, on the other hand, live by deceit. Telling the truth is not an obligation; they say whatever they want to serve themselves.

12:6   In life we basically learn about two kinds of people, helpful ones and harmful ones. Verse 6 describes people who use words to ambush and kill their victims, and also people whose words rescue and protect the innocent. Consider your own speech; does it harm or help people? Verse 6 reminds us that even everyday conversation such as gossip can kill while encouragement can offer hope for life.

12:7   Since Hebrews believed that a man's life continued to exist through his descendents, it was crucial to have sons who would carry on the family name and manage its property. A man who did not produce sons or lost them (such as Job) was a man considered cursed by God. Wicked men would soon "be no more" while the "house" or "dynasty" of the righteous would survive for countless generations.

12:8   The two passive verbs in verse 8 are unusual; we are not told specifically who praises and who despises here but we can guess it is people in general. Even bad people recognize good ones. The word for wisdom in this verse is less common (appearing six times as a noun and eight as a verb in the book), but seems to refer to applied wisdom or putting into practice the good things that are learned. Verses 10:5 and 16:20 also make use of this term.

12:9   Translators have problems with the wording of the first half of verse 9; does the ordinary man have a servant or is he a servant himself? The contrast in this verse is between one who is not honored though he is worthy and one who boasts about himself and is unworthy. One man is gainfully employed (may even employ others) and thus not a liability to others, while the other who lacks bread and thus cannot contribute to others in need, considers himself too highly. Verse 11 complements this verse.

12:10   Verse 10 can be used as a proof text for being kind to animals as well as advice on how to manage flocks and herds. Since wisdom and righteousness go together, the good farmer is also wise. The wicked in comparison are poor farmers, lacking the wisdom to see that well-fed animals work harder and bring higher prices in the market. They are cruel even to their own livestock, not realizing that cruelty to animals also harms their owners.

Verse 11 ends the three-verse pericope on the wise, hard-working, and kind farmer. Except for its last two words, this verse is identical to 28:19.

Protestants didn't invent the so-called Protestant work ethic; in ancient Israel hard work was a virtue which paid its own rewards. The man who frittered away his time on useless projects and vain enterprises eventually frittered away his life.

Verse 12 is somewhat unclear in Hebrew but the root meanings of its seven Hebrew words include "desire," "wicked," "net," "evils," "root," "righteousness," and "give." The last word was translated into Greek as "firm" (one more letter than the Hebrew). It is interesting that the next verse's trap corresponds to the "net" of this verse.

The gist of this verse is that wicked men catch all kinds of bad things in their nets, finding what they want and reaping what they sow. The word "root" in the second half of this verse seems to have little relationship with any words in the first; at best we have a mixed metaphor.

The sins of the tongue are self-incriminating. Sooner or later, as Ecclesiastes 10:20 says, you will regret unwise things you said. Prosecuting attorneys must prove before a judge and jury that a criminal's story does not hang together. Through intense cross examination the attorney reveals inconsistencies and exposes the deceit in the testimony of the accused. Remember the rabbinic maxim which says if you always tell the truth, you don't have to remember what you said.

Verses 13 and 14 are a pair linked by the idea of speech. Their theme is getting what you deserve or reaping what you sow; what you say brings either curse or honor just as what you do with your hands can be noble or shameful. Even though generally the less you say the better, there are times when it is wise and right to speak (cf. 15:23).

Verse 15 is an often quoted proverb hardly needing any elaboration. We all know people who see themselves incorrectly, in fact, does anyone see himself as others see him? While some people have too humble a view of themselves, others who are arrogant have an inflated self-image. What can be more frustrating than dealing with someone whose mind is made up, choosing what is wrong despite all kinds of efforts to persuade him otherwise? Are we like that kind of person? Do we have ideas that godly people have told us are wrong? Do we listen to advice?

12:16 Some people are thin-skinned. The smallest criticism or slightest annoyance sends them into a rage. The kind of person described in verse 16 is almost impossible to live with; his extreme reaction to annoyance is far more repulsive than the original provocation.

It takes grace to ignore some insults; some of the best examples of Christian charity I have seen are people who have lived with undeserved, cruel criticism. This ability to turn the other cheek is a gift from God.

12:17 The first half of verse 17 equates the telling of truth with the execution of justice while telling lies promotes injustice. Each of us contributes to law and order when we tell the truth and reduces it when we don't. The truth of this verse applies to many situations in life besides courtroom testimony. How honest are we on income tax forms, expense accounts, in private as well as public life? How do our actions aid or reduce law and order for others?

12:18 Words can wound or heal, says verse 18. We all would condemn murder without hesitation, but how severe would be our judgment of words which cause almost as much harm? Think of character assassination or slander, words which can pierce the psyche as decisively as a sword pierces flesh.

The second half of verse 18 emphasizes the healing that good words can bring. The tongue is a powerful instrument; like a surgeon's knife it can bring healing while it cuts away disease.

12:19 Sometimes we despair of the truth of verse 19; we can't really believe truth will win out against lies. That is because our perspective is too limited.

> Tho' the cause of evil prosper,
>   Yet 'tis truth alone is strong;
> Tho' her portion be the scaffold,
>   And upon the throne be wrong . . .

is what James Russell Lowell said in his hymn "Once to Every Man and Nation." From God's perspective of eternity truth will outlast falsehood. Eventually the father of all lies and his followers will be no more.

Verse 20 seems to say the goal of evil men is deceit; joy comes only to those who do good. The contrast here is between not only the wicked and the good but also between what their aims in life are.

The key word in the second half of this verse is *shalom,* reminding us of the beatitude, "Blessed are the peacemakers" (Matt. 5:9).

Isaiah said, "There is no peace . . . for the wicked" (48:22; 57:21). We say, "there is no rest for the wicked." Verse 21 offers the same thing in somewhat generalized terms. A life in constant disagreement with the laws of God will bring constant hardship and crisis, but a life lived according to the precepts of Proverbs will bring happiness and fulfillment.

Most of the words in verse 22 have been used in former chapters (cf. 11:20 for "the LORD hates"; 12:2 for "pleased"; vv. 17 and 19 for "lies"; and vv. 13 and 19 for "lips." This verse includes the last reference to God in this section.

The proverb in verse 23 is like 13:16 and 15:2. We've all been in situations where the conversation is dominated by those with the least to say and where people who had something substantial to contribute were forced into silence. This proverb commends the wise man who uses few words while it rebukes the fool for his "blurting folly" (NIV).

Hard work versus laziness is contrasted in verse 24 as it was in verse 11, and will be again in 13:4. Given enough time, the lazy man will become a slave to the diligent one. Hard work means being a self-starter (not a clock-watcher), a shrewd investor of time and strength, a hearer and responder when opportunity knocks, and a stick-to-it kind of person.

"Worry" or "anxiety" in verse 25 is an unusual word which is used only three times as a noun and six times as a verb in the Old Testament. The word implies "sorrow" and "fear" which exact their toll on one's peace of mind and physical health. Today doctors are just beginning to estimate the terrible effects stress has on the physical body, yet look at the same truth expressed in this ancient book! "An anxious heart weighs a man down" (NIV) physically as well as emotionally.

12:20

12:21

12:22

12:23

12:24

12:25

How much better to be kind and use ones words wisely in order to cheer or build someone up.

The lesson of verse 25 repeats what was said in the opening verses of chapter one.

12:26 The contrast in verse 26 is between the good advice of a righteous man and the misleading advice of a wicked one. The wicked man can't lead anyone to the right road since he himself is lost, but unlike the bumper sticker which says "Don't follow me, I'm lost too," the wicked encourages others to become lost with him.

12:27 Verse 27 is difficult because its verb used in the first section is used only once in the Bible. Greek translators chose a word which looked similar to this one in their translation. The words in the second section of this verse also seem scrambled. It seems that the contrast here is between the lazy and diligent and also what they do. The lazy man's work results in nothing while the diligent man gets a rich reward. The verse reminds us of 11 and 24 with the same theme.

12:28 The Greek translation of verse 28 provides a true antithesis while the Hebrew does not. The Masoretes recognized the problem and took the word "to" in the second half to mean "no" or "not," thus providing the following reading: "The road or path not of death." The verse parallels "road" and "path" while it contrasts "life" and "death." What is missing in this translation is a counterpart for "righteousness."

Verse 28 is just one more verse which expresses the theme of two ways of life. Note how Jesus used the same images in the straight, narrow way versus the broad way (Matt. 7:13–14).

13:1 In verse 1 the word "rebuke" appears the first of three times in Proverbs (13:1, 8; and 17:10). Outside Proverbs it is used less than twelve times as a noun and almost that many times as a verb. Proverbs never uses the word as a verb.

The language of this verse echoes what was said in the opening verses of the first chapter of the book, especially with the use of the word "son."

13:2 The first part of verse 2 sounds like 12:14. Its theme may be the most prevalent one in the book; you get what you deserve. The Hebrew includes the mixed metaphor of a "righteous man who eats the fruit of his lips." The righteous man's appetite is for good things and he will receive them; the wicked man hungers for violence and he will receive that.

Verses 2 and 3 both express the theme of right talk (see also 12:6, 13, 14, 18, 19, 22). What we say often gets us into much more trouble than what we do. Consider people who buy things at too high a price because they said yes too soon. Think of people who have lost credibility because they have betrayed confidences. Think of what James says about the power of the tongue (3:1 – 12). The simple chorus children sing is a powerful reminder:

Be careful little lips what you say,
  for the Father up above
is looking down with love,
  so be careful little lips what you say.

The first treatment of the theme of laziness was in 6:6 – 11; most recently it appeared in 12:24 and 27. The principle is simple; if you want things you must work for them. Wishful thinking will never replace hard work. In our country almost any material thing can be attained by someone who is willing to work hard for it. He may have to do without some things in order to get others, but his work will result in "desires that are fully satisfied."

The language of verse 5 is strong; honest people don't just avoid lies, they hate them. The wicked are not simply to be pitied; they actually stink. One verb that describes the wicked is the same one that Moses used in reference to the putrid Nile (Exod. 7:21) and rotting manna (Exod. 16:20), and one the preacher used to describe dead flies in a bottle of perfume (Eccles. 10:1). The effect wicked men have on their family or community is to make everyone smell bad.

Wisdom as a protector is the theme of verse 6, as it was of 2:11 and 4:6. Picture truth or wisdom (as 18:10) as a fortress or tower. Behind its stout walls you are safe. False-hood, by contrast, is a flimsy, hastily built shelter full of cracks and holes, bound to collapse with the first heavy blow. The word for "downfall" or "overthrow" is another word which appears almost exclusively in Proverbs. Six of its nine Old Testament occurrences are in this book.

Verse 7 seems to be merely descriptive, neither condemn-

13:3

13:4

13:5

13:6

13:7

ing nor condoning action. It does not say pretending to be either rich or poor is bad, but is instead perhaps a warning that people are not always what they seem to be. One possible interpretation of the verse is that some wealthy people pretend to be poor because of false humility or a bid for sympathy. Poor men, on the other hand, may pretend to be rich because they don't want to feel inferior. We all know wealthy people who shop in second-hand stores and poor people who drive big cars they can't really afford.

Another level of meaning in this verse suggests that those who are rich in worldly goods might be poverty-stricken in a social, personal, and spiritual sense. Others who are economically poor might have lives filled with happiness, security, friendship, and faith in God.

13:8   "Poor people fear no thieves" is a modern adaptation of the proverb in verse 8. If you don't have anything it won't be stolen. You won't even have to spend money on fire insurance if what you own has no value. Riches can even be a curse in the sense that generally it's the rich who are kidnapped for ransom.

13:9   The image of a lamp appears throughout Scripture (e.g. Ps. 119:105 and Jesus' parable of the candle under a bowl in Matt. 5:14–16). The warning that wicked men will have their lamps "snuffed" out is found in Job 18:5–6, 21:17, and Proverbs 20:20 and 24:20. The illustration reminds us of Jesus' parable of ten girls with oil lamps in Matthew 25:1–13. Lamps and light represent life; this verse teaches that the righteous will have a long, satisfying life while the wicked will suffer hardship and meet an early death.

13:10   "Quarreling," mentioned in verse 10, is a variety of trouble referred to only rarely (Prov. 17:19, Isa. 58:4). "Arrogance" or "pride" here means a big ego or an inflated opinion of oneself. An inflated view of one's own opinions cannot help but cause trouble, especially when it conflicts with the strong views of another person. Wise men, on the other hand, are open to new ideas. They welcome advice and are prepared to change their minds in light of new information.

13:11   "Easy come, easy go" is the modernization of verse 11. The contrast here is between those who get rich quick and easily lose it all and those who slowly accumulate wealth and watch it grow. Some men gain and lose hundreds of thousands of dollars on the stock market. Others win and lose in gambling casinos or risky business deals. People who are not used to large sums of money and suddenly inherit a fortune often spend it quickly and have little to show for it. Money management is a skill acquired through the "little by little" gathering and wise use of money.

The verb "quickly gained" in this verse is questionable. Its Greek translation is like its counterpart in 20:21, but the Hebrew actually uses "vanity" to suggest illegally gotten wealth (cf. 10:2; 21:6; 28:20, 22). Here the verse is a clear warning to crooks and a promise of blessing to honest and frugal men.

Verse 12 is a simple declarative statement without warning or advice. Hope is beautiful, but if it is never fulfilled one's hope can soon turn to bitterness. A wish come true, however, is "a tree of life." The applied lesson of this verse teaches us to deal cautiously with the hopes and wishes of others, especially children. We must keep our promises, doing everything we can to make hope flourish in others while avoiding action that might produce roots of bitterness. **13:12**

Verses 1 and 10 already spoke of taking advice, and verse 13 repeats their lesson. The words here ("word" and "command"), however, suggest religious instruction just as *torah* or "law" did in 1:8 and 6:23. Verse 13 is a good proof text to quote for the importance of heeding Scripture; he who scorns it "will pay for it" while he who respects it "will be rewarded." **13:13**

Two incongruent images are used in verse 14, "a fountain of life" and "death traps." Wisdom both nourishes and protects you. Drinking from its fountain will help you survive the terrors of desert life and alert you to any dangers there, even helping you avoid "snares of death." **13:14**

"The way of the transgressor is hard" is a common quotation of verse 15. This is unfortunate since "hard" in the sense of difficult is not what the word means. "Hard" here means strong or firm, referring to the callous behavior of wicked people. Some translations use a word like "ruin" to describe the way transgressors take. The man who is set in his evil ways, callous and indifferent to the wise instruction of others, is on a path to ruin. **13:15**

The two halves of verse 16 are not exactly antithetic; while "sensible" contrasts with "stupid" and "planning" with igno- **13:16** rance," the verbs "acts out" and "exposes" are not opposites. A better contrast with similar phrases is given in 12:23.

13:17   The messengers in verse 17 are like employees; every businessman yearns to hire reliable, industrious, and intelligent people. He wishes, at all costs, to avoid hiring men who will make trouble, stir up mischief, or fail to give a day's work for a day's pay. Trustworthiness is so valuable in a worker that it actually "brings healing" to the job.

13:18   Verse 18 repeats the theme of taking or rejecting advice. People in Old Testament times must have been much like people today; advice wasn't willingly received then either. Yet "ignoring discipline" in those times reaped the same "poverty and shame" as flouting the law does today. How many times must we hear the same lesson before we begin to apply it to our lives?

13:19   Verse 19, like 16 also has two halves that seem unrelated. The first part of 19 is like verse 12, while the second part is like verse 18. Perhaps verses 18 and 19 should not have been separated; the wise man of 18 who accepts good advice also has his "longing fulfilled" which is "sweetness to his soul." The fool, on the other hand, who ignores discipline and "detests turning from evil" wins for himself failure, disgrace, and disappointment.

13:20   Verse 20 is a neat little verse; well-balanced and trips easily off the tongue in Hebrew or in English. The repetition of "wise" is obvious here, but repetition of the Hebrew root which means "friend" with one pronunciation and "ruin" with another is obvious only to those who read Hebrew.

Two modern proverbs sound like verse 20: "Birds of a feather flock together" and "Like begets like." You become like those you spend time with. Examine your friendships and take a hard look at the television programs you watch and books you read. Do you really want to be like those people you watch and read about? Are your friends the kind of people you want yourself to become?

13:21   The first part of verse 21 repeats the misapplied lesson of verse 15; "the way of the transgressor is hard." Bad people in this world seem to have an uncanny amount of "bad luck," but the truth of the matter is, "misfortune pursues the sinner." Job's friends mistakenly applied this truth to Job's situation, but the error was easy to make. Sinners generally do bring about their own problems by the wrong they do.

Verse 22 speaks about cosmic justice in the sense that eventually the meek will inherit the earth (Matt. 5:5). Other proverbs teach the righteous will become rich and the wicked poor; this is just one more expression of that truth. God's blessing rests on those who please him. He will see to it that they live long and that children will inherit what they have worked so hard for. The wicked, either through lack of progeny or because of their own foolishness will forfeit what they have. Consider also the parable of the talents in this context (Matt. 25:14–30, especially vv. 26 and 28).   13:22

The Hebrew in verse 23 is difficult. Literally it reads, "Much food toiling poor people; and there is sweeping away with no justice." The word "toiling" is questionable, appearing elsewhere only in 21:4 where we find standard translations choosing between "plowing" and "lamp."   13:23

The verse seems to focus on the distribution of food; poor men may sweat and toil to produce much, but all of it may be for nothing if it is not dispensed properly. It seems waste, inequitable distribution of farm goods, and improper remuneration was an ancient as well as modern problem.

Verse 24 is the basis of "Spare the rod and spoil the child." It is also the first of many verses in Proverbs on this theme (cf. 19:18; 22:15; 23:13–14; 29:15, 17).   13:24

The Bible definitely recommends physical discipline of children. Spanking, for instance, is proof of a parent's love for his child in the sense that he cares enough for the child to discipline him. It is far better for a parent to be accused of corporal punishment than to be accused of ignoring or not caring enough about his children. The "rod" in this verse is not merely a figure of speech; but the combined weight of parallel passages in Proverbs supports its literal meaning.

Chapter 36 ends with the familiar theme that righteous men will be rewarded with full stomachs while wicked ones will go hungry. Full or empty stomachs mesh easily with other results of righteous or wicked living; having plenty to eat with long life, happiness, and fulfilled hope while hunger accompanies early death, disappointment, and despair.   13:25

Verse 1 of chapter 14 charges women with the responsibility for the building up or destruction of homes. Although   14:1

the Hebrew word for "house" and "home" is the same, "home" is the preferred word here. A house is not always a home and this verse does not speak of house construction, masonry, or carpentry but of home building; the knitting together of family and the day-by-day routine of creating a happy and comfortable place for a family to live. The last twenty-two verses of Proverbs expand the illustration of a wise woman who "builds her house." Foolishness, on the other hand, seeks to tear down "with her own hands" all that wisdom has established.

14:2   Verse 2 is a bit different from other "fear of the LORD" verses. That phrase comes second, not first, in the opening line. Walking in integrity is a demonstration of obedience while following crooked ways is a demonstration of disobedience to the Lord. Consider John 14:15 in this context: "If you love me, you will keep my commands."

14:3   Verse 3 contrasts the speech of the wicked to that of the wise. How do a wise man's words protect him? Apparently against the proud talk of the fool in false accusations, slander, misleading counsel, or even ungodly advice. Wisdom, we are taught, will protect us from all of that foolish talk.

14:4   Two words in verse 4 make the meaning of this verse uncertain. One word is "barn," traditionally translated "clean." The other word is "empty," a slight change from the Hebrew which reads "manger." Two possible interpretations include: (1) No oxen make an empty barn while some oxen make a full barn, and (2) No oxen produce a small crop while many oxen produce a large crop. The "clean crib" (KJV) of some translations might mean a barn empty of grain or crops, or even "clean" because no animals are there to feed and care for.

The lesson in either case seems to have something to do with investing. You must buy, care for, clean up after, and be responsible for draft animals because they are absolutely vital for farming a lot of acreage and reaping a substantial harvest. The broader application of this lesson suggests wisdom in preparation for any lifetime endeavor, whether that means getting more education, buying more machinery, or investing in more farm animals.

14:5   The translation of verse 5 should read "A reliable witness never *lies*;" suggesting the repetitive nature of the Hebrew version of this verse. Lies are a mixture of what is true and false; what a truthful witness offers includes only what is

true. Our courts make all witnesses who take the stand swear
to tell the truth, the whole truth, and nothing but the truth,
but an unreliable witness may tell the truth sometimes, and
offer a lot that is certainly not the truth.

Proverbs 8:9 taught wise men have rapport with wisdom
while scornful men do not. "Mockers" or "scornful ones" are
afflicted with a kind of spiritual myopia; their ego is so big
in their own eyes that they fail to see what is actually in front
of them. Their minds are closed to everything except what
they have already determined is right. Their search for wisdom is vain because they don't look in the right places and
don't recognize treasure when they stumble across it.

14:6

Proverbs 13:20 introduced the theme of verse 7; since
nothing is gained by consorting with fools, why waste time
with them? Stay away from them; their companionship only
results in "suffering harm."

14:7

The ultimate deceit is self-deceit, verse 8 says. The fool
thinks he knows everything; a misguided certainty which will
only lead him to disaster. The wise man, on the other hand,
is more introspective about what he does. Life confronts us
with so many decisions in so many kinds of relationships. We
must make so many choices. We need God-given wisdom to
know how best to proceed in each circumstance or with every
opportunity.

14:8

Verse 9 is difficult to understand because its translation is
somewhat uncertain. The word "sin" can also mean "sin offering." Fools mock, but do they mock at sin or the liturgy of
the sacrificial system? We aren't sure. Proverbs doesn't include much teaching about the formalities of Israel's religion.

14:9

Another problem in this verse is a word which looks like
"between" or "among," but which also can be translated
"understand." The Hebrew syntax of this word is quite unusual, but a literal translation reads: "Fools despise sin, but
among upright ones is acceptance." The contrast here is between fools who carelessly engage in sin while good people
find acceptance with God by responsible living.

Verse 10 says no one can truly say to someone else, "I
know how you feel" or "I know what you're going through."
Only the person who actually suffers or rejoices can inti-
mately speak of those experiences. We may try to sympathize
or understand, but we cannot enter fully into the joy or pain

14:10

111

of others. Every heart carries its own special burden or is lightened by its own special joy. One experience that is, in fact, totally private is death. No one, not even one's family, can participate fully in that experience.

14:11   Chapter 12:7 also taught what is in verse 11 even though "house" in 12:7 should probably read "home." Here it seems to be more literally "house" with implications of "home." The evil man who uses foolish methods of construction or poor principles of design is inviting his house to fall apart. If he uses poor methods and principles in building a home and rearing children, he is also inviting ruin.

The good man's home will have well-behaved children who bring honor to their parents. Those children will be numerous (a sign of blessing and wealth in that society) and live long; their work will be productive and prosperous. Real estate agents who advertise "home for sale" are guilty of false advertising; what they offer for sale are houses only. Homes cannot be built by carpenters or masons but only by God-fearing parents.

14:12   The road that "seems right" in verse 12 teaches us to be wary of ways that seem to be right because they are so convenient. The broad road which leads to destruction is right in front of us while the narrow one which leads to life everlasting is harder to find. It takes effort to leave the mainstream and pull off from that highway to hell (cf. 3:5; 7:27; and 16:25).

14:13   The phrases of verse 13 are linked together in Hebrew by the words "but its end," and the word for "sorrow" or "grief" is a rare one, used elsewhere only in 10:1, 17:21, and Psalm 119:28. The verse sounds like it belongs in Ecclesiastes (cf. Eccles. 2:2). The author indirectly speaks here of the ultimate fate of every man (cf. Luke 6:25b). Every life ends with death; that certainty overshadows all emotions, experiences, or plans. Of joy and sorrow, the more enduring emotion in this life is sorrow.

14:14   Although the second half of verse 14 is somewhat unclear, its meaning corresponds with 1:31, 12:14, and other verses which teach man gets what he gives and reaps what he sows.

14:15   Verse 15 is almost a word-for-word translation of the original. Faith is wonderful, but faith in the wrong thing or person can be eternally disastrous. People who simply say "have faith" have not thought things through enough. Faith must be placed in the right things and persons in order to effect good in ones life. Verse 15 says fools who "believe anything" are people who have no discretion. Prudent men, on the other hand, think things through before they act.

Though the words in verse 16 are different from those in verse 15, both verses express the same theme of wrongly placed belief versus confidence in the Lord. We are reminded here of Alexander Pope's words: "Fools rush in where angels fear to tread." Courage and an adventuresome spirit may be admirable at times, but only a thin line separates them from recklessness and unnecessary risk-taking.

14:16

The meaning of the first half of verse 17 is clear, but the second part is somewhat vague. The adjective "crafty" in the second line does not describe "wiser people" as much as people who plan or plot or scheme. The word is used both in a positive sense in 1:4; 2:11; and 3:21, and in a negative sense in 12:2; 24:8; and Psalm 37:7. The use of "crafty" as negative seems to make more sense here; "an evil schemer is hated," yet this would make the verse non-antithetical (most verses in chapters 10–15 are). The use of "calm" (TEV) derives from the Greek translation which may have come from an entirely different Hebrew text than the one we know.

14:17

Whatever the second line says, the first is perfectly clear. Impatience, foolishness, and a quick temper usually go together (cf. v. 29).

Verse 18 is another reminder that we reap what we sow and inherit the fruits of our own actions. The results of living in this verse are an "inheritance of folly" or a "crown of knowledge." It's hard to imagine a father specifying in his will that his ignorant son should inherit the family's store of folly, but that, figuratively speaking, is what happens. A wise son, on the other hand, gets to wear the crown of knowledge which is also passed on from generation to generation.

14:18

It is easier to understand verse 19 eschatologically than in terms of the here and now. Evil men bow down in the presence of the good? Too often we see just the opposite happening. Wicked men trample all over the righteous. Robbers and rapists terrorize communities. All over the world evil is secure on the throne while truth stands shaky on a scaffold. Proverbs generally does not discuss end times, yet this is one verse that definitely does (see also Phil. 2:10).

14:19

14:20   Verse 20 expresses the unfortunate truth that greed is a
more compelling trait than generosity; people are more eager
to have rich friends than poor ones. The simple observation
neither condemns nor condones, but perhaps helps us by "telling it as it is." Do we avoid poor neighbors? Do we covet
attention from the rich? Do people want *our* attention because
we have money? Have we bought our friendships?

14:21   Verses 20 and 21 belong together. Verse 20 was merely an
observation, while 21 is the lesson we should draw from it.
Jesus often spoke about the rich and poor, demonstrating by
his own actions how best to relate to them. Often he seemed
to go to extremes by avoiding the rich to befriend and help
the poor (see especially Luke 6:20–26).

14:22   The two words "love" and "faithfulness" that we discussed
in 3:3 appear also in verse 22 with all their rich meaning. The
Hebrew word here for "work for," "plan," or "devise" is interesting too because it means "plow" or "think up." The modern idiom "furrowed brow" beautifully connects these ideas.
The word implies both mental action, such as thinking or
planning evil or good, as well as physical action such as plowing or stirring up evil or good.

14:23   A different word for "poor" is used in verse 23, perhaps
purposely by the author to set apart this "poverty" from that
described in verses 20 and 21. In the debate that rages today
about Western affluence versus world hunger many who have
much tend to accuse those who do not of laziness, while those
who "have not" tend to accuse the rich of avarice. There are
reasons for poverty other than laziness just as there are reasons for wealth other than hard work and wisdom. The "poverty" in verse 23 (used as a noun eight times in Proverbs and
five elsewhere and as an adjective thirteen times in Proverbs
and six elsewhere) is generally the kind of poverty that comes
from sloth or imprudence, while the term in verses 20–21
refers more to people who are oppressed or locked into harsh
circumstances.

Proverbs uses these different terms many times to illustrate different lessons. For further study on the poor consider
the following:

(1) The destitute or lonely poor: 13:8, 23; 17:5; 18:23;
19:1, 7, 22; 22:2, 7; 28:3, 6, 27; 29:13; 31:20.

(2) The oppressed poor: 3:34; 15:15; 22:22; 30:14; 31:5, 9.

(3) The lazy poor: 6:11; 11:24; 21:5, 17; 22:16; 24:34; 28:22.

The use of three words for fool or folly in verse 24 creates some ambiguity of meaning. The verse (like verse 18) uses the metaphor of a crown as the reward for wisdom, so the antithesis of this statement somewhat suggests itself in fools who reap folly by their foolish behavior. **14:24**

Verse 25 sounds like verse 5 plus a little more. A faithful witness not only tells the truth; his testimony also results in saving lives. Literally he might save innocent people from the death penalty (cf. 1 Kings 21:10), or symbolically, from a New Testament point of view, his true testimony about man's destiny and need for Jesus Christ might save his soul for eternity. This symbolic meaning may be more than what Solomon meant, yet certainly is not more than what the Holy Spirit might have meant when he included this proverb. **14:25**

Verses 26 and 27 are two more "fear of the LORD" verses. In verse 26 a right attitude toward God brings confidence and security while in verse 27 it brings deliverance and life. **14:26–27**

The most basic level of meaning here is literal; one's actual physical safety, security, or even longevity is assured by serving God. Yet another level of meaning is also appropriate here; if Paul or Peter had quoted this verse they would have surely applied it to spiritual life. Reverence for the Lord also assures you of eternal safety, security, and longevity; a promise infinitely more important than its literal meaning.

A teacher who has no students is like a king who has no subjects; their titles are worthless. Since their titles are worthless, so is their influence or power; no one honors or fears them. The proverb is a simple statement of fact, a reminder of worldly vanity and empty pomp. Take heed lest you too present yourself as a kingdomless king. **14:28**

Some verses which speak about anger or patience (14:17; 15:18; 16:32; 19:11) include the semitic idiom of a long or short nose, or long or short breath. In verse 29 the wise man also has a long nose or is patient, while the stupid one is short of breath. Everyone must strive to lengthen temper in order to become more resilient to life's ups and downs. The word for "temper" here also suggests the pliability of metal. **14:29**

A paraphrase of the verse might suggest that if you bend or flex in response to life you are wise, but if you remain rigid and unyielding you will break under pressure and be a fool.

14:30   Verse 30 is ancient advice on psychosomatic conditions. A healthy mind produces a healthy body, while sickness in the mind such as jealousy actually causes physical illness. If we worked harder at solving emotional problems many of our physical ones might also go away.

14:31   Verse 31 uses two more words for "poor" (cf. vv. 20, 21, and 23). Unlike the word used in 23, the terms in 31 refer to people who are inextricably stricken with poverty. They cannot in any way be blamed for their sorry condition, thus those who oppress them are actually guilty of sinning against God.

Other uses of the first word are in 10:15; 19:4; 21:13; 22:9, 16, 22; 28:3, 8, 11, 15; 29:7, 14. Uses of the second word are in 30:14; 31:9, 20.

The teaching in this verse foreshadows the words Jesus spoke in Matthew 25:45: "Whenever you refused to help one of these least important ones, you refused to help me." The rabbis said God created the poor for the benefit of the rich in order that the rich might have someone to give alms to.

14:32   The Hebrew word for integrity is *TM* while death is *MT*. "Death" is the word used in verse 32 in Hebrew texts, but Greek translators read "integrity." If "integrity" is correct, a nice antithetic parallel exists between six key words in the verse: wicked versus righteous, downfall vs. refuge, and evil vs. integrity. If "death," on the other hand, is used, then the possessive pronouns attached to it must refer to the wicked. The verse thus would read: "But good people trust or hope for their (i.e. the wicked's) death." Either the righteous anticipate deliverance from evil when wicked men die, or death is the righteous man's escape from a wicked world. Verse 32 is another expression of the teaching that man reaps what he sows.

14:33   The Greek translation of verse 33 (used in the TEV and footnoted in the NIV) produces a better reading than the original Hebrew; a good antithesis in the Greek makes wisdom known to the discerning but not known to the heart of fools. The Hebrew, on the other hand, says wisdom not only reveals herself to the discerning; "even among fools she lets herself be known" (NIV).

Verse 34 is another well-known verse. The word "disgrace"   14:34
in the second line is unusual; the Hebrew word for it is usually
translated "mercy" or "faithfulness." Here, however, the word
carries its Aramaic meaning (see also 25:10 and Lev. 20:17).
The word "nation" (a translation of two Hebrew words) implies much more than a government or political entity here.
The word can also refer to individuals or groups of people
aside from geographic or ethnic considerations. Righteousness exalts any group of people, while sin is a disgrace to
them.

The proverb of verse 35 includes two categories: employer-   14:35
employee relationships and proper wages for quality of work.
The man who pleases his boss by working hard is wise; his
"king" or employer will delight in him and reward him for his
efforts. The man who "shames" his boss, however, by poor
efforts, is likely to make him so angry he will lose his job.

Verses 1, 2, and 4 of chapter 15 all refer to speech. Verse 1   15:1
is well-known; "A soft answer turns away wrath." The proverb suggests self control; many an argument can be stirred
up or defused by the kind of answer a man gives (see also
v. 28).

Verses 12:23 and 13:16 describe the fool who speaks even   15:2
when he has nothing to say. The wise man, on the other hand,
who speaks more infrequently often has more to say; his
tongue "commends knowledge" says 15:2. Many of us have
a hard time keeping our mouths shut. We feel compelled to
offer an opinion or give a personal illustration on every subject. We should resist that temptation and force ourselves to
listen rather than speak. "Gushing folly" only makes a fool
more foolish; we are forced to listen to his words while we
miss out on the potential contribution of the wise man he has
silenced.

Verse 3 is a wonderful proof text for the doctrine of the   15:3
omniscience of God. Our God sees and knows everything,
both good and evil. If you are good you will be comforted by
that fact, but if you are evil you should be warned by it. The
eyes of the Lord keep watch on all.

The "deceitful tongue" of verse 4 is a rare term, appearing   15:4
only twice in the Old Testament (here and in 11:3 where it is
translated "dishonesty" and "duplicity" in the NIV or TEV).
The verb "crushes" appears four times in Proverbs and three

times elsewhere. The proverb is a colorful illustration of the effects of a "healing" or "deceitful" tongue on others. Scripture does not recommend flattery or something less than honesty, however. It says instead that what we say should always be tempered with kindness rather than cruelty.

15:5   Verse 5 reminds us of earlier chapters of Proverbs which included a father's advice to his maturing son (cf. e.g., 1:8). Remember here how the book speaks in generalizations; a father is older, and therefore wiser. What he has to say to his son is valuable advice; only a fool would ignore it. Of course there are exceptions to the rule, but for the most part, following the advice of parents is a good idea.

15:6   Verse 6 offers two possible interpretations. One suggests the righteous who are wise are also shrewd investors of money; hard times do not reduce them to poverty. They have carefully distributed their assets so that daily fluctuations of the economy do not disturb them. Wicked men who are fools, on the other hand, are not wise money managers. They all too often put all their money in one business venture, and when that fails, lose all they've invested.

A second interpretation of this verse is a reminder to the wicked that the Lord has ways of leveling things out, redistributing ill-gotten wealth, and of interrupting a sinner's economic progress with unexpected and expensive crises. A rabbinic homily says, "The door which is not opened for the beggar will open for the doctor" (Pesikta Rabiti, 42b). A modern adaptation of this is: "If you don't give it to the Lord, you'll give it to the doctor."

15:7   Wise people say worthwhile things, says verse 7; they spread knowledge. Fools spread something else, perhaps the "firebrands or deadly arrows" of 26:18 or the "gushing folly" of 15:2.

15:8   Verse 8 forcefully indicts the hypocrisy of wicked men who offer sacrifices to the Lord, reminding us of other Old Testament passages such as 1 Samuel 15:22, Psalm 40:6–8 (quoted in Heb. 10:5–7), Psalm 51:16–17, Proverbs 21:3, Isaiah 1:11–17, Jeremiah 7:22–23, Amos 5:21–24, and Micah 6:6–8. Yet so many of us find it easier to tear our garments rather than mend our hearts. Being right inside is so much harder than saying what is right. Even offering the right words in prayer is simpler than living out the kind of lives we pray for. God is not mocked; he will reject the sacrifices of the wicked and welcome the prayers of the righteous (see Ps. 19:14).

Notice in verse 9 that the Lord hates the sin, not the sinner. How hard it is for us to make that distinction; even David in some Psalms gives way to unmitigated anger against his enemies. "I hate them with total anger," he writes (139:21–22), hardly separating the wicked from their deeds. Yet, says verse 9, the Lord "detests the way of the wicked," not the wicked themselves.

15:9

Verse 10 is the first of three consecutive verses which are not antithetic parallels. The second line in each verse instead expands or enlarges the meaning of the first.

15:10

Verse 10 promises punishment, even death to people who "leave the path" of good and resist correction. Sinning is bad enough, but refusing to acknowledge sin is unpardonable. This refusal ultimately leads to rejecting God's offer of pardon through Jesus Christ, and so to eternal damnation. All of us are sinners; through Christ some of us have confessed it, been forgiven, and are fighting not to repeat it.

Verse 11 is another "how much more" proverb (see also 11:31, 19:7, and 21:27). The lesson of this verse is much like that of verse 3; the eye of the Lord is everywhere. If he can see into Sheol and Abaddon (cf. Rev. 9:11), the darkest places of death and destruction, then surely he can also see into the hearts of men.

15:11

Both verbs in verse 12 express what a fool does *not* do; he does not take correction and does not consult the wise. A most accurate barometer of spiritual maturity is one's willingness to accept criticism. The worst athletes, artists, or students, for instance, are those most resistant to criticism. The ones who accept it and act on it are the achievers, excellers, and winners. How much do we resent the slightest attempts of others to give us advice? How often don't we rationalize it away by thinking "He doesn't know what he's talking about," or "If she's so smart why isn't she doing any better"?

15:12

Faces betray feelings, says verse 13. Sensitivity to facial expression is a talent worth pursuing, especially by pastors, teachers, and counselors. No matter what a person says, what's inside will show on his face.

15:13

15:14   We've heard the theme of verse 14 before, as recently as verse 12; wise men seek knowledge while fools are content with foolishness. Remember how proverbs speaks in generalizations; all men cannot easily be divided into two categories. Yet it is true that those who search for wisdom generally become wiser and richer than those who have given up the search in favor of safety, mediocrity, and their own limited perspective.

15:15   Verse 15 does not contrast poor people and happy people as much as poor people who are unhappy and poor people who are happy. It is possible to be poor and also happy. The difference is determined by one's attitude toward life. Wealth doesn't bring happiness, in fact, according to an old friend, "Wealth only makes misery more comfortable."

This verse is not a true contrast; although "bad days" are opposite of "good life," "poverty" is not opposite of "happiness." Both parts of the verse are true but the second half doesn't necessarily follow from the first.

15:16   Verse 15 is partially explained by verse 16, which is also the first of many "better than" proverbs (cf. 15:17; 16:8, 19, 32; 17:1; 19:1, 22; 21:9, 19; 25:7, 24; 27:5, 10; and 28:6). It is also another "fear of the LORD" verse (cf. 1:7).

The proverb teaches that poverty isn't bad; in fact, it's good if coupled with reverence for God. By contrast, wealth is no blessing if it is accompanied by trouble. The Hebrew word for "trouble" here is even stronger in other contexts, carrying with it the meaning of tumult, catastrophe, and disaster.

15:17   The finest meat is found on the tables of the rich while vegetables are normal fare for the poor. Yet the menu is inconsequential, says this proverb. What is important is who you eat with; those you love or those you hate and whether they love or hate you. The best thing, of course, is to have both good food and good friends to share it with (cf. 17:1).

15:18   Verse 18 speaks about patience (cf. 14:17, 29; 16:32; 19:11; 29:22) and impatience, or a hot temper. The word for "argument" or "dissension" here is almost exclusive to Proverbs (used fifteen of eighteen times in this book). The man who stirs up dissension is hot tempered, easily irritated, and itching to pick a fight. The peacemaker, on the other hand, is patient, longsuffering, and calm; a man who eases tension rather than adds to it.

Two words, "hedge" and "thorns," describe the problems the lazy will have to face. Since these words appear only twice in the Bible, their exact meaning is uncertain. Still, we can safely say verse 19 teaches man reaps what he sows. In this particular case the lazy man who fails to do his job right the first time by clearing a proper path now finds the work even more difficult the second time around; thorns and a hedge block his way. The honest man, by contrast, has prepared well by working hard. The road he travels is one he can make good time on; it is not only free of obstructions but smoothly "paved."

Bringing joy and despising are not exact opposites, but the message of verse 20 is clear; a wise son brings joy to his parents while a foolish one does not. The verse does not teach though, that a wise son pleases only his father while a fool despises his mother. The proverb merely uses poetic language for emphasis here; a less poetic but more literal reading would say: "A wise son pleases his parents but a fool despises them." Chapter 10:1 is very similar to this verse but with better parallel construction.

Verse 21 is parallel to 10:23; the illustration one of a wise man straightening out the road he plans to use. The more time and effort he spends in the beginning building the way, the less effort will be needed later on as he travels on it. The wise man does himself a favor when he works hard to build a solid foundation for his house or studies his lessons well as a youth; his life will be the "straight course" of a man of understanding.

Verse 14 of chapter 11 advised seeking many opinions be- fore taking an important step; here verse 22 offers the same advice. It adds to this that many plans fail because of "lack of counsel"; many advisers will often succeed in making plans that work.

Appropriate, timely words were valued by the sages; two verses along with verse 23 that express this idea are 23:16 and 25:11. The proverb here stresses the importance of two things: the right word and the right time for that word. The right word at the wrong time can be worse than no word at all; expressing sympathy to a widow months after the death of her husband is poor timing. Instead of comforting her, these untimely words may only succeed in reopening emotional wounds.

The wrong words at the right time, on the other hand, can also be disastrous. Think of the times you knew you had to say something but found yourself helplessly searching for the right words. What you had to say needed polishing, but timing was so critical that even improper words were better than no words at all. What a joy to be able to say exactly the right thing at the right time!

15:24   Verse 24 seems a bit ragged in Hebrew, but most modern translations neatly present the opposing elements of the proverb: upward versus downward, and life versus death. We are back to the familiar theme of choosing between two paths in life; one leads upward toward life while the other descends to the grave.

15:25   The word for "destroy" or "tear down" in verse 25 is a rare one (used twice in Proverbs and twice elsewhere) which seems to mean uproot; a nice contrast to "protecting" or "establishing" in the second line. In Hebrew "house" means home, family, and domestic concord in general (cf. 14:11 and its comments). The property of the widow is also the boundary mark of 22:28 and 23:10. Widows, like the poor and fatherless, were especially vulnerable to the abuses of crafty and cruel men, therefore the LORD himself promised to protect their rights and property.

15:26   Thoughts which please the LORD in verse 26 are like the words compared to honeycomb in 16:24. God hates what is bad and loves what is good. Since he hears as well as sees everything, is he not able to read our innermost thoughts even before they become words?

15:27   Children whose fathers live by greed and dishonesty must have a hard time. Evil men bring trouble into their families even though children may be innocent.

The second half of this proverb is vaguely related to the first. Accepting bribes is another kind of dishonesty which can have troublesome effects on everyone. Consider the effects on government or big business, for instance, when evidence of bribes becomes public knowledge. Good life, says this proverb, comes to those who "hate bribes."

15:28   The second half of verse 28 is like verse 2, but the first half emphasizes the necessity to think before you speak (cf.

v. 23). The person who hesitates to speak may say less, but what he says will be considerably more valuable. All of us think faster than we talk and talk faster than we write. Anything we say can be improved by a little more thought. Rhetoric is not a bad word. It is really a lost art.

The Lord distances himself from the wicked so that he cannot hear them, but he is also far away from them because they have distanced themselves from him. The great gulf between them prohibits any communication. Yet that gap does not exist between God and righteous men; according to verse 29 he hears their prayers.

15:29

Verse 30 sounds like verse 13a which included the Hebrew idiom "good face." Verse 30 uses "bright eyes" or "cheerful look." The look belongs to someone who hears good news and is at peace with God. The man who is truly happy is affected clear down to his bones, says the second part of this verse; the Hebrew idiom says his bones become greasy with fat. The idiom makes sense when we remember the arid conditions of Solomon's country. Drought was a curse while moisture was a blessing. Fat or greasy bones were connected in his mind with wealth and happiness, while sickness and poverty accompanied dry bones.

15:30

Consider the joy and relief that comes upon receipt of a long-expected letter bearing good news; that's the kind of happiness this verse describes.

Verse 31 is another straightforward injunction to keep our ears open to instruction because in the long run it will do us a lot of good. Literally the verse reads: "The ear that listens to the advice of life will reside among the wise." Obedience, life, and wisdom belong together.

15:31

The first half of verse 31 is very similar to the last half of verse 32; people who respond well to correction are at home with the wise and gain understanding. The man that resists correction, on the other hand, hurts himself; the Hebrew literally says "he hates his own soul."

15:32

The two halves of verse 33 seem unconnected. The first half is a "fear of the LORD" passage which ties in with the motto of the book (cf. 1:7). The theme of the second half, "humility comes before honor" (NIV), is better known in King James English as "Pride goeth before . . . a fall" (see also 11:2, 16:18, 18:12, and 29:23).

15:33

11

Synonymous Proverbs

Proverbs 16:1–22:16

Some scholars think there is a break between chapters 15 and 16; prior to 16 antithetical parallels dominate while now they become widely scattered. Although the first two verses of chapter 16 are contrasts, for the most part we will now be dealing with synonymous parallels (two lines which say the same things in different words) or synthetic parallels (the second line elaborates on or extends the idea of the first).

Verse 1 of chapter 16 is difficult to understand in Hebrew. **16:1** A literal translation gives us: "The preparations of the heart belong to men. But the answer of the tongue is from the LORD." Despite its unusual metaphors, however, the verse says what is taught in verse 9 and 19:21; man may make his own plans but God's purpose prevails despite all of them.

The author of this verse firmly believed in the sovereignty of God. While man has freedom to exercise his will or make his own plans, he says, God still "has the last word" (TEV). The final verse in this chapter repeats that certainty; "the lot is cast into the lap, but its every decision is from the LORD" (NIV).

Even the most violent criminal rationalizes his sin to him- **16:2** self; somehow we all manage to talk ourselves into doing what we want to do. Verse 2 says it's only when we measure our motives against a standard of righteousness such as the Bible that we begin to see the error of our ways. God is not fooled by our chicanery or casuistry. He judges motives. If we have pure motives then we will do what is right since pure motives will usually produce right action.

16:3   Verse 3 reminds us of Psalm 37:5; both verses begin with the Hebrew word "commit," which means "roll." The acrostic psalm uses the word because it begins with the third letter of the Hebrew alphabet, but here the word is used because it best describes the nature of our commitment to the Lord. "Roll over" to the Lord or commit to him all your plans and they will succeed.

A number of proverbs teach how the Lord frustrates the plans of the wicked; in contrast to that we see here how the Lord encourages the plans of the righteous. The crucial thing is choosing the right plan; one which God will sanction and bless.

16:4   Verse 4 includes a truth many find difficult to accept. To accept it and even appreciate it we must somehow extricate ourselves from earth-bound thought patterns and view people as God does; we are rebels occupying his planet. He has sent to us a most generous offer of peace in the form of his son, but we have rejected and spurned that offer. What will the Lord of the universe do now? He will destroy those who remain unresponsive to his offer. He has known this would happen right from the beginning; the wicked were made for the day of destruction.

16:5   The "proud of heart" in verse 5 who are an "abomination to the LORD" in older translations are "what the LORD hates" in newer ones. That phrase is used often in Proverbs 3:32; 6:16; 11:1, 20; 12:22; 15:8, 9, 26; 17:15; 20:10, 23; and 21:27), plentiful reminders that evil will not go unpunished.

16:6   Two familiar phrases, "love and faithfulness" and "fear of the LORD," appear in verse 6. Sin does not go unpunished, yet here we have the beautiful reminder that though righteous men also sin, God's love and faithfulness have provided a way of atonement. Furthermore, fearing the Lord is the way they must follow to help them avoid further sin.

16:7   Verse 7 is a beautiful reminder that when you please the Lord you also love your enemies. They in turn find it difficult to repay kindness with hostility. The end result is peace, even though it is unclear whether you or the Lord makes friends out of enemies. Perhaps it's both. A rabbinic proverb asks, "Who is a hero? He who turns an enemy into a friend" (Abot de Rabbi Nathan, chapter 23). When the love of Christ flows through Christians to others, the most hardened unbelievers find it difficult to hate.

Verse 8 sounds much like 15:16 except that here it's better to have little "with righteousness" than much "with injustice." Verse 15:16 said it was better to have little "with the fear of the LORD," than much "with turmoil."

16:8

Wealth that is acquired through dishonest means results in at least two problems; a bad conscience and fear that one's dishonesty will be exposed, resulting in shame and poverty. Proverbs says it is far better to have little than to have much accompanied by guilt and fear.

Verse 9, like the first and last verses of this chapter, also speaks of God's sovereign control over the plans of men. This wonderful truth offers confidence and hope to every believer; no matter how poorly we plan our lives the Lord will make good of them by directing our steps.

16:9

The king speaks "as an oracle" in verse 10, a word translated from a Hebrew word which means something bad in every other context it appears. This "divination" is expressly forbidden in Deuteronomy 18:10 and appears as a negative action in Numbers 22:7 and 23:23 (Balaam), I Samuel 15:23, all three major prophets, and many minor ones (Isa. 44:25; Jer. 14:14; Ezek. 13:6, 23). Does the word in verse 10 really mean the king speaks something wrong or forbidden? Most translations believe not and thus translate the word as a positive exception to the rule. Other translations which remain more faithful to the traditional usage of the word link this verse with verse 9. The result is something like this: "the king may speak divination but God directs actions which he says are just." Now verse 10 sounds like verse 33; what looks like pure chance from our limited perspective is really firmly under God's control (see also 19:21; 16:1, 9; and 20:24).

16:10

Chapter 11:1, like verse 11, both speak about God's hatred of crooked scales and unjust weights. Even though the "scales and balances" of Solomon's day are different from the units or measurement we use today, the same kind of greed which prompted one man to rob another then is still operative today. The biggest victim today may be the government which gets cheated out of taxes.

16:11

When we say, "He keeps two sets of books," we are using different words to express the Biblical term of "diverse weights" (KJV at 20:10, 23). Apparently the reasoning of men who use such weights says it is better to steal a fraction of a penny from two million people than to steal thousands of dollars from a few, but Proverbs is clear about such a fallacy. The Lord *abhors* dishonest weights and scales.

16:12   Verses 10, 12, 13, 14, and 15 all speak about kings; a little cluster of verses in a sea of miscellanea. Verse 12 suggests two interpretations; either a king does not tolerate evil from his subjects or life is intolerable when kings do evil. Both ideas make good sense and fit the second half of the verse. Every government needs the submission, loyalty, and trust of its citizens in order to survive; if these are withdrawn regimes topple. Likewise a ruler must be a man of integrity or his people will lose faith in him and throw him out. Governments that work are a combined effort of those that rule and are ruled.

16:13   Verses 13 and 12 are definitely a pair. Verse 12 says what a king hates while 13 says what he likes. What he likes is honest advisers. Mutual trust is the foundation of any successful regime; if a king can't depend on the words of those closest to him all will soon be lost.

16:14   Verses 14 and 15 are also a pair; 14 speaks of a king's wrath while 15 describes his favor. One means death while the other promises life. Both verses reflect the tyranny of a king; the power of life and death he exercises on the basis of hardly more than a whim. We are reminded here of two episodes in the life of David; one in which David ordered the death of an Amalekite who brought news of the death of Saul and Jonathan (2 Sam. 1:1–16). The other is David's command to kill the assassins of Ishbosheth (2 Sam. 4:5–12).

16:15   Verse 15 speaks of a king who is so pleased "his face brightens" (NIV). His favor is so important to his subjects that it is compared to the promise of a "rain cloud in spring." His favor means life to a dry and thirsty land.

16:16   Verse 16 reminds us of the first chapters of Proverbs with their discourses on wisdom. Proverbs 3:13, 14; 8:10, 11, and 19 all compare wisdom to gold or silver, finding wisdom more precious than precious metals. Verse 16 is also one of more than twenty "better than" proverbs.

16:17   The prominent theme of two roads or ways reappears in verse 17. Most references to roads in earlier chapters stressed

the symbolic meaning of road to mean life, but here the concrete imagery of the Hebrew is preserved. Rough road means
trouble here, while smooth road suggests easy going. Watching one's step means not only being careful about where you
put your foot but also about what you say and what decisions
you make.

The generalizations in verse 18 is so familiar it hardly needs explanation. The   16:18
lesson is beware of pride and arrogance; the higher you climb
the farther you might fall. The modern equivalent of this proverb might be "The bigger they are the harder they fall."

The generalizations in verse 19 are that poverty, humility,   16:19
and honesty are partners while wealth, pride, and dishonesty
also go together. Though the arrogant may be rich for a time,
a day will come when they will have to forfeit their wealth.
Only those who are "lowly in spirit" will escape the awful
destiny of the proud.

Verse 20 is a typical synonymous parallel; those who pay   16:20
attention to God's teaching also trust in him. Both "instruction" and "LORD" are objects of these sentences; giving heed
to both result in the promises of prosperity and happiness.
Any words in these parallel sentences might be exchanged
with their counterparts without much change in meaning. The
wise father never doubts that what he teaches his son is in
full accord with Biblical precepts.

The noun for "pleasant" in verse 21 is used elsewhere only   16:21
in Proverbs 27:9 (other forms of it are used in Prov. 9:17;
16:24; 24:13; and 27:7). The word means "sweet" like the
honeycomb sweetness of verse 24. Verses 21–24 all expand
the theme of good and right speech. The last half of verse 21
suggests a teacher whose words are so sweet that they increase the appetite of those who listen to them. The words
do not flatter or trick those that hear them; rather the motivation for using them is the noble one of making learning
pleasant.

Understanding is like an inexhaustible fountain or cistern;   16:22
there is no end to what a wise man can learn. Since fools are
unteachable, however, it's a waste of time to invest in their
education. It is highly unlikely Solomon would accept the idea
that all men are created equal and thus deserve education at
government expense.

16:23   The Hebrew idiom in verse 23 is interesting; brains of intelligent people tell their lips what to say thus adding persuasion to their words. Many people talk without thinking and spout hollow words, but how much wiser it would be to have one's mouth serve the brain. The words of these lips carry weight and substance in the classroom, court, or marketplace.

16:24   Kind words are like two benefits of honey, verse 24 says. Other benefits of honey include its rareness, natural sweetness, golden color, and purifying agents, but here the verse stresses its sweetness and healing qualities. Kind words are like honey; they flavor life with goodness and health. The word "honeycomb" in this verse appears elsewhere only in Psalm 19:10 where it is compared to the word of God.

16:25   The proverb of verse 25 is exactly the same as 14:12. Why? A casual view of Scripture might suggest such repetitions are accidents; the results of scribes who simply forgot what they had included and copied over again. Another view of Scripture might suggest such verses are so worthwhile that they were repeated to ensure their truths were not overlooked. After all, we have four gospels. This verse like Judges 17:6, 18:1, and 21:25 stress the cardinal sin of self-deception which leads to self-destruction.

16:26   Verse 26 is a fundamental truth; the need for food will motivate even lazy men to work. A sad truth, however, is that throughout history and many parts of the world today many industrious, creative workers are inextricably locked into a life of drudgery because the doors of opportunity are locked against them. Hunger "drives them on" but is never appeased.

16:27   Verses 27–30 expand the theme of the abuse of language. Here as in 6:12 and 19:28 the "man of Belial" appears. In this verse he "digs" (KJV) a trap to catch others or burns people with his words (NIV). James expanded this image of the tongue as the source of fire which quickly gets out of control (James 3:5–6).

16:28   The term for "gossip" in verse 28 is used only three other places; Proverbs 18:8 and 26:20, 22. This despicable sin not only separates the gossip from his friends but also drives a wedge between people who are close friends. Saying bad things about others, questioning what they do with raised eyebrows, or making subtle accusations against them with innuendo all succeed in turning people away from each other. God despises the insidious work of the gossip.

Verse 29 says wicked men are even bent on destroying re-   16:29
lationships with their own neighbors; abusing trust and seeking to exploit it for their own ends. Treating strangers poorly
is bad enough, abusing neighbors is intolerable.

The verbs in verse 30 are unusual descriptions of body   16:30
language, yet their meaning is clear. A man who "winks with
the eye" and "purses his lips" is simply not to be trusted; his
words say one thing while his facial gestures indicate something else. Think, for instance, of the backslapping, smooth-
talking salesman. An honest pitch doesn't need more than its
own truth to generate enough enthusiasm to make a sale;
backslapping makes the whole thing look suspicious.

Verse 31 introduces the theme of gray hair as a symbol of   16:31
age, honor, and respectability. Long life as the reward for a
good life is a recurrent theme of Proverbs, but gray hair implies more than just old age. In ancient times, people respected and revered old people as well as parents. Change
came slowly and technological advances were almost nonexistent. Everyone assumed old people knew more than young
ones and many years meant an accumulation of much wisdom
(cf. Job 32:4–7). That assumption has suffered considerable
erosion today.

Verse 32 is a fine synonymous parallel with a "better than"   16:32
format. One modern translation (TEV) especially illustrates
the rhythm, cadence, and alliteration of the original: ". . . better to be patient than powerful. . . . better to win control over
yourself than over whole cities."

Controlling one's temper is more difficult for some people
than others. The verse is a reminder to all to control anger,
but it is more than that. It is also a warning to everyone who
would become so impatient in the pursuit of goals to use
violence (like a warrior), or improper means in order to achieve
them. It is an indictment to all who conquer others while
failing to conquer themselves.

Verse 33 is a succinct reminder that God is in control of   16:33
the affairs of men. We may cast lots, but God's will prevails.
We are reminded here of some examples of casting lots; the
selection of Achan as a thief (Josh. 7:16–20), Jonathan as the
soldier who had eaten during a fast (1 Sam. 14:41–43), Jonah
as the prophet who had offended his God (Jon. 1:7), and
Matthias as the replacement for Judas (Acts 1:23–26).

Does this mean the Bible advocates making difficult decisions by means of the lot? The traditional answer to this question is one I agree with; today we have so much more revelation that we need not resort to the lot. Remember too, even Proverbs recommended the use of multiple counselors (11:14, 15:22, and 24:6). Still a situation might arise where Scripture is silent, counsel is divided, and a believer might want to use something like the lot in connection with prayer, that God might make his will made known through it.

17:1   Verse 1 of chapter 17 is much like 15:17; the people you eat with are more important than what's on the menu. The same point might be made about neighborhoods; better to live in a small house with friendly neighbors than in a palace with hostile ones all around. The lesson also applies to jobs; better to receive less pay in a fulfilling atmosphere than more pay under cutthroat conditions. It's all a matter of values; if peace of mind is important, then a dry crust won't seem so bad. If the banquet is important then be prepared for the trouble that may accompany it.

17:2   Today undeserving children still inherit fortunes. Yet inheritance laws are different from what they used to be. A person today can leave his estate to whoever he chooses; disinheriting an undeserving child is not unusual. Monarchies also are rare today where the future king must be the oldest child of the current ruler regardless of his qualifications. History is riddled with examples of wise kings who had to leave their kingdoms to foolish sons. It is much better that the power and the wealth go to those who are most like the ones who gained it in the first place — an ideological rather than a biological dynasty.

17:3   Verse 3 is a kind of three-way comparison of silver, gold, and the human heart. All three must be tested or purified by a crucible, furnace, or the Lord. The first half of this verse is repeated in 27:21, but the point here is the last phrase; just as silver and gold are tried by fire, so is man's heart tested by God.

17:4   Several modern proverbs suggest the lesson of verse 4; "Like begets like," "It takes one to know one," or "Birds of a feather flock together." We are most attracted to people who are like ourselves. Crooks and liars are like that too; they are most comfortable around people who cheat and lie. Perhaps the lesson here suggests we look more closely at people around us to see if they reflect what we ought to be.

Verse 5 warns against becoming too happy about the misfortune of others, even if they are enemies. We must never mock, insult, or take pleasure in the misfortune of poor people, and must resist the impulse to gloat even when our enemies meet with disaster. Both parts of this verse include motive clauses; the first that God is your maker as well as maker of the poor so to scorn them is to scorn his creation. The second clause includes the warning that if you gloat over the misfortune of others the same thing might happen to you.

17:5

Verse 6 speaks of the mutual joy that grandchildren and grandparents share in each other. True piety exists when parents and children in each generation honor and respect the other. Generation gaps and misunderstandings must have existed in Solomon's day or a verse like this as a model of what should be might not have been written. The lesson is clear; family members need each other for support and encouragement, no matter what their difference in ages.

17:6

Differing translations and commentaries on verse 7 suggest problems in its translation. The difficulty focuses on the adjective modifying the speech (or lips) of a fool. Does the word mean excellent, or fine, or arrogant, or proud? Greek translators chose a word which means faithful, implying something like "excellent" instead of "proud." Their translation makes the couplet a contrast. Another choice, "arrogant" (NIV), makes the verse a parallel. A colloquial paraphrase of the verse favoring this second choice sounds like this: "A ruler has no business being a liar, and a fool has no business being proud" (cf. v. 4).

17:7

Other advice in Proverbs against giving and taking bribes (vv. 23 and 15:27) makes the words of verse 8 sound strange even if later verses (cf. 18:16; 19:6; and 21:14) seem to support the giving of bribes. How can something be spoken against and recommended in the same book?

17:8

We should first of all note that verse 8 describes the way things are rather than how they ought to be. Second, the matter of bribery must be defined in terms of motive. Note the word is often translated "gift." When does the word shift its meaning from gift, gratuity, or tip to bribe? It probably changes when we become aware of the motive behind giving a gift; it becomes a bribe only when you expect something illegal to be done for you. In many lands, however, public servants depend on such gifts for daily bread just as waiters and waitresses expect tips to supplement meager wages.

Verse 8 simply says some people, whether right or wrong, give gifts to motivate others to help them succeed at whatever they're doing.

17:9 The truth of verse 9 is more succinct in 10:12 where we might read the paraphrase: "Love draws a veil over others' faults." The Hebrew word for "love" ends the first half of verse 9 while the word "hate" opens the second. Forgiving sin promotes love between people while nurturing differences prompts separation.

17:10 Verse 10 is an extreme way of saying that wise people accept correction while fools refuse to accept criticism (1:7; 13:13, 18), even after a "hundred lashes." People who are wise are also sensitive; their consciences are tender and their wills are pliant. Fools, on the other hand, are stiff-necked and unresponsive.

17:11 Verse 11 is another version of you reap what you sow. Grief comes to those who sow evil while long life is the reward of those who sow good. The "rebellion" of the evil man in this verse is like the word used by Ezekiel to describe the "rebellious house" of Israel. The trouble this rebellion stirs up may be domestic or international, but as a rule, troublemakers die young.

17:12 A mother bear robbed of her cubs is vengeful and dangerous, yet dangerous as she is, she's no match for meeting a fool in pursuit of foolishness. Not all fools are dangerous while probably most angry bears are, nevertheless people lacking sense can be devastating. Consider meeting a fool with a knife, or gun, or even behind the wheel of a car; a mother bear could be less dangerous.

17:13 Returning evil for evil is wrong but understandable; repaying good with evil is totally unacceptable. Evil will never leave the "house" of the man that does this; "house" meaning more than the building he lives in. "House" also means family, domestic relations, and even successive generations. Repaying evil for good is so insidious it creeps from one generation to the next.

17:14 The proverb of verse 14 uses the marvelous image of a dam breaking under pressure to illustrate human relationships that rupture because of quarrels and disputes. A leak in a dam begins with merely a damp spot. Eventually this starts to glisten with wetness, then a trickle of water escapes. In time a rivulet begins to flow until finally a torrent pours out, destroying the dam and endangering fields and homes below it. Quarrels which break out between friends are like those damp spots in dams; if they continue to grow in intensity they will succeed in destroying relationships forever. If neither party involved in a dispute bends enough to propose settlement or peace, the breach may become bitter and permanent.

Jesus' teaching in Luke 12:58 expands this proverb: "If someone brings a lawsuit against you and takes you to court, do your best to settle the dispute with him before you get to court. If you don't, he will drag you before the judge, who will hand you over to the police, who will put you in jail."

The Hebrew version of verse 15 includes a nice play on words; the first half has "condemn" and "wicked" from the same root while "innocent" and "acquit" are from another root. One translation (NAB) highlights this play on words with the use of the verbs "condemn" and "condone," but a more faithful rendering of the Hebrew would sound something like: "incriminating the just and justifying the criminal." The point is, God hates such abuses of justice which condemn the innocent and acquit the guilty. 17:15

Verse 16 is another warning against investing money in fools or people it will be wasted on. Most people would agree with this verse in principle, but its application might prove to be more difficult. Who exactly is a fool, my child or yours? No parent wants to make that kind of judgment. Educators, too, hesitate to make such a decision, preferring rather to talk about factors such as heredity, educational opportunities, peer pressure, individual maturation, or environment. Still, somewhere in all of this, either parents or the government must decide when more money for education becomes just plain poor stewardship because fools such as "underachievers" (today's education label) are draining their funds. 17:16

Most scholars agree verse 17 is a synonymous parallel instead of a contrast between friend and brother; both are there when you need them. Friends are sometimes even closer than 17:17

relatives (cf. 18:24; 27:10), but hopefully relatives are also friends. Both, in any case, are needed for support and encouragement, especially during hard times.

17:18 The warning of verse 18 is an echo of chapter 6:1–5 and its extensive treatment on the risks of cosigning (cf. also 11:15). Only the man who "lacks judgment" will pledge his possessions as security for someone he hardly knows.

17:19 Verse 19 moves along with a kind of rhythm; sin and trouble go hand in hand. You can't have one without the other. The second half includes the idiom "high gate" which doesn't make much sense in English but literally reads "He who makes high his door . . ." This image may literally refer to people who show off their wealth by building huge homes with grand entrances, or may figuratively refer to the mouth of a braggart which pours out all kinds of proud words. Either usage suggests someone who brags and thus, according to this verse, "invites destruction."

17:20 Verse 20 is still another proverb with the theme, you reap what you sow. Over and over the sages state this lesson, perhaps hoping that if it is repeated often enough, we'll obey it. Verse 20 says what you have in your heart and on your tongue determines what will happen to you; perverse hearts and deceitful tongues will only reap trouble and hardship.

17:21 Verse 21 is a synonymous parable on the theme of disappointed parents. Notice here (as in other verses on this theme) that parents may be disappointed or even unhappy because of foolish children, but that Scripture does not condemn or censure them because of it. The Bible seems to recognize the fact that parents can only go so far and no further in raising children. If children, despite good training insist on being foolish, then parents can no longer be blamed. Parents, on the other hand, who have been blessed with children who choose to be wise ought to be thankful without bragging; that choice too is out of their hands.

17:22 The Hebrew word translated "medicine" in verse 22 occurs but once in the Bible (cf. Hos. 5:13 for the related verb). It could also mean "shows on your face" (a guess based on 15:13 which is similar to this verse). Both meanings suggest Proverbs' often stated connection between spiritual and physical health; a cheerful heart promotes health while a dispirited one prompts illness.

136

Verse 8 discussed the importance of motives in gift giving;   17:23
if one's motive is to win undeserved favor then a gift becomes
a bribe. Verse 23 explains this kind of bribe given in secret
by men who are evil, resulting in the perversion of justice.
This kind of gift is wrong. It can only result in rich men
getting what they want from the law while poor men who
can't afford to pay bribes go wanting. Both givers as well as
receivers of bribes are guilty of perverting justice says this
verse; there is nothing quite so dishonorable as a judge who
is "paid off" to deliver a favorable verdict.

"He bit off more than he could chew" or "His eyes were   17:24
bigger than his stomach" are two modern adaptations of the
second part of verse 24. Literally we read here "the eyes of
the fool are on the ends of the earth," meaning possibly the
foolish man's sight is directionless. The phrase might also
mean the fool dreams a lot instead of making realistic plans.
He might also make plans which are too idealistic or imprac-
tical, but in any case it takes a disciplined mind to make plans
that work, and a determined person to work those plans. The
discerning man operates within boundaries while the fool
does not.

Verse 25 is another reminder of the grief foolish children   17:25
cause their parents. The verse is both a reminder to children
to become wise and thus please their parents as well as a
consolation to parents whose bitterness is shared by others
who also have unwise children.

Verse 26 like 15 refers to the perversion of justice. Abuses   17:26
such as punishing innocent men or whipping honest officials
must have been common enough to prompt proverbs on the
subject.

Verse 27 says wise people stay cool and keep their mouths   17:27–28
shut, in fact, such self-control is viewed as wisdom even if it
is exercised by a fool (v. 28). It's one thing to be a fool, another
to broadcast that fact to the world. Asking stupid questions
or bringing up irrelevant data only succeed in proving one's
ignorance.

The Hebrew idiom translated "restraint" or "calm" in
verse 27 is "cool of spirit," a close reminder of our modern
idiom, "keeping one's cool."

We have all met people like those in 18:1; social misfits   18:1
reveal themselves by playing devil's advocate or taking op-

posite views on issues, not because they really believe it, but because they want attention focused on themselves. Their primary motive, says this proverb, is not the free exchange of ideas and opinions which might profit everyone. It is, instead, merely selfishness; grabbing center stage for their own glory. How "unfriendly" are we in the expression of our own opinions?

18:2   Verse 2 describes another kind of anti-social behavior; this kind of person sabotages any meaningful discussion with extraneous facts and irrelevant arguments because he is too foolish to want to settle anything. He's the one who interrupts meaningful Bible study with offbeat questions like where did Cain get his wife or how did Noah get all those animals on his ark? He doesn't really want to learn anything important because he's much more concerned about showing how clever he is.

18:3   Verse 3 includes two pairs of things; sin belongs with shame as dishonor goes with disgrace. The series starts with sin which leads to shame (or contempt). Shame is just a step away from dishonor which leads to disgrace. We should avoid sin for more reasons than just fear of dishonor, but for some the warning might be enough. Sin is a road which progresses downward; the consequences of walking it are progressively more severe.

18:4   Verse 4 may be understood as either a synonymous parallel or an antithetical one. If the lines are synonymous, then deep thoughts are also wise thoughts, but if they are antithetical (as the "but" in the NAB, indicates), then man's thoughts are like deep water in a well, while wisdom flows like a bubbling brook. Like Jeremiah's analogy of springs and cisterns (Jer. 2:13), standing water may be stagnant, but flowing water is pure. Is the sage indirectly suggesting the man who would be wise should draw from the brook of wisdom rather than the stale, tired cistern of his own mind?

18:5   Verse 5 (like 17:15 and 26) decries injustice in the courts. Showing partiality to the wicked is just as bad as depriving the innocent of justice; both succeed in destroying the law which was designed to protect every man's rights.

18:6   Verses 6, 7, and 8 all expand the theme of correct use of the tongue. Verse 6 simply says a fool's mouth gets him into trouble. The "beating" he earns (used only one other time in 19:29) is a literal whipping from his father, employer, or even enemy. His words are so stupid, so careless, and so provocative that others become angry enough to come after him with fists. Only an insensitive person would push others that far.

Verse 7 repeats the lesson of 6 in different words; fools bring trouble on themselves by what they say. This time, however, the self-destructive nature of his words brings about his ruin. The argument he deludes himself into believing is so riddled with flaws that it ends up destroying him. **18:7**

Verse 8 and 26:22 are identical; the only two places where the Hebrew word for "tasty" or "delicious" occurs (the KJV translated it "beatings" but almost all later versions follow the Greek which suggested something delicate). The point is, gossip seems so "delicious" to us that we are powerless to resist it. Hearing bad things about others is so tasty that we gulp it right down into our memory. How much better off we would be if our appetite was as keen to hear good things about others. **18:8**

Shoddy workmanship in constructing something is tantamount to destroying it, says verse 9. Lazy people look for short cuts; they don't use the level and square as often as they should and don't tighten bolts as much as they should. The end product is not only inferior but potentially dangerous; think of a car with faulty brakes or a house with inferior wiring. **18:9**

Verses 10 and 11 go together; the first describes the refuge of the righteous man while the second describes the stronghold of the rich man. These verses do not imply good men aren't rich or even that poor men are good. What the verses do say is that righteous people trust the Lord while rich people trust their riches. Most of us today have adequate food and housing. Many of us even have put enough money aside so that we are sure we will have enough to live on until we die. For the most part then, our trust for the future is not in the Lord as much as it is in Social Security or retirement programs. Our stronghold is much like the "fortified city of the rich"; we imagine it to be "unscalable." **18:10-11**

That's a faulty assumption. There are problems and difficulties in life that money cannot shield us from; the ultimate crisis being death. The rabbis say, "Shrouds have no pockets," meaning death cannot be bought off. How much better to find safety inside the strong tower of the Lord.

18:12   Pride versus humility is the subject of verse 12 (see also 3:34, 11:2, 15:33, 16:18, and 29:23). Outward appearances are so often deceptive; people whose hearts are proud are not really superior, while those who are humble are not necessarily inferior. How difficult it is to remember this lesson; consider how often we evaluate people on the basis of what they look like instead of trying to find out what's inside. How thankful we should be for a God who looks past our public image in order to deal with what is in our hearts. What does he find there, humility or arrogance?

18:13   Verse 13 advocates good manners as well as common sense. How can you give an intelligent answer if you don't hear the question, and how can you show respect to someone you don't even listen to?

18:14   Verse 14 tells us something medical experts are just beginning to give credence to: people who want to be healthy heal more quickly than those who are too depressed to want to get well. Some people almost wish themselves into dying; the battle to live implies such agony and pain that they give up emotionally, spiritually, and eventually physically. A "crushed spirit" will hardly promote healing in one who is ill.

18:15   Verse 15 is another call to wisdom or knowledge, similar to so many other verses in Proverbs that recommend a life of wisdom, industry, righteousness, piety, and thus prosperity.

18:16   Verse 16 is another verse that describes rather than commends what should be in the world of business and politics. Gifts to the right people *do* open doors, that's simply a fact. Is it right? Probably not; if buying your way in is the only way to get anywhere in life, then the poor will never achieve anything. If the "great" are only accessible through gifts, then they will become like the corrupt judges of 17:23, indifferent to the pleas of the poor.

18:17   We say "There are two sides to every story" as a modern adaptation of verse 17. If you read advertisements for only one brand of automobile you might never consider buying anything else, but if you compare the claims of other car manufacturers you might not be too sure about any one of them. The point of verse 17 is to listen to both sides of an argument before you decide what is right; don't make a de-

cision until you've heard more than one opinion. Witnesses
in court aren't the only people whose testimony ought to be
examined closely for accuracy; children too need to be questioned sometimes in order to extract truth from seemingly
contradictory accounts of an unpleasant incident.

Verses 17 and 18 belong together, even though hopefully
a court wouldn't have to resort to lots to determine who was
right in a dispute, especially in life-and-death matters. Con-
tractors who present sealed bids on a project are an example
of lots which "settle disputes" today, as are court cases which
are sometimes settled by a blind choice of one verdict from
among several equal ones. As long as litigants involved in a
case agree to this system none can object to its results.

18:18

Verse 19 presents some problems in translation. Some
translations (RSV and TEV) follow the Greek, Syriac, Aramaic,
and Latin with the use of "help" and "like" ("a brother *helped*
is *like* a strong city"), while the Hebrew (also KJV and ASV)
uses something like "offended" and "than" ("an *offended*
brother is more unyielding *than* a fortified city"). The differences in the first half are apparent; happily the second half
of this verse is clearer. The Hebrew which likens the disputes
or quarrels between brothers to "the barred gates of a citadel"
makes the verse a synonymous parallel, while other versions
based on the Greek make the comparison an antithetical one;
helping a brother is like a strong castle, "but quarreling is like
the bars of a castle" (RSV). Still another translation reads:
"A brother is a better defense than a strong city, and a friend
is like the bars of a castle" (NAB).

18:19

Verses 20 and 21 speak of the man who finds satisfaction
in his own words; but the verses are not making an indirect
reference to writers or public speakers. What they say, in
simple terms, is that what you say is what you are (cf. 4:23);
another variation on the reap what you sow theme.

18:20–21

Verse 21 identifies two consequences, life and death, which
result from what we say. We must also accept the consequences of what we don't say. In the New Testament salvation
is contingent on confession by mouth of Jesus Christ as Lord.
Failure to confess is tantamount to denial (Matt. 10:32; Rom.
10:9–10, 1 John 4:15).

Most ancient versions add "good" to "wife" in verse 22 so
that only if a man finds a *good* wife will he find what is good.

18:22

The Hebrew never said it that way; it says finding a wife is finding something good. In general wives are assets to men. They are also absolute necessities if men want children to bear their name. One gets the impression there were few bachelors in Old Testament times; perhaps most men realized the inherent blessings of God-sanctioned matrimony.

18:23   Verse 23 is another statement of the way things are, not the way they should be. The poor man who is wise speaks with humility; proud words would certainly reap disfavor. Yet rich men are never given license to answer harshly or with rudeness no matter how much money they have. Arrogance is no man's prerogative.

18:24   The point of verse 24 is the contrast between friends who do not last and friends who do (cf. 17:17). The verse is not quoted in the New Testament, but a nice application of it may be seen in comparing friends who may abandon a companion "in adversity" to Jesus Christ, "a friend that sticks closer than a brother."

19:1   Verse 1 of chapter 19 makes a contrast between honest poor men and dishonest foolish ones. "Poor" in this verse is an honorable term which does not imply sloth or stupidity, but neither does the verse say all poor people are honest. The proverb simply teaches that honesty is best, even if it results in being poor.

19:2   Two Hebrew words in verse 2 deserve comment; the word "soul" in older translations ("zeal" in newer ones) did not have theological implications like it does today. Originally it meant simply air or breath; what goes in and out of your nose. When a man "breathed his last" or "gave up the ghost" he ran out of this "soul." Later the word gathered additional meanings such as neck or throat with their emotive responses of appetite (6:30) and enthusiasm. We still use the word "spirited" to describe a lively horse or vigorous presentation, but the most common meaning of the word remains "self" (8:36), "life" (7:23), or "person." The New Testament parallel of this word is the Greek *pneuma* (Acts 2:4; 7:14 in KJV & RSV).

    The other word we should note here is "haste" (appearing for the first of four times in this book [21:5; 28:20; 29:20] and six times elsewhere in the O.T.). The word implies the foolishness of making snap decisions; "missing the way" by acting in haste. Some people say smart carpenters, for instance, measure three times and cut once, while foolish carpenters (acting in haste) measure once and cut three times. The verse reminds us of the need for careful thought as well as deliberate planning (cf. e.g. 17:24).

If we have done a good job we must give God glory, says verse 3, while if we have done poorly we must take the blame ourselves. Although this seems unfair at first, a deeper consideration of God's character should set our thinking straight. God does not wish to lead his people into folly or sin; it is counter to his character. What he wants for us is what is good; we may rage against him for bad things that happen to us in life, but in most cases it is our "own folly" that has ruined us.

19:3

Verse 4 was said in different words at 14:20 and will be repeated in verses 6 and 7 of this chapter. Unfortunately, in life people will tend to gravitate to the rich while they avoid the poor. Their motivation is greed; people who fawn upon the rich do it because they hope they can get something from them. They're the same ones who avoid the poor who they think are always trying to get something from *them*.

19:4

Our responsibility is to avoid this discrimination based on greed; and instead to act on the basis of New Testament teaching: "It is more blessed to give than to receive" (Acts 20:35).

Sooner or later liars will be found out and brought to justice, says verse 5 (cf. 12:19). Deuteronomy 19:16–19 said a priest had to investigate any allegations against a person; if his accuser proved to be a liar he would suffer the punishment that would have come to the accused. Verse 5 may hint at this legislation, but for the most part repeats the maxim in its own words that crime doesn't pay.

19:5

Today bribery in highest levels of business and government makes the truth of verse 6 all too familiar. While most of us will never occupy such important positions of influence, we must still heed the words of advice. What about our increasing fascination with "born again" actors, actresses, rock stars, athletes, and other newsmakers? Is our adulation and excessive praise calculated to "curry favor" with rulers and make friends with "people who give gifts"?

19:6

Verse 7 is the only verse in Hebrew from chapters 10–22:16 that has three lines instead of two. Three explanations are possible: (1) The structure is an exception to the rule, (2) One line is missing from what was originally two separate verses,

19:7

or (3) the extra line was added by some scribe along the way. Whatever the reason, the third line is so cryptic that all translations have to add another line to make sense out of it.

The point of the verse is clear however, saying much the same thing as verses 4 and 6 of this chapter. The poor are shunned by strangers, friends, even relatives, still, they shouldn't embarrass themselves or others by constantly asking for loans or handouts. Rich people, on the other hand, ought to treat the poor not with indifference but with firmness mixed with genuine concern.

19:8   Just as evil and folly bring their own rewards, so wisdom and knowledge reap rewards. The proverb in verse 8 doesn't really say people who love wisdom "prosper" in the sense that they make more money than fools. Prosperity here really refers more to peace of mind, self-satisfaction, and fulfillment; good pay is just a side benefit to other basic senses of accomplishment.

19:9   Verse 9 reads exactly like verse 5 except for the last verb; here false witnesses will eventually "perish," there they "will not go free."

19:10   Chapter 17:7 said fools and eloquent speech don't belong together; chapter 26:1 says honor and fools don't fit together either. Now verse 10 teaches luxury or "the good life" doesn't belong with fools. Like the numerical proverbs of 30:21–23 which list things that just are not right, this verse says luxury belongs to noblemen (not fools) just as slaves should not rule. If slaves do rule it is unfortunate, but on the other hand there is no reason today why a fool can't become wiser through study and why a slave can't become a businessman through hard work. It is fools and slaves who expect and demand what they don't deserve that get society or a nation in trouble.

19:11   Verse 11, like 14:29 and 16:32, teaches the lesson of self-control versus impatience. The way a person reacts who is attacked by criticism is a good measure of his wisdom and spiritual maturity. The truly wise man exhibits patience and a willingness to overlook offenses.

19:12   Chapter 16:14–15 reminded us of how tyrannical some monarchs can be; the epitome of rich men who answer rudely (18:23). Yet rulers can also be extremely charitable dispensing favors and scattering gifts. Verse 12 seems to warn against kings who are fickle; he who dispenses good things may also turn on you and devour you (cf. 20:2). Remember the rabbi's prayer in "Fiddler on the Roof"? "Lord, bless and keep the czar — far from us!"

Some women make life good for husbands (18:22) and some have a long list of virtues (31:10–31), but verse 13 warns us some may also be naggers who ruin their husbands. Aside from warnings about the seductress in chapters 5–7, this is the first of several verses which talk about unhappiness in marriage (see also 27:15 21:9, 19, and 25:24).

19:13

The man in this verse seems to be afflicted with two problems, a foolish son and a nagging wife, although the problems may be related. The "constant dripping" of the complaining woman reminds us of the ancient Chinese water torture.

Happily, verse 14's prudent wife follows the verse about the nagging one, surely no coincidence on the part of the writer. The two verses frankly state there are two kinds of wives, those who help and those who hurt. Yet life is never as simple as that. We have another generalization here which means the teaching is most often true, even though wives who are "good" one day may be "naggers" the next and vice-versa. Still, the lesson can easily be applied to today.

19:14

Those who are unmarried ought to ask God for guidance in finding mates. The decision is critical, yet by oneself a person has little chance of making the right choice. Those who are married ought to ask themselves whether they are naggers, complainers, or spouses who build up and encourage their mates.

The first warning against laziness given in 6:9–11 was followed by more advice in 10:4, and later will be said again in 20:4, 13 and 23:21. Laziness must have been as much a problem in ancient times as it is today. Verse 15 speaks of sleep brought on by laziness which is especially deep, hardly a nap or even the refreshing slumber one experiences after a hard day's work. This sleep is rather the unconscious oblivion one succumbs to after long periods of avoiding work. This lazy man's conscience has become so dead that he isn't even aware that he's letting life's precious opportunities pass him by.

19:15

The format of verse 16 is similar to many others we've seen. Literally it reads, "He who *keeps* the rules *keeps* his

19:16

life" (cf. two "loves" in 17:19, two "finds" in 8:35 and 18:22, and two "keeps" in 21:23).

The laws or rules mentioned here probably do not refer to Levitical laws, although breaking some of them could certainly reap the death penalty. Rather rules here probably mean teachings or maxims regarding dishonesty, bribery, intolerance, impatience, prejudice, pride, lust and laziness which so often are taught in these proverbs.

19:17   If oppressing the poor is a reproach to God their maker (14:31; 17:5), then being kind to them is "lending" to God. The Lord doesn't need loans from us, of course; rather we must think of this gift to God as an investment. The dividends on this stock will surely be substantial as he "rewards" us.

19:18   Verse 18 encourages the proper discipline of children. Sometimes a child may be particularly incorrigible, but God assures parents here that there is hope in his continued discipline.

The second half of verse 18 can be read two ways. It can say don't beat children to death, or else if you don't beat them they will become undisciplined people who will ultimately destroy themselves. In other words, either too much beating or too little beating can kill children; either *you* kill them with too much or *they* kill themselves because of too little. The Hebrew literally reads, "and unto his death do not lift up your soul." The uncertain meaning of that idiom makes the teaching of this proverb unclear; we can only be sure it commends strong discipline.

19:19   Verse 19 also includes some uncertain words in its second half. The problem is not the Hebrew as much as our translation of it. The Hebrew suggests either "repeat" or "add," most translations using "repeat" while others (JB and NEB) use "add." The message of the first half of the verse seems clearer; hot-tempered men sometimes keep their emotions under control because they want to avoid the humility of having to apologize if they should lose control.

19:20   Verse 20 might be called the key verse of the book because it neatly summarizes what Proverbs is all about. In only a few words are the distilled essence of the book: "Listen to advice and accept instruction, and in the end you will be wise" (NIV).

The first verses that spoke of God's sovereign control of this world were 16:1 and 9. Verse 21 repeats that truth which is wonderful assurance; God is so in control that somehow he can make good out of even our bad decisions and foolish errors. Some translations use "devices" instead of "plans" here, suggesting man plots and schemes evil things. Whatever word is used, the teaching is clear. God's purpose prevails. 19:21

Verse 22 may be only the second place in the Old Testament where the classic Hebrew word for "loving-kindness" or "loyalty" is given its opposite meaning (cf. 14:34). Strangely enough the same word can also mean "disgrace" (Lev. 20:17), the exact opposite meaning. Still, whichever meaning is chosen makes good sense (See 3:3 et al for the "loyalty" choice and 15:27 for the "shame" of greed choice). 19:22

Verse 23 refers to two themes in its first half; the fear of the Lord and long life (See comments on 10:27 for verses on the fear of the Lord and 3:22 for those about life). Fearing God brings long life plus the promise of contentment and security. What more could a man ask? Happiness, security, and long life are benefits which cannot be bought. 19:23

Verse 24 is one of the more graphic pictures in the Book of Proverbs. The lazy man "buries his hand in the dish" means that even though he reaches out for a handful of food he doesn't have the strength or willpower to lift it to his mouth. The hand sinks deep into the common bowl. 19:24

Verse 25 introduces a new theme; punishment is an object lesson for others. Seeing another person publicly punished for his crime can serve as a warning to others. Smart people who see what happens to "mockers" will work to avoid both sin and its punishment. 19:25

Ignoring parental advice is bad enough; verse 26 speaks about children who actually abuse their parents, treating them like enemies to be driven off the land. Events like this must have happened in ancient times in order for such a proverb to have been written, but we have no record of it (Mark 7:10–11 may come close to this, cf. also 2 Sam. 15). 19:26

The Hebrew imperative "stop" is actually a rhetorical device designed to say just the opposite, "do *not* stop learning." When you stop learning you begin to forget. Constant energy is needed to resist ignorance and all its associated vices. 19:27

19:28   "Under oath" means nothing to the corrupt witness; he lies if and when it suits his purpose. His object is to escape the law, even to "mock it." The second half of verse 28 says evil is "meat and drink" for the wicked, without it they could not survive. What good is life to them without violence, sex, swearing, suggestive talk, or alcohol? Wicked men "gulp" evil while they make fun of what is right.

19:29   Verse 29 is a neat little proverb which says punishment is for scorners while beatings are for fools. The proverb teaches man reaps what he sows, although what the fool reaps here is much less severe than the death other verses speak about.

20:1   Another theme of Proverbs is temperance, verse 1 of chapter 20 being the first verse we have read about alcohol. The verse names two kinds of alcohol, wine and beer (the second often translated "strong drink"), beverages made from grapes and grains. Either brew could lead to intoxication and foolish behavior. Other antialcohol passages include 23:20–21, and 29–35, 31:4–5.

20:2   The Hebrew in the first half of verse 2 is the same as 19:12a except for a different word for "anger" (cf. also 16:14 where we are warned to keep clear of any angry king). Thankfully we do not have to worry about the capricious tyranny of kings such as the one mentioned here, whose "wrath is like the roar of a lion."

    The proverb nevertheless is relevant to our situation in the sense that we would be wise to stay clear of any angry person, king or commoner. Although few people today can impose death on people they are angry with, they can nonetheless cause real pain and suffering. Stay clear, warns this proverb.

20:3   Self-control is the teaching of verse 3. Earlier verses warned against the folly of quarreling (17:14, 19), and now this verse says wise men not only will avoid fruitless arguments but will also work to resolve them. Successful human relationships are like so many other things in life; there are so many ways to damage them but only one way to build them up. Almost anyone can start an argument, but it takes a truly wise man to resolve issues, avoid strife, and make friends out of enemies.

20:4   The two themes of laziness and reaping what you sow are included in verse 4. Reaping what you sow is the major theme though. The right time to plow and plant in the Middle East is during rainy winter. It's a chilly, messy, muddy chore, but if a man misses the right "season" for planting he will reap "nothing" at harvest time.

Verse 5 refers indirectly to counseling or drawing out the deepest thoughts from inside a person for therapeutic reasons (see also 18:4). Some things buried deep inside a person ought to be left there; dredging up old hates and prejudices may only cause more problems. Other thoughts, however, ought to be brought to the surface so they can be examined and dealt with. It takes a truly wise man to know which memories ought to be urged to the surface and which ones should be left alone. The wise counselor knows how to ask the right questions.

The two attributes of loyalty and faithfulness (cf. 3:3) are seldom seen, although counterfeits of these, like any other imitations of valuables, exist. The man who exhibits fidelity as well as abiding love is likewise rare; many who claim to have these virtues are guilty of false advertising.

The application of verse 6 is all too evident; we should ask how do others see us? Do we produce as much as we talk? How well do we demonstrate integrity as well as fidelity in our commitments to business and marriage? How well do we keep our word in small matters such as promptness, keeping appointments, or finishing a job we agreed to do? See Psalm 15:4b for more teaching on this subject.

Children who have parents they can't respect are to be pitied; it is a blessing to have parents you can respect. Parents teach so much more by their actions than by their words; their values indeed are ever so much more powerful than moralizing by mouth. Consciously as well as subconsciously children are able to spot hypocrisy in parents.

Verses 8 and 26 both use the word "scatter" or "winnow." In verse 8 the king scatters evil with his eyes, somewhat like a man who directs a bright light into a closet full of cockroaches. The bugs seek darkness as evil people do and will scatter in all directions away from light. In such a way a just king drives away wicked men from his court. The verse is a warning to wicked men to stay clear of a righteous king; trying to fool him will only result in severe punishment. Consider what happened to two women who claimed ownership of one live baby in 1 Kings 3:16–27.

20:9   The obvious answer to the rhetorical question in verse 9
("who can say he is clean and without sin") is no one. No one
is without sin. This verse indirectly supports the doctrine of
total depravity; all have sinned and come short of the glory
of God.

20:10   The literal translation of verse 10 reads, "A stone and a
stone, an ephah and an ephah" to explain dishonest weights
and measures. We have noted this theme before, in 11:1 and
16:11, and will read it again in verse 23.

20:11   Verse 11 suggests what we say is not necessarily what we
do. Verses 6 and 9 said people do not always live up to their
own claims; their actions prove what is in their hearts. So it
is with children; it isn't what they say that proves their goodness as much as what they do.

20:12   Verse 12 says both hearing and seeing are good ways of
determining truth. Sometimes hearing isn't enough; your eyes
tell you something else. One sense may say a child is good,
but the other will disagree. A man may say he is innocent,
but a king's eyes (his detectives) might prove him wrong. On
the other hand, if what you hear agrees with what you see,
you have enough evidence to determine truth. God has given
two "gates" or senses by which knowledge can enter, the eyes
and the ears.

20:13   Verse 4 and now 13 include the mixed themes of laziness
and reward. Laziness results in poverty while hard work generally produces wealth. Remember Proverbs' tendency to gen-
eralize; surely there are other factors which influence a man's
wealth besides hard work or laziness. Consider, for instance,
the influence of inheritance, education, opportunity for ad-
vancement, or the type of government he lives under.

20:14   The humorous little exchange in a market place recorded
in verse 14 sounds so familiar; we all can relate to the words
of a buyer. In Hebrew the verse says a buyer says, "It's bad,
it's bad," yet the very thing he demeans becomes the subject
of boasting later to his friends. Stores which advertise "sec-
onds" or "irregulars" at "half price" or "greatly reduced prices"
know exactly what they're doing. Buyers may brag about the
bargains they got, but as a rule sellers are sharper than buyers. Consider the words of an old rabbinic proverb: "When
a fool goes to market, the merchants rejoice."

Verse 15 (like verses in chapter 8) is another comparison of wisdom and wealth. "Lips that speak knowledge" here are rarer and more precious than gold or rubies. In the market place of life buyers must know what they are looking at. The ability to differentiate between what is cheap and what is valuable can mean even more than money in the pocket.

Other proverbs warned against cosigning for debts of strangers and verse 16 continues the teaching. Apparently this practice was common; cosigners perhaps charged a small fee for their service figuring it was worth the risk. Still, we aren't certain of this. The verse sounds more like advice to lenders who should demand collateral from cosigners who are stupid enough to enter into risky deals. The verse is repeated in 27:13.

Verse 17 reminds us of what Lady Folly told her victim in 9:17; "food eaten in secret is delicious." The proverb warns against stealing but also against its consequences. Stolen bread that tastes so good soon begins to feel like sand.

The Old Testament occasionally draws a comparison between sex and food; sex may be the suggested "food gained by fraud" in verse 17. Other passages which make this comparison are Genesis 39:6–7, Judges 14:14, 2 Samuel 13:5, Proverbs 6:26, 9:17, and 30:20.

The wise man struggles to make long-range plans, seeking advice and counsel from others to help him. In times of war, for instance, he relies heavily on spies, war historians, and military strategists (cf. 11:14, 15:22, and Luke 14:31).

Don't tell secrets to anyone you don't trust, says verse 19. People who give away secrets often pass on erroneous, even damaging information. On the other hand, this verse says "avoid the man who talks too much." The advice may be just as hard on the listener as the gossip. Confidentiality is a priceless commodity today in an age of electronic listening devices and computer memory banks. Only true friends should be entrusted with secrets.

Verse 20 is a serious reminder of the fifth commandment; whoever curses one of his parents will have his "lamp snuffed out." That image may be more gentle than the one used in 30:17 (where children who curse parents are eaten by vultures or have their eyes pecked out by ravens), but the point is the same. Exodus 21:17 says it clearly; whoever curses his father or mother must be put to death.

20:21   Verse 21 is like 13:11; things which are inherited are not appreciated like things which come as a result of hard work. Some children are actually cursed by inherited wealth; money "quickly gained at the beginning" destroys personal initiative and stunts growth. In the end they are worse off than people who have worked hard for their money.

20:22   Verse 22 includes a teaching that initially sounds more like the New Testament than the Old. The Old Testament taught punishment should be "an eye for an eye and a tooth for a tooth." Jesus, on the other hand said, "Turn the other cheek and go the second mile, pray for those who abuse you, and count it an honor to suffer for my sake." Only God should exact vengeance on wrong-doers. Still, Romans 12:19 which says, "I will take revenge, I will pay back, says the Lord," is a direct paraphrase of Deuteronomy 32:35.

20:23   Verse 23 is similar to verse 10 except for verse 10's weight and volume measures versus the weight and the scale measures of 23. Not only could the weight be over or under the standard, but the scale itself might be inaccurate, perhaps with a fulcrum that the dishonest merchant could adjust to his own advantage. The point is, God "detests" any methods used to cheat and rob others.

20:24   Several verses speak of God's control over the affairs of men (16:1, 9; 19:21). Verse 24 states the truth in the form of a rhetorical question: How can anyone understand his own way if all his steps are directed by the Lord?

20:25   Verse 25 warns us to be very careful when we make a promise. The enthusiasm of the moment may not reflect a realistic assessment of our ability to carry it out. Sometimes people pledge money or make faith promises for more than they can possibly give. This is dangerous because it forces some people into breaking vows. Verse 25 advises practicality and realism in the matter of making vows. Judges 11:30–39 is a graphic warning against foolish promises; Jepthah was forced to sacrifice his own daughter because he made a rash vow.

20:26   The king who winnows or scatters the wicked also runs over them with the threshing wheel, says verse 26. The order of punishment ought to be reversed; first the farmer threshes and then he winnows. Still, no matter what the order, the king is the one who is able to separate the chaff from the wheat and the guilty from the innocent. Then the wicked are destroyed by the "wheel."

The figure of speech in verse 27 is noteworthy; the lamp of the Lord is like the conscience or spirit of a man. God has placed a small light in each person to remind us when we do wrong which we call conscience. Ancient people called this a lamp; something placed inside man to keep things from getting too dark or to prevent him from becoming too evil. Someone who had a "seared" (1 Tim. 4:2) conscience was a person whose lamp had been extinguished.   20:27

The terms "loyalty and faithfulness in verse 28 (cf. 3:3 and 20:6) are used to characterize good government. The king who exhibits love and faithfulness is safe; his throne is secure.   20:28

We expect different things from young people than old ones. We may admire physical strength in young men, but old people who have gray hair exhibit a different kind of strength; (1) they have survived youth (an accomplishment in and of itself), (2) they have reached the age of rest and relaxation, and (3) they have acquired the wisdom of old age.   20:29

Verse 30 must be understood in its context; its strong recommendation for "blows" and "beatings" might otherwise be misinterpreted. This verse, on the heels of verse 29, continues the theme of maturation or growth toward the acquiring of wisdom. People learn at different rates, some faster than others. Verse 30 says those who constantly resist the right way have to be beaten or flogged by life or even other people before they learn.   20:30

Just as God controls nature, so he directs the hearts of kings, says verse 1 of chapter 21. Just as ancient farmers opened and closed water gates to control the flow of irrigation, so God's sovereign will directs kings. While kings and rulers may often seem absolute in power and authority, history reveals that God is in control. Think of how Cyrus of Persia, for instance, was used by God to effect the return of Israel's exiles to Palestine. Or consider how God "hardened Pharaoh's heart" to spur on the Israelites to freedom. Consider the census of Caesar Augustus which caused Mary's baby to be born in Bethlehem. God is in control.   21:1

21:2   Except for two synonyms verse 2 is exactly like 16:2 (though a man's ways seem "right" or "innocent" to him, his "motives" or "heart" are weighed by the Lord). Apparently this is another proverb the Spirit felt we needed to read more than once.

21:3   Although God gave his people an elaborate sacrificial system in the Pentateuch, he never intended external sacrifice should be given without internal commitment. From the beginning he demanded right attitudes; broken and contrite hearts rather than dead animals. Verse 3 says doing what is right and just is even *more* acceptable to the Lord than sacrifice (cf. 15:8 and its references).

21:4   The Hebrew of verse 4 reads literally, "the plowing of the wicked is sin." The Greek, using the same consonants with a different vowel reads, "the lamp of the wicked is sin." There are two possible interpretations here. The first one based on the Hebrew says that even when the wicked do something good or productive like plow a field they sin because they don't do it to the glory of God. They may be good farmers but because they are in rebellion against God all their work is wicked.

The second possible interpretation may be a variation on the sowing and reaping theme. Since wicked men sow conceit and arrogance their fields will yield only sin. The word which is translated "plow" is a strange spelling for a noun that occurs only three times elsewhere (Prov. 13:23; Jer. 4:3; and Hos. 10:12), whereas "lamp" is much more common. One translation (NIV) suggests "haughty eyes and a proud heart" *are* the lamp of the wicked.

Whichever translation is used, the verse certainly links together arrogance, conceit, and sin; all are wrong in the eyes of the Lord.

21:5   Verse 5 is an antithetic parallel similar to those we saw in chapters 10–15. Here the contrast is between one who is careful and one who is hasty ("hasty" being a pejorative term in 19:2; 28:20; and 29:20, while "diligent" is commendatory in 10:4; 12:24, 27; and 13:4). Timing, of course, is the important thing. Only the "diligent" or wise man knows when to act and when to hold back. More often than not, says the proverb, it's better to make plans than throw away time and money on something you haven't thought through enough.

Verse 6 is another proverb on the theme that crime doesn't
pay (see also 10:2, 11:4; and 15:27). The translation which
likens men with ill-gotten treasure to "jaws of death" (TEV)
comes from the Greek rather than Hebrew which says something like "seekers of death." The same image was used in
13:14 and 14:27.

21:6

As in other passages with uncertain words, the main thrust
of this verse is still clear. The wicked will eventually get what
they deserve; those who get rich by illegal means will pay for
it in the end with their lives.

Verses 6 and 7 both teach that wicked men will eventually
be punished. Their evil is even more explicit here; "violence"
actually "drags them away" (NIV). They don't just cheat or
sin once in awhile; they "refuse to do what is right" even
when they know it is sin.

21:7

Two unusual Hebrew words cause some uncertainty in
verse 8. The word translated "crooked" or "devious" appears
only in this verse. Fortunately its meaning is clear enough to
cause little dispute. The word for "guilty," however, is not so
clear, although traditionally the verse has been translated to
mean the way of the sinner or "guilty" is crooked. The meaning of the verse is still obvious; the crooked way of the guilty
is contrasted with the upright way of the innocent.

21:8

Of all the proverbs that are repeated, this one in verse 9
seems least deserving. Yet verse 9 *is* repeated, in 25:24 as
well as 21:19.

21:9

The "corner of the roof" which sounds like hyperbole is
probably a literal description of the flat roofs people in Palestine slept on in hot weather (cf. Matt. 24:17; Luke 5:19;
and Acts 10:9). The verse probably does not recommend divorce though, as much as it does prudence in dealing with a
bad situation. Just as it is wise to steer clear of an angry king
(20:2), so verse 9 advises staying a safe distance away from
a quarrelsome mate until some of the anger passes. Note the
verse doesn't say the angry wife should go to the roof. The
house is her territory; his is the city gate or the field. If he
invades her turf and thus provokes her anger, he invites his
own banishment to the roof.

You would think even wicked men would treat their neighbors with kindness, yet verse 10 says evil people hate everyone around them. They hate relatives, friends, associates —

21:10

even themselves. The whole world is an enemy to be outwitted or taken advantage of.

21:11 Chapter 19:25 taught how public punishment of criminals might deter others from crime. According to verse 11 this public thrashing not only confirms doing what is right for the wise, but also may succeed even in teaching the fool. This kind of fool in verse 11 is the teachable type, his foolishness consisting of inexperience or naiveté (cf. comments at 1:4).

21:12 Many translations (JB., NIV, TEV and others) capitalize "Righteous one" or insert "God" as the subject of verse 12 even though the correct subject may really be "righteous man." Still, if "righteous man" is the true subject, does he "bring to ruin" the house of the wicked? God would seem more likely to cause that. You see the dilemma of translators even though the general teaching of the verse is clear; crime simply doesn't pay.

21:13 Verse 13 and other verses which speak about the unequal distribution of wealth raise a question which this brief commentary is hardly able to answer. Why do some people have so much while others have so little? That question may seem less relevant to North Americans or Europeans who do not live in conditions of extreme wealth and poverty like most other people in the world. Still, the world-wide problem is acute today.

Some people are suggesting it is sinful to be rich, quoting for authority New Testament verses which condemn greed, self-indulgence, and the love of money. Yet Proverbs includes a remarkable number of verses which say wealth is a sign of God's blessing upon men who work hard, make wise plans, and use their talents.

Verse 13 commends charity to the poor, yet this does not mean that rich men should share all that they have with the poor. Such a practice might only succeed in stifling creativity and initiative, thereby robbing the rich as well as the poor of the opportunity to improve themselves.

Proverbs is not legalistic; it does not tell us exactly how much to give or exactly who to give it to. It does, however, urge us to be sympathetic and caring about the needs of others, since "but for the grace of God, there go I."

21:14 Verse 14 doesn't commend bribery as much as good sense. If someone is angry with you, and your offer of peace (no matter how it is cloaked) is sincere, then the price of the gift is small in comparison to the cost of continued fighting. The man who brings flowers or candy to an angry wife may settle a quarrel better than a thousand logical arguments.

Justice in action makes good people happy and bad people afraid. Good people are happy because one less murderer, thief, or rapist roams the streets. Evil men are afraid because their deeds might now be exposed. They will have to stop their wicked ways or else risk being caught and punished.

21:15

Verse 16 includes a graphic description of someone who wanders from the path and gets lost. The man who leaves the secure path of understanding actually ends up "in the company of the dead," the Hebrew here suggesting something like the "congregation of the ghosts." The proverb is a striking reminder that we get what we deserve in life.

21:16

Verse 17 is a warning against people with "champagne taste on a beer budget." Luxuries are for the already rich, not for those who just act like they are. Wealth, like poverty, has a way of compounding itself. "The rich get richer while the poor get poorer" is a modern equivalent to this proverb; even if poor people try to emulate the rich they'll only succeed in getting poorer.

21:17

Verse 18 is a promise to good people that someday all the wicked things others have done will serve to "ransom" or set them free. Consider 11:8 in this context; righteous men will be rescued from trouble which will instead come upon the wicked.

21:18

Verse 19 goes one step further than verse 9; here the man with a quarrelsome wife is urged to live in a desert rather than simply a corner of the roof. The point, however, is the same. Stay clear from an angry spouse until the anger cools down.

21:19

Verse 20 is another generalization which equates wisdom with wealth ("stores of choice food and oil"), and foolishness with an empty larder. Wise people plan ahead and so have plenty to eat, while foolish people "devour all they have" without thinking at all about the future. If you are rich don't necessarily think you are wise. If you are poor, examine yourself, maybe you have made some stupid moves.

21:20

Verse 21 includes a lavish use of rich terms: "righteousness," "loyalty," "life," "love," and "honor." Surely the good life belongs in abundance to those who obey God.

21:21

21:22 Brains are better than brawn, says verse 22; real strength depends on what goes on in your head. Young people may have strong arms and legs, but old people have strong "heads." We are reminded here of David's general, Joab, who used wise logistics to conquer a city thought to be impregnable (see 2 Sam. 5:6–8 and 1 Chron. 11:4–6).

21:23 Verse 23 includes more advice on the wise use of the tongue (cf. 12:13 and 13:3), repeating the verb "cares for" or "guards" for emphasis; "he that guards his lips guards his life."

21:24 Verse 24 lists four synonyms ("conceited," "arrogant," "proud," and "inconsiderate") to describe the man called "mocker," each slightly different from the other. "Conceited" and "inconsiderate" are from the same root while "arrogant" is a rare word used elsewhere only in Habakkuk 2:5. "Proud" is translated in other verses as "scorn" or "mocking." What a picture to describe the man who sets himself up as his own authority against God!

21:25 Verses 25 and 26 may not be so closely related as the print in some translations indicates (no space between verses). Lazy people, to be sure, often become so poor that they have to depend on others to survive, yet verse 25 simply says sluggards kill themselves by not working. When we say "he killed himself" we associate that with overwork, but this verse couples that phrase with inactivity. People who won't work may eventually have to die of starvation.

21:26 Verse 26 is interesting, commending charity right after two descriptions of men who don't deserve charity at all. Who wants to give "without sparing" to sluggards or covetous men? Surely poverty for these men is a willful thing rather than a result of unfortunate circumstances. Why should thrifty, hardworking men sacrifice so that lazy, greedy ones can be more comfortable?

Still, the lesson here is clear; those who have shouldn't pass judgment on those who have not before they give. We are commanded to give "without sparing," that is, without holding back despite the status of the recipient.

21:27 The initial Hebrew words of verse 27 are the same as 15:8 except for "the LORD." The teaching is similar too except for the added statement that wicked men offer sacrifices to the Lord out of "evil intent." Surely ignorance, even self-deception can be tolerated more than outright evil. These motives might include deceit, pride, or the hope that God somehow can be bought off.

Verses 19:5 and 9 dealt with the matter of perjury like verse 28 now does. A false witness who "is not believed" in one translation (TEV) seems to be an inaccurate rendering of "shall perish," unless the idea here is that a false witness offers such unbelievable testimony that he is likely to get thrown out of court.

21:28

The second half of the verse also presents problems, although clearly it is a contrast between true and false testimony. False testimony will destroy itself in time along with those who listen to it, while true testimony "lives on" by affirming itself.

The Masoretes who added vowels to the consonants of the Hebrew text had problems with one word in verse 29 which is variously translated as "are sure of" (TEV), "brazenfaced" (NAB), "air of confidence," or a "bold front" (NIV). The original text suggests "establish."

21:29

Still, despite its irregularities, the main thrust of this verse is unaffected. Evil men have to put up a front to make people believe them, while what a good man says carries its own weight. In the long run it takes a lot more effort to be dishonest than it does to tell the truth.

The structure of verse 30 is interesting. It includes three negatives: no wisdom, no insight, nor any plan can succeed if it is against the Lord. Another way to say this verse is that no one is wise, bright, or clever who is opposed to the Lord. Wise men, by definition, are on the Lord's side.

21:30

Victory in battle comes from God, not from chariots, horses, or war machines. This teaching of verse 31 is repeated in many other passages such as Psalms 20:7, 33:17, 127:1; Hosea 1:7; and Zechariah 4:6. History is filled with vivid examples of wars which were won or lost because of seemingly trifling incidents. The exodus of Israel through the Red Sea is a classic example of how weakness won over strength because "horses and chariots" were no match for the Lord.

21:31

Personal honor or a "good name" was of utmost importance to Israelites in ancient times. Today people who go broke in one city move to another, unmarried mothers leave town to have their babies, and embezzlers make amends. Everyone is given so much leniency to start over that one wonders how

22:1

important "good names" really are. Verse 1 of chapter 22 says a man's honor is to be valued above all material possessions, even silver or gold.

22:2   The truth of verse 2 seems so obvious that we might be tempted to skim over it. Still, there is a powerful lesson here. Since all people are created by God, both rich and poor alike, all are therefore objects of his concern. Since God cares for all people, so must we — regardless of their social or financial status (See also 14:31 and 29:13).

22:3   Verse 3 is much like 14:16 in meaning, although worded differently. The prudent man here is cautious; he recognizes danger and pulls back. The fool, on the other hand, is oblivious to risk and keeps going. In the end he will "suffer" for his carelessness.

22:4   Verse 4 is another "fear of the LORD" verse, set up in Hebrew almost like an algebraic equation: $(a + b = x + y + z)$. Obedience plus humility equal riches, honor, and life. All these terms are crucial in Proverbs; this verse encapsulates the entire book.

22:5   The Bible teaches we should stay far away from the path of evil. If we don't even come near the place of evil we probably won't be tempted by it, and if we aren't tempted we probably won't fall. Verse 22 says the one who avoids evil "guards his soul," unlike the one who strays onto paths of the wicked only to find himself trapped by its nets and thorns.

22:6   Verse 6 is a favorite of people today who are concerned about proper parenting, yet the ancient Greek translation does not include this verse. The verse is also somewhat difficult to understand because it includes both a rare word and unusual idiom.

The rare word is "teach," "train up," or "start" (cf. NEB). It is not the word used in 1:3, but one that appears only twice in Deuteronomy 20:5 and once in 1 Kings 8:63 (parallel to 2 Chron. 7:5). It means "dedicate" and its noun form is the name of the Jewish feast of Hanukkah. The unusual idiom in this verse, translated "the way he should go," really says in Hebrew "on the mouth of his way."

Problems in interpretation, however, really do not originate from these words. Instead, differing views center on the applied meaning of the phrase "the way he should go." Does this mean teach a child the way he *should* go (KJV and tra-

ditional view), or the way *he* goes? The second view says if
you encourage a child to pursue the things he's most inter-
ested in, then he will really excel in them later in life.

Both views say what a child learns stays with him when
he grows up. The question is, what shall we teach him; what
he wants to learn or what we think he *should* learn? The
traditional view seems to fit in better with other verses about
childrearing in Proverbs, although the second view is possible.

Verse 7 neither condemns nor condones money lending.   22:7
Instead, it simply says that if you borrow you become a slave
to the lender. That, in itself should be enough to make someone hesitate before asking for a loan. Rich men and "lenders"
are on top, while poor men and "borrowers" are at the bottom.

The proverb in verse 8 obviously teaches the theme of reap-   22:8
ing and sowing; that very figure of speech is used. Here we
are told people who sow wickedness will reap "trouble" and
their way of oppressing others will come to an end.

In Hebrew the man who gives bread to the poor is also   22:9
"good of eye," meaning his eyes tell people what he is like
inside (cf. Luke 11:34). Verse 9 clearly teaches charity without
any comments on the worthiness of recipients (as 21:25–26
did). The "poor" here are destitute because of circumstances
not necessarily because of sloth or stupidity.

Like other verses that pile up synonyms (21:30; 22:4),   22:10
verse 10 lists three results of getting rid of a mocker: you
spare yourself arguments, quarreling, and insults. An old rabbinic proverb says something like this: "When a fool leaves
the room it seems as though a wise man entered."

Verse 11, like many others, strongly suggests the author-   22:11
ship of Solomon (cf. 8:15; 14:28, 35; 16:10, 12–15; 20:8, 26,
28). What king wouldn't love to have men of "pure hearts"
and "gracious speech," serve under him? To such men this
monarch promises actual "friendship."

God is the protector and defender of truth, says verse 12.   22:12
It will survive while false words will be "frustrated." The
proverb is a forerunner of the later promise that someday all
lies and the father of lies will suffer the sting and shame of
defeat.

Verse 13 includes such preposterous excuses for the lazy   22:13
man who doesn't want to work, that we almost want to laugh.
"I can't go to work because there's a lion outside!" "Someone

might murder me!" Still, these excuses are no flimsier than the ones people use most often to avoid work; they only sound preposterous to someone who isn't making them up.

22:14   Verse 14 includes the first warning against adultery since its extended treatment in early chapters. The word "pit" appears only here and in 23:27 where its meaning is the same. A kind of sensual meaning is hinted at by this word; the way God punishes men who anger him is to let them fall into the "pit" of an adulteress. Those he loves are spared this evil.

22:15   Verse 15 includes still another reminder that corporal punishment produces a better child. Foolishness must be beaten or spanked out of little ones so that wisdom can be learned. "Folly" is such a serious flaw that serious steps must be taken to drive it far from childrens' hearts (cf. 14:8;. 17:12; 19:3; 24:9; and 27:22).

22:16   The man who "gets rich" or "increases his wealth" in verse 16 probably does so by both oppressing the poor and bribing the rich. The verse doesn't say bribe, yet the implication is clear. Poor people are the ones who need gifts, not rich ones. Giving to the poor, however, seems to reap no profit so gifts become not evidence of generosity as much as manipulative greed. The warning here is clear; he who oppresses the poor will himself become poor.

PART THREE

The Sayings of the Wise
Proverbs 22:17—24:34

12

Thirty Wise Sayings
Proverbs 22:17–24:22

Verses 17–21 introduce a new section titled "Sayings of 22:17–21 the wise" or "Thirty wise sayings." The first verse advises "pay attention," "listen," and "apply your heart"; strong imperatives similar to the ones expressed in earlier verses such as 1:2–6, 2:1, 3:1, 4:1, and 5:1.

Our way of saying the idiom of verse 18 (keep these sayings "in your heart") might be to "learn them by heart." The Hebrew literally advises us to "keep them in your belly" and "fix them on your lips." In ancient times the scarcity of books and literacy made the skill of memorizing almost a necessity. Still, despite the availability of Bibles and people who read today, memorizing proverbs and other portions of Scripture to tuck them away in our hearts remains an excellent practice.

The NAB includes the name of the Egyptian scribe, Amen-em-Ope, in verse 19; apparently because of two extra words in the original which literally mean "even you." This inclusion is highly speculative, however. We do have some information about an Egyptian wisdom catalog which is divided into thirty sections and credited to this Amen-em-Ope. The Egyptian document is incomplete, however, including only seventeen of thirty sections, each section being much longer than the individual verses or clusters of verses in Proverbs. Furthermore, many of the Egyptian proverbs sound more like verses outside this section of Proverbs than like those in it. Generally the bulk of evidence disproves rather than proves the dependence of Proverbs on Amen-em-Ope.

The word "thirty" may appear in verse 20, however; the Hebrew letters that spell thirty may also (with different vowels) spell "excellent" or "former." The author who said he wrote "thirty sayings" of counsel and knowledge may really have written "excellent sayings" or even sayings which weren't "formerly" written down. If "thirty," on the other hand, is an accurate translation, perhaps the number has something to do with the number of days in a month; coincidentally, Proverbs has thirty-one chapters, one chapter to be read each day of the month.

Verse 21 contains an interesting phrase to describe the person who is taught "true and reliable words." This person, says the sage, learns so well that "he can give sound answers to the one who sends him." This probably means that, when the time comes, the student will give the same answer as the teacher might have given.

22:22–23   The editors of many modern translations (including the NKJV but not the KJV or NEB) have grouped the "sayings of the wise" into thirty sections, each section a cluster of verses on the same theme (the TEV actually numbers the paragraphs). Yet a closer examination of these sections shows they aren't as tidy as they look; for example, verses 22:28 and 23:10 are too similar to deserve separate entries, and 23:29 – 35 seems disproportionately long even though it sticks to one theme.

The first cluster of verses (22 and 23) speaks against exploiting the poor. The Hebrew here literally translated says "taking advantage of the disadvantaged," making use of repetition for emphasis. This poetic device is also used in the warning against "exploiting the poor because they are poor" and God's defense of the poor which includes "arguing their arguments" as well as "plundering those who plunder them."

The Egyptian proverb most like verse 22 says:

> Guard against robbing the oppressed
> And against overbearing the disabled.*

Verse 23 has no parallel.

22:24–25   Verses 24 and 25 are linked together by the conjunction "lest," or, "or else." The teacher here strongly advises against

---

*This and all translations from the Egyptian are by John A. Wilson in *Ancient Near Eastern Texts*, ed. James B. Pritchard, Princeton University Press, 1955, pp. 421 – 24.

associating or "making friends" with "hot-tempered" or "easily angered" people. Other passages such as 15:17–18 warn against people like this; it is too easy to "learn his ways" and thus become "ensnared in sin." As is common to human nature we catch on to sin faster than we do to righteousness. Verse 24 says stay clear of this kind of evil.

Verses 26 and 27 are a warning against cosigning, a repetition of the teaching of 6:1–4. You may be a debt-free responsible citizen, but if you co-sign for someone who skips town or fails to pay back his loan the creditors will come looking for you. Paying back the money may leave you so destitute that "your very bed will be snatched from under you." You will have to live up to your cosigner commitment. **22:26–27**

Verses 26 and 27 have no Egyptian parallel since the institution of lending was virtually nonexistent there.

Verse 28 sounds like a piece of legal advice; don't move the "boundary stone" or "marker" (see also 23:10). An Egyptian proverb which parallels this verse is less pithy; it is four verses long and includes a warning against oppressing widows (cf. 15:25). **22:28**

Ancient people must have shared the problem of crooked farmers who moved markers in their fields in order to increase their acreage. The problem becomes critical within the context of inheritance, each Israelite having acquired property initially when the nation entered Canaan and divided up the land (Josh. 14:1). That land stayed in the same family for generation after generation, rarely if ever was it sold. Consider then, how easily one's property might shrink over the course of hundreds of years, especially if a dishonest neighbor was inclined to nudge boundary markers in his favor.

The way to influence kings or impress employers, says verse 29, is to do a good job. Gifts, bribes, or even boasting achieve little by comparison; those in charge generally know who is most productive. **22:29**

The Egyptian proverb that sounds most like this one says:

> As for the servant who is experienced in his office,
> He will find himself worthy (to be) a courtier.

Verses 1–3 of chapter 23 say that what you do at a banquet or elegant dinner tells others what kind of person you **23:1–3** are. The ruler who hosts a dinner has a sharp eye on his guests. Some are so awed by the elegant surroundings and rich array of food that they will probably miss out on the real purpose of the evening. Others will overeat, thereby revealing greed and overindulgence. Wise men, however, will eat with moderation and restraint, constantly aware of what the host is asking of them.

The term "restrain yourself" (TEV) or "don't stuff yourself" (LB) is literally "put a knife to your throat" in Hebrew. The meaning, however, is clear. One must be cautious and wise in the presence of superiors (see also 19:2's discussion on "soul").

23:4–5   The Egyptian proverb which parallels verses 4 and 5 includes this passage:

> Cast not thy heart in pursuit of riches . . .
> Do not strain to seek an excess . . .
> Their places may be seen, but they are not . . .
> They have made themselves wings like geese
>   and are flown away to the heavens.

The lesson of these verses in Proverbs is that happiness doesn't necessarily come with wealth. Even though a man may become exhausted trying to get rich, what he has amassed could disappear by tomorrow. "Have the wisdom to show restraint" in making money, says the proverb.

23:6–8   Verses 6–8 and 1–3 are similar in meaning. Both sections use the rare word "delicacies" (KJV "dainties"), although the settings for eating them are quite different. The earlier passage described guests at the table of a ruler or important man, while here we see guests at the table of a stingy man. Why does this second kind of person even have guests? Is he offering them dinner out of a sense of duty, to repay a social debt, or is he trying to bribe them?

Several linguistic problems appear in this passage. Does the Hebrew "evil eye" really mean stingy, or something else? Verse 7 is unclear too. The Greeks translated it "For eating and drinking (with him) is as if one swallowed a hair. Do not have him join you or eat bread with him." "Vomit" in verse 8 should be taken figuratively, not literally. It means that the whole course of events is nauseating. "It's enough to make you sick" might be the modern parallel here.

There is no Egyptian proverb which parallels these verses.

The brief lesson of verse 9 sounds like what we read in 23:9 18:2. Save your breath, says the sage, don't waste your advice on a fool. He won't listen to you anyway. The Egyptian parallel to this verse is more a warning against revealing secrets, specifically to fools.

Verses 10 and 11 teach the same lesson of 22:28, although 23:10–11 there the warning against moving boundary stones stressed heredity and antiquity while here it emphasizes the rights of the oppressed. It is so easy to take advantage of weak people and so easy to abuse those who cannot fight back. Wicked men know homes without fathers are easy marks, yet verse 11 says men who would attack them should think twice. The "Defender" of widows and fatherless children is no ordinary lawyer; he is God himself. He "will provide the legal aid" against anyone who tries to steal their property, and he WILL WIN the case.

Two words here deserve additional comment. The word in verse 10 is "fatherless," not "orphan," since by definition an orphan is parentless. "Widows and fatherless" are frequently used together in the Bible, both terms designating the absence of male leadership in the home.

The other word is "defender," elsewhere translated "redeemer." The ancient word refers to the closest relative responsible for the welfare of a widow and her children. How beautiful to think of God taking the place of both a lost husband and father as well as the legally responsible relative or friend in the lives of defenseless people.

Verse 12 is most characteristic of Proverbs, and central, 23:12 really, to all wisdom literature within and beyond Israel. From this verse on to the end of the "thirty sayings" section, there are no verses which parallel proverbs in the Egyptian document, "The Instruction of Amen-em-Ope" (with the possible exception of 24:11).

Verses 13 and 14, like other child-discipline verses (13:24, 23:13–14 29:15 and 17) encourage occasional spanking. Children may think they're going to die from such treatment, but the paddling should produce just the opposite effect. Discipline will save children by forcing out of them the very foolishness that might lead them to an early grave (the Hebrew word in verse 14 is *she'ol*).

It is doubtful that the teacher's word for "rod" is figurative here (as in Isa. 11:4). Scripture does endorse physical punishment, even if that means using a wooden stick on a child's bottom. Wisdom literature is also timeless in the sense that what is recommended here does not change in the New Testament. Children needed spankings then just as much as they need them today.

23:15–16   "My son," which introduces verses 15 and 16, brings us right back to the opening chapters of Proverbs. In some respects these verses in the "thirty sayings" represent the whole book, especially in their general statements about wisdom. Just as the parents of a fool grieve (10:1; 17:21, 25; 19:13), so parents who have wise children rejoice. Their hearts are glad because their children have their mouths under control.

23:17–18   Psalm 37:1 – 11 may be the classic passage urging believers not to envy sinners, but there are also four verses in the Book of Proverbs which teach that lesson: 3:31, 24:1, 19, and now verses 17 and 18. None is exactly like another, yet all use the key word "envy."

We are so often tempted to envy people who have more than we do. Some are rich with material possessions they have acquired through dishonest means, yet this avenue to wealth is not open to God's children. Even in poverty we must learn to be content with what we have, knowing that if our ways are pleasing to the Lord that, by faith, we will receive the kind of reward that will make life's riches pale by comparison.

23:19–21   Both "drunkards" and "gluttons" in verses 20 and 21 are rare words, yet their meaning is certain in this context. Verse 19 is a general admonition for sons to be wise but verse 20 gets down to specifics; don't associate with people who eat or drink too much. Verse 21 tells us why: alcohol and gluttony are expensive and debilitating.

As a general rule Christians do not abuse alcohol; overeating is something else. Alcohol may affect the mind in a way that overeating does not, but the two vices are very much the same. Is eating a necessity or a hobby? Would you rather eat out or give to the poor? How many "great places" do you know about for food? "Gorging on meat" is just as serious a sin as "drinking too much wine"; both are gluttony.

Verses 22–25 are not as closely related as verses in other 23:22–25
paragraphs, yet they do go together well enough to be considered one "saying." Three of the verses speak of parents, for
example. Verse 23 is the exception yet what it advises are
what parents most want for their children; truth, wisdom,
learning, and understanding.

Verse 22 includes the contrast between a child's birth and
his mother's old age, a rather unusual association of ideas.
The teaching perhaps suggests we should honor our parents
from the time we are born till the day they die.

Verses 24 and 25 use two words for happy five times, and
three words for parents (father, mother, and begetter) five
times. The device stresses the importance of the fifth commandment and the wonderful results of obeying it. Discipline
isn't meant to make a child miserable but to make him wise.
Parents who discipline their children are blessed correspond-
ingly by wise children who bring them joy.

Verses 26–28 are a mini-representation of the extensive 23:26–28
anti-adultery passages of chapters 5–7. "My son" introduces
this section of a father's advice to his son. The proverb may
be a warning against two kinds of loose women, the unmarried prostitute as well as the unfaithful wife. Still, the distinction doesn't matter much; all sex outside of marriage is
forbidden.

The prostitute traps her victims the same way the woman
in 7:6ff did; she "lies in wait like a bandit." The latter half of
verse 28 is somewhat unclear in traditional versions which
say something like "she increaseth the transgressors among
men" (KJV). Does she add to her clients, or add to her bag of
tricks to lure them in?

Verses 29–35 is the longest series of verses on the same 23:29–35
subject that we have encountered since we started the miscellaneous section at 10:1. In fact, it is the most comprehensive description of alcohol's bad effects in the entire Bible.
The description of a drunk here is so graphic that one wonders if the author himself had experienced drunkenness.

Verse 29 asks six questions: who is miserable, and has
sorrow, strife, complaints, bruises, and bloodshot eyes?
Verse 30 answers the question; "those who linger long over
wine" (NASB). Alcohol affects people in different ways. A re-
laxed, happy stage may exist for awhile, but "lingering over

wine" or too many for the road can quickly lead to irresponsible words and actions. Sometimes drinking produces anger or belligerence, even "strange sights" or mind-confusing things. But more often than not prolonged drinking will eventually lead to numb insensibility.

Verse 31 commands us to resist wine's allure which consists of sight, taste, and feel. Don't let its color, sparkle, or texture tempt you, says the sage.

Verse 32 tells what happens after the effects of wine wear off; what went down so smoothly now "bites like a snake and poisons like a viper." Everything hurts; bloodshot eyes and "needless bruises" are the results of beatings acquired when the drinker couldn't feel them. Woe, sorrow, strife, and complaints follow.

Verse 34 reflects a basic Hebrew aversion to the sea; its undulations reminding them of the wobbly legs of a drunkard. If it is hard to keep ones balance on deck, how much more difficult it must be to perch on the rigging far above the rolling motion of the waves.

Verse 35 is most tragic. After all these horrible after-effects of overindulgence, the drunkard finally manages to come to long enough to say, "when will I wake up so I can find another drink?" The easiest course is to resubmerge himself in the non-sense world where alcohol is king.

24:1–2   Verses 1 and 2 of chapter 24 are another warning against envy (cf. 23:17–18). The earlier passage said don't envy the wicked; obedience to God will pay off someday. The reason for not envying given in these verses is more immediate and practical. Why court evil, even if it seems to reap easy riches? Violence begets violence; such behavior is totally inappropriate to the people in God's family. The best course of action is not even to become familiar with such people. Their conversation is constantly on ways and means of making trouble for others while making money for themselves.

24:3–4   Verses 3 and 4 include three parallel lines plus a kind of coda. By wisdom, understanding, and knowledge, homes are built, established, and furnished. Furthermore, these homes are "filled with rare and beautiful treasures," meaning the fruits of the Spirit that live in those who acquire wisdom.

This metaphor of the house reminds us again of Jesus' parable of men who built houses on rock and sand (Luke 6:48).

The theme of verses 5 and 6 says brains are better than   24:5-6
brawn and wisdom is better than might (cf. 21:22). Verse 6
applies this teaching to the waging of war saying simply,
Don't go charging into battle without a plan. Other applications of the teaching might include: don't bite off more than
you can chew; don't start something you can't finish; and look
before you leap.

Two themes which seem to contradict each other appear in   24:7
Proverbs; one kind of fool has nothing to say in an intelligent
discussion while another kind speaks even though he has
nothing to say (12:23; 13:16; 15:2; 18:2). Perhaps the two
are not contradictory at all; both fools have nothing *worthwhile* to contribute. Verse 7 says wisdom is "too high" for the
fool who sits at the gate and says (or should say) nothing.

Only a few bad mistakes can give someone a bad reputa-   24:8-9
tion, yet the person who does bad things soon begins to be
obsessed by evil. Someone whose thoughts are continuously
evil is sick, but thinking this way is one habit we all too easily
acquire. Only God can control our thoughts, making them
captive to the mind of Christ, and purifying them of all wicked
and vain things. The process of good or evil starts in the
mind, expresses itself by mouth, and puts itself in action with
the hands. Those who would worship God "in spirit and in
truth" must enter his sanctuary with both clean hands and a
pure heart (Ps. 24:4).

Verse 10 is as cryptic in Hebrew as it is in English. The   24:10
gist of its meaning is not entirely clear but seems much like
the teaching of Jeremiah 12:5 (NIV):

> If you have raced with men on foot
>   and they have worn you out,
>   how can you compete with horses?
> If you stumble in safe country,
>   how will you manage in the thickets by the Jordan?

Although the second half of verse 11 is difficult to under-   24:11-12
stand, its meaning is probably much like that of the first half.
Its idiom is strange but its lesson seems quite simple; "rescue
anyone headed for death" or in the words of a popular hymn,
"Rescue the Perishing."

Verse 12 is the Old Testament counterpart to the question
"who is my neighbor?" Scripture answers here essentially the

173

way the parable of the good Samaritan did — everyone is my neighbor regardless of how well I know him. I may wish to turn away from someone who is in deep trouble, but the Lord will still hold me accountable for how I respond.

Verse 12 sounds a bit ominous with its warning that God not only sees what we do, but "weighs the heart that perceives it." Even our motives are known to God.

24:13 – 14   Honey has two qualities which prompt the writer of verses 13 and 14 to say, "Eat honey." Honey is "good" and it is "sweet." So is wisdom "good" and "sweet" to the soul. In fact, this "soul honey" is so desirable that it fills the one who eats it with a "future hope" which "will not be cut off." So relish wisdom as you would honey.

24:15 – 16   Verse 15 includes a few problem words such as "wicked" and "house." "Wicked" appears in a strange syntax here, while "house" is a rare form meaning something like "resting place." Perhaps the warning here is to the "outlaw" or wicked man "who lies in wait" and represents a threat to the righteous or honest man's "resting place" or peace of mind.

The sixteenth verse adds a threat to the warning, saying it's pointless and dangerous to try to harm the righteous because, in the end, you will meet your own destruction. The theme is a familiar one in Proverbs but what is new here is its form of command rather than warning; "Do not lie in wait," and "do not raid" are unmistakable imperatives.

24:17 – 18   An earlier verse which warned against mocking the poor or taking pleasure in someone else's misfortune (17:5) was somewhat easier to obey than the command of verses 17 and 18. Here we are told we may not rejoice or gloat over the misfortune of our enemies. How do we reconcile this passage with other portions of Scripture such as the songs of Moses and Miriam (Exod. 15) and numerous psalms which rejoice in God's triumph over enemies (e.g. 136:10, 17 – 22)? The difference is one's attitude; diligently resolving to praise God for his victory rather than the defeat of our enemies. The best solution would be to turn our enemies into our friends.

The New Testament carries this thought one step further. "Love your enemies," Jesus said, "and pray for those who persecute you" (Matt. 5:44, NIV). God never rejoices in the death of a sinner, so gloating over the defeat of an enemy would surely anger him (Ezek. 33:11).

Verses 19 and 20 are the third warning against envy in 24:19–20 this section (23:17; 24:1). Here we are told our future is bright because we love the Lord, but the wicked man has no future at all. The figure of speech used in verse 20 is of a lamp being "snuffed out" (cf. 13:9), representing the brightness of life and hope being extinguished in the sinner. Such a person has no future at all.

Verses 21 and 22 are like a summary of the thirty sayings. 24:21–22 The Book of Proverbs begins and ends with the phrase "the fear of the LORD" as does the conclusion of this "thirty sayings" section. Here the father tells his son to "fear the LORD *and* the king."

Mention of the king here alludes to the system of government in the days of Solomon and the sages. Ancient Israel was a theocracy ruled by God through a king. Rulers were divinely appointed and responsible to God for not only leading a country politically and socially, but also spiritually.

The meaning of "rebels" is somewhat unclear in verse 22; does disaster fall *on* them or does it come *from* them? Perhaps "rebels" shouldn't be used here at all; the RSV suggests disaster comes from God and the king upon those who do not fear them.

13

Further Sayings of the Wise
Proverbs 24:23–34

Verses 23–24 include a collection of miscellaneous proverbs titled "Further Sayings of the Wise." The first half of verse 23 introduces the "sayings," while its second half leads right into the teaching of verses 24 and 25.

The theme of fair judgment in verses 23; and 25 was stated **24:23b–25** before (cf. 17:15; 18:5; 28:21). Here we are warned specifically against partiality or prejudice, or, in the words of the Hebrew idiom, not to "respect faces." Think, for instance, of racial prejudice; judgment based almost entirely on looks rather than merit. Verses 24 and 25 name the rewards of judgment; cursing and denouncement to those who judge unfairly and rich blessings to the one who is fair.

The rules apply to all of us, not just black-robed officials. Every one of us makes judgments, many times a day. What Scripture forces us to ask ourselves is are we prejudiced? Do we accuse the righteous and acquit the guilty? Are we so fair that we reap blessings from others instead of rejection?

A kiss is a sign of affection, friendship, trust, and com- **24:26** mitment. Verse 26 says people appreciate an honest answer as much as a kiss from a friend. The words may not be what you want to hear, but because they are honest you will be grateful for them (cf. 27:6).

"First things first" is our modern equivalent of verse 27. **24:27** The proverb stresses the importance of good planning, especially within the context of settling onto new property. "Get your fields ready," the verse says, "then build your house"; good advice to Israelites who received property through conquest and weren't sure of its suitability for farming. Only

177

after they farmed it would they know if it would be productive enough to consider building on it.

24:28–29 Verses 28 and 29 deal with integrity in legal testimony as well as retaliation. False witness in court was apparently so severe a problem in Bible times that the ninth commandment was written to stop it. In those times (before computers, lie detector machines, or forensic medicine) life or death matters or at least questions of honor depended solely on the truthfulness of witnesses. False testimony could have disastrous results.

Verse 29's "doing to him as he has done to me" is exactly opposite the spirit of the golden rule ("do to others as you would have them do to you" Luke 6:31.) It is not our business to punish others for what they have done to us; revenge belongs to the Lord (cf. 20:22).

24:30–34 Verses 30–34 make up another long section which is a kind of lesson from life or folksy tale with a moral. The story comes straight from a farmer's field in Palestine. From the first verse we know exactly what kind of farmer owns it; he is lazy and stupid. His land is overrun with thorns and weeds, the stone wall around it "in ruins."

The initial lesson here is easy enough to pick up. What do others see when they look at our property, junky garages, peeling paint, and obvious needs for repair? Do our sloppy, lazy habits make us so careless that others are appalled by the evidence of neglect?

Verse 32 goes on with the "moral of the story"; a verbatim quote from Proverbs 6:10–11: "A little sleep, a little slumber, a little folding of the hands to rest — " (NIV). What begins with just a little nap eventually becomes a way of life. The end result of such a lifestyle is, the sage says, "poverty which will come on you like a bandit and scarcity like an armed man" (NIV). The lesson is obvious; work hard and you won't go hungry.

PART FOUR

More Proverbs of Solomon Copied by Hezekiah's Men

Proverbs 25–29

V erse 1 of chapter 25 is valuable not only because it tells us something about how chapters 25–29 took form, but also how editors and copyists worked to gather and record ancient proverbs. Hezekiah was a good king; peace and prosperity prevailed while he was on the throne. Such conditions made it possible for art, literature, and true religion to thrive. Although these proverbs were written many years before by Solomon, he knew nothing about the Book of Proverbs as we know it today.

25:1

Verses 2–7 all make some reference to the king. Verse 2 seems strange at first though; how can matters which are "concealed by God" also be the "glory of kings"? To understand we must first recognize that in ancient Palestine the king was patron not only of the arts but also of the sciences, so, hand in hand with wisdom in the more philosophical sense went wisdom in the natural dimension. Really to discover something about the world around us is not to feel triumph over God but to give him additional honor because the discovery generally leads to new areas which invite exploration.

25:2

The Hebrew word for "conceal" in verse 2 and "unsearchable" in verse 3 link the two verses. As God's thoughts are hidden from the king, so the king's are hidden from us. This "unsearchable" quality may either refer to the superior wisdom of a monarch or else his unaccountable whims; thinking or acting as he pleases without explaining his actions to anyone. Such a monarch is to be feared as well as honored.

25:3

Verses 4 and 5 belong together, the first a proverb and the second its application. Both verses begin with "take away" or

25:4–5

"remove"; remove dross from silver and you will have something valuable enough for the silversmith to work on. In much the same way removing the impurities, or wicked men, from a king's palace will allow wise men to rule through him. How does a king spot such impurities, or evil advisers? Hopefully "The king . . . knows evil when he sees it" (20:8, TEV).

25:6-7   Scribes who originally divided the verses of Proverbs may have made a mistake when they included verse 7 in with verse 6; clearly the last line of verse 7 belongs with 8. Some newer translations (e.g. NEB, NAB, and NIV) simply incorporated this line in with verse 8, thereby doing away with the problem.

Verses 6 and 7 are linked by the word "before" or "in the presence of;" both the verses speak of pride and presumption. They were paraphrased by Jesus in his illustration of a wedding guest who presumed to take a higher seat at the table than what he deserved (Luke 14:8-10).

25:8   The proverb in verse 8 is a warning against hasty legal action. "You'll hear from my lawyer" or "I'll sue you" should always be difficult words for a Christian to say, for if a "neighbor puts you to shame" in court you may lose both your honor as well as the case. Better to "drop the matter before a dispute breaks out" (17:14) or settle out of court (Luke 12:58) than run to a lawyer with all the attendant grief and expense.

25:9-10   The Hebrew in verses 9 and 10 seems a little awkward, but the essence of this proverb is that when you argue against someone in court you yourself become vulnerable; "he who hears it may shame you." Are you "shamed" because you have attacked your brother openly or because your suit against him betrays what he formerly said in confidence to you? Perhaps both actions are responsible. How much better to go the route of Matthew 18:15: "If your brother sins against you, go to him and show him his fault. But do it privately."

25:11   Verse 11 includes the well-known image of "apples of gold in pictures of silver" (KJV). A "word aptly spoken" is compared to this image which is so beautiful in its simplicity that no more words are necessary.

Rabbi Ibn Ezra once said a proverb has three characteristics: few words, right sense, and fine image. Lord John Russell said a proverb contains the wisdom of many and the wit of one. Archer Taylor said a proverb is characterized by "shortness, sense, and salt."[1] The proverb in verse 11 matches these definitions well.

"Gold" connects verse 12 with the preceding verse; here an 25:12
earring or ornament of "fine gold" is compared to a "wise man's rebuke." The "rebuke" is also a "word aptly spoken" but goes one step further as the theme of this verse links up with others which teach about accepting criticism and taking advice.

A trustworthy employee is like a cold drink on a hot day 25:13
says verse 13 with its image of "coolness of snow at harvest time." A faithful messenger can always be depended on to arrive when he is most needed. His masters find him refreshing.

The image of "clouds and wind without rain" in verse 14 25:14
is especially meaningful to people desperate for moisture to save their crops. To the farmers of ancient Palestine, clouds black and bulging with promise yet devoid of moisture were infuriatingly unproductive. They were like people who boast and brag, promise and predict, but never produce. We all know the type. But rather than think of them, ask yourself, "Do I make a pretense of being more than I am? Do people get an inflated picture of me? Am I a wind bag?"

The Hebrew of verse 15 includes the intriguing image of 25:15
a "soft tongue which is able to break a bone" to illustrate how patience can persuade rulers far more effectively than violence (cf. 15:1, 16:15). It takes time for bone to be softened to the point where even a tongue can break it, and sometimes it takes long years of diligent work to bring about changes in an administration, government, or church.

The word which means "surfeited" links verses 16 and 17; 25:16–17
"too much" honey will make you vomit just like "too much" dropping in on a neighbor will make him sick. Too much of anything, regardless of how good it is, can be revolting.

"Familiarity breeds contempt" is the modern equivalent of verse 17; don't make a nuisance of yourself by spending too much time at the home of a friend. Wisdom is knowing when you are welcome and when you are not, sensitivity to the feelings of others being the key.

[1]From *The Proverb*, Cambridge, Mass., 1931, pp. 7–8, 95.

25:18   Verse 18 includes another warning against false testimony, here likened to a "club, sword, or sharp arrow" directed against a neighbor. Of these three weapons only a club is unusual. It is mentioned only two other times in the Bible and is related to the verb "scatter." Certainly lying about another man wounds him; he can be beaten, stabbed, or cut by words which are just as cruel as weapons.

25:19   The "bad" or "loose" tooth and "lame foot" of verse 19 are apt illustrations of someone that fails you when you need him most. Eating and walking, basic functions in life, are dependent on teeth and feet. Someone you depend on for help in a time of trouble is also crucial. What a disappointment to discover he or she is unreliable.

25:20   Problems in the Hebrew of verse 20 make us uncertain whether the singer has a sad heart or sings songs to someone who has a sad heart. Although the second is most often used, both meanings illustrate singing that is neither appropriate nor timely. Instead of soothing the troubled soul like oil (Isa. 1:6), this singing is like robbing a man of a coat on a winter's day, or pouring "vinegar on soda." Sensitivity to the feelings of others is the key here.

25:21–22   Since verses 21 and 22 are quoted in Romans 12:20, most people probably think Paul wrote them instead of Solomon. The lesson of mercy here, however, is hardly limited to the New Testament. Moses, in fact, taught early in Exodus 23:4–5 that you should help your enemy's donkey out of the ditch. David's treatment of Saul also is a vivid example of mercy toward someone who persecutes him. This thread runs through the ministry of Christ and is particularly pronounced in the beatitudes (Matt. 5:3–10).

The "coals of fire" or "burning coals" in verse 22 aren't difficult to understand if we realize that treating an enemy with "food to eat" and "water to drink" actually makes him see his own shame. Kindness is so unexpected that it burns into his conscience, teaching him a lesson no violence could. Such action is the noblest of all because it succeeds in saving the enemy while it destroys his enmity.

25:23   The gossip or "sly tongue" of verse 23 is obviously the kind of talk that only serves to harm others. Like the "north wind that brings rain" this kind of behavior can only succeed in producing the "angry looks" of fractured and broken relationships.

Verse 24 is identical to 21:9, emphasizing the importance of removing oneself from an angry spouse until he or she has cooled down enough to talk out a problem.

Receiving good news by letter from a friend or relative in a faraway country is, verse 25 says, like the gift of cold water to a desert-weary man. Such news is a relief, a blessing, and a special gift to people who might have prayed for weeks or even months for others in special need.

The image in verse 26 is of a good person who is like a spring or well which is contaminated by the pollution and poison of wicked men. It takes a while for a spring to cleanse itself, and once a good man has capitulated to evil his honor may never be restored. Before it is pure again, many who drink from it may suffer or even die. The righteous man who would be pure and refreshing to others must never "give way to the wicked."

The first half of verse 27 is clear but the second half doesn't seem to fit in with it. A wooden translation of the Hebrew here reads: "the searching of their honor, honor." If we repeat the "not good" of line one in the second one we read, "it is not an honor to seek one's own honor." The problem is the phrase still is not analogous to the first half, unless the author meant here that trying to be too honorable might be just as sickening as eating too much honey. Is he saying, perhaps, that the person who is truly honorable or praiseworthy won't covet the praise of others?

The last verse of chapter 28 teaches patience; self-control is like a city that is well fortified while a lack of self-control is like a city without a wall. Learning to accept insult, defeat, and disappointment without taking offense will only help you in life; a short fuse and hot temper can only result in getting you into more trouble while increasing your vulnerability to the attacks of others.

Proverbs often speaks of impropriety: the gold ring in a pig's snout, a slave who rules, a fool who eats rich food, or the wife who is quarrelsome. Verse 1 of chapter 26 picks up this theme by likening a fool who receives praise to "snow in summer" or "rain in harvest"; neither is appropriate. In fact, fools who are encouraged might be just as destructive as snow or rain out of season. The lesson is simple; do not give praise to a fool.

26:2   The references to birds and animals in Proverbs (vv. 2, 3, 11, 13, and 17) may not indicate Solomon's rural upbringing as much as his wide-ranging zoological interests. First Kings 4:33 says Solomon "talked about animals, birds, reptiles, and fish."

We have a saying, "Sticks and stones can hurt my bones, but names will never harm me." Verse 2 somewhat disputes that saying; an "undeserved curse," like a hex or "evil eye" brings a lot of "hurt." Words were very meaningful in Solomon's day; blessings as well as curses carried a lot of weight. Like the flutter or darting of restless birds, so curses (even undeserved ones) cause anxiety, restlessness, and fear in the person who is cursed. The irony is, the one who utters the curse often forgets about it much sooner than the person who is cursed.

26:3   Verse 3 includes a neat three-way analogy, the moral of the story coming with the third in the series. Just as whips are for horses and halters for donkeys, so rods or paddles are made for fools.

26:4–5   Verses 4 and 5 include one of the most interesting paradoxes in Proverbs. One verse says "don't answer a fool according to his folly" while the other says "answer a fool according to his folly." If you don't answer you won't run the risk of being a fool, but if you do answer you'll prevent him from thinking he is smart. Perhaps the real lesson here is no matter what you do, you won't win in your dealings with a fool. Some Jewish proverbs also reflect this proverb's frustration with fools: "A fool can ask more questions in an hour then ten wise men can answer in a year"; "The biggest foolishness of the fool is this: he thinks he's smart"; or, "when a wise man talks to a fool, two fools are conversing."

26:6   Two ideas of former proverbs are combined in verse 6. The reliable messenger of 25:13 and the unreliable messenger compared to a "lame foot" in 25:19 are like the man who "cuts off his feet" in verse 6 when he uses a fool to deliver a message. Certainly such action is destined for failure; only wise and reliable men ought to be trusted to deliver messages.

26:7   Verse 7 also uses the word "legs" although these legs are limp and lame, not "cut off" like those in verse 6. This proverb teaches the impropriety of offering wisdom to a fool; he is just as powerless to understand or make use of it as lame legs are to walk.

The man who is foolish enough to tie a stone into a sling- **26:8**
shot is doing something just like that when he praises a fool,
says verse 8. Misusing a weapon may result in personal injury
just like misusing words of honor may permanently damage
the fool as well as the one who praises him.

The second part of verse 9 is exactly like verse 7, but what **26:9**
the first part means isn't clear. Most translators agree it says
something about a drunkard with a thorn, but what that
means includes several possibilities: (1) The drunkard is so
insensitive to pain he doesn't even feel a thorn in his hand
just like the fool is so insensitive to wisdom he doesn't know
when he says something wise. (2) The drunkard who carries
a thorny branch in his hand waves it around as dangerously
as a fool spouts proverbs (a little knowledge is a dangerous
thing). (3) The man who is so inebriated that he can't pull a
thorn out of his hand is like a fool who doesn't know how to
apply the proverb he has on his lips. No matter which meaning you choose, the point of this proverb is that proverbs don't
belong in the mouths of fools.

The Hebrew of verse 10 is unclear although certainly the **26:10**
proverb is a warning against employers who hire fools or "any
passers by." The one who uses such indiscrimination is like
"an archer who wounds at random;" hiring fools is just one
more way of encouraging them.

Peter used the same figure of a "dog returning to his vomit" **26:11**
to describe apostate believers (2 Pet. 2:22) as verse 11 does
to describe fools who persist in foolishness. Although this
image is repulsive, so is the fool and reprobate Christian;
both persist in returning to disgusting habits and beliefs.

The only thing worse than a fool, says verse 12, is someone **26:12**
who is proud. Such a person is too proud to listen to anyone
else, even someone who tells him he is a sinner. The person
who will not admit sin sees no need for a Savior. Pride or
self-deception is Satan's most powerful tool. The ones who
least think they need deliverance are the very ones who need
it most.

Verses 13–16 all speak about the "sluggard," the first **26:13**
sounding much like 22:13. This man is worried about two
kinds of lions, one "in the road" and another that "roams the
streets," yet both sound like far-fetched excuses to explain
why this loafer won't leave his house to go to work.

26:14   Verse 14 compares the sluggard's movements in bed to a door swinging on its hinges. He looks as if he might be getting up to do something productive, but then he falls back on the pillows. He simply lacks the ambition, drive, or self-discipline necessary to swing out of bed and head for work.

26:15   Verse 15 is much like 19:24; this lazy oaf is so stupid he might starve to death because he can't even bring food from the dish to his mouth.

26:16   Verse 16 uses the phrase "wise in his own eyes" to describe a person who is also a sluggard. This one thinks he is so smart that he can outwit anyone (the meaning of "seven" men), when actually he is totally incapable of measuring up to their "discreet" answers.

26:17   A person who grabs a dog by the ears (the Greek reads "tail") is asking for trouble in much the same way as someone who "meddles in other people's business," says verse 17. Only a fool would try to insert himself between fighting participants. They might turn on him like angry dogs despite his attempts at peacemaking.

26:18–19   Humor is a delightful gift from God but it can be misused, says the proverb in verses 18 and 19. The man who "deceives his neighbor" and says he was "only joking" is like a crazy person with deadly weapons. Even if this man *was* just playing a trick, it was hardly funny. Good humor does not laugh at another man's discomfort. The prankster here shows insensitivity as well as poor moral judgment.

26:20   The comparison of fire without wood and a quarrel without gossip is one lesson that's hard to miss; you can't have one without the other. Verse 20 is the first of three proverbs with the theme of gossip, this one saying it is like "fuel" to a quarrel.

26:21   Verse 21 continues the theme of gossip with the use of the "wood-and-fire" image. Here however are added the image of charcoal-to-embers and quarrelsome people-to-arguments. Trouble-makers or quarrelsome people actually *kindle* strife, a Hebrew word which means "heat up." Even today we tend to connect the same ideas of fire and burning to angry people; consider a "heated argument" between people who are "hot under the collar" or have "fiery tempers."

26:22   Verse 22 is identical to 18:8. Here, however, it fits in better with preceding verses. The lesson is clear; even though gossip is evil and malicious its "choice morsels" are all too often irresistible.

Although verse 23 was once very difficult to understand, archeological discoveries along the Syrian coast which have shed light on a number of problem areas in the Bible have also cleared up this verse. Older translations which once talked about "silver dross" on a "potsherd" now are rendered "coating of glaze over earthenware" with a simple change in word division. Now the image makes sense; people dipped their pottery vessels in glaze or slip in order to make them shiny.

The shiny pots are compared in this verse to "fervent lips with an evil heart," the Greek translation reads "smooth" instead of "fervent" or "fiery," but whatever the meaning is of this uncertain word, the lesson of the proverb is clear; the hypocrisy of these lips is like veneer laid over a heart that is cheap and profane. Jesus' illustration was of whitewashed tombs (Matt. 23:27).

Verses 24–26 expand the theme of verse 23 and its warn- ing against a hypocrite. All three verses describe how clever this "malicious man" is, "disguising himself with his lips," using "charming speech," and "concealing his malice by deception." The essence of hypocrisy is disguise; showing one thing on the outside while being something else inside. This man speaks words of flattery from a heart that seethes with hate.

Yet happily he is eventually exposed; people begin to see through his lies and unmask his wickedness. Hopefully this action will result in his repentence, forgiveness, and restoration.

The image of a man who digs a pit to trap someone, then falls into it himself is found in Psalms (7:15; 9:15; 57:6) as well as verse 27. This is "dynamistic retribution," the natural tendency of things to get even. The stone that rolls back on the man who displaced it also teaches that if we disturb the natural order it will retaliate. This second image is somewhat reminiscent of Sisyphus, the ancient king of Corinth who had to spend eternity rolling a boulder up a hill only to have it roll down before he reached the top.

The theme of an evil tongue which has appeared in the last twelve verses ends here with verse 28, serving as a final warning that "lying tongues" and "flattering mouths" bring hurt and ruin. We aren't sure whether the liar or his victim suffers "ruin" here; the first half of this verse suggests the victim, but verse 27 and others say the liar himself comes to ruin.

27:1   The first verse of chapter 27 is often quoted; "Do not boast about tomorrow, for you do not know what a day might bring forth." Don't take life for granted, warns the verse in an almost ominous tone, certainly don't brag about things that may never happen. The verse is *not* an indictment against long-range planning (e.g. 24:6), however it is a warning against a cock-sure attitude toward controlling all the events in our lives.

27:2   The lesson of verse 2 is obvious yet hard to put into practice. A person who praises himself doesn't give praise at all. He exhibits pride. Praise by definition must come from others, yet think of how many times in seemingly innocent ways we praise ourselves. Little allusions to who we know, where we've been, or what we have are all manifestations of pride.

27:3   The stones and sand of verse 3 were images ancient Israelites were thoroughly familiar with; their heaviness and burden apt comparisons to the load of trouble caused by a fool. In fact, even desert sand that blew into faces, and rocks that had to be cleared off the land before it could be farmed were not as aggravating as the "provocation of a fool." This provocation, says the verse, "is heavier than both."

27:4   Verse 4 uses the same structure as verse 3. Here anger is "cruel" and fury "overwhelming," but "who can stand before jealousy?" Perhaps jealousy too is "heavier than both," involving as it does both anger and wrath.

27:5   Verse 5 is a "better than" proverb which explains the delicate task of criticizing in love. Often we are not sure about what to say to a person we know is doing wrong. Should we rebuke him openly or hold our tongues in silence? Verse 5 says if our love for that person is genuine we should correct him (cf. 28:23).

27:6   Verse 6 in Hebrew is a perfect antithetical parallel. Friend is paired against enemy, wound against kiss, faithful against deceptive. Kisses may come from an enemy while wounds come from a friend, yet how easily we would accept the kisses and reject the wounds despite their sources. We are so afraid of pain! Consider here the lesson of so many proverbs about the wise man who learns to accept criticism.

27:7   Verse 7 may speak about eating but that isn't its only meaning. People who are full reject honey while those who are hungry would be satisfied even with something bitter. Is the sage here trying to illustrate life's inequalities; people who have so much they don't want anymore versus others who are so needy they would rejoice at even a handout? Surely there is a way to reconcile some of these extremes today.

Verse 8 has an "as . . . so" or "like . . . is" format which compares a "man who strays from home" to a "bird that strays from its nest." One Bible commentator says this proverb is "a comment on the malaise of rootlessness."[2] A man that leaves home doesn't necessarily misbehave, although he might. The real problem is that in moving away he has severed all connections that make him a responsible member of society. He no longer feels an integral part of family, community, or nation.

27:8

One of the most tragic effects of a mobile, transferable society today is that people no longer have a place they can call home because every few years they must sever bonds of friendship, abandon familiar surroundings, and adjust to new patterns of life. Surely this rootlessness is a contributing factor to anti-institutionalism and the breakdown of the family.

The Hebrew of the second half of verse 9 is so unclear that any translation must be viewed with caution. Although a variety of interpretations are offered, the one that seems most reasonable makes the second half of the verse synonymous with the first. The verse thus sounds something like this: "perfume and incense bring joy to the heart" like "the counsel of a friend brings sweetness to the taste."

27:9

Verse 10 is obviously longer than most proverbs and could probably have been divided into two verses. The first part talks about friendship and the responsibility we have to cultivate friends from generation to generation.

27:10

The second half of the verse reminds us that when we get in trouble we should seek help from someone who is physically close. Blood relatives who are miles away can offer far less than neighbors who are close by. The verse might also refer here to brothers who are alienated in affection from each other in contrast to friends that are like brothers of the heart. A modern commentary on this proverb is "You can pick your friends but you have to take your relatives" (cf. 18:24).

[2]William McKane, *Proverbs,* p. 612.

27:11   The first line of verse 11 sounds like so many other proverbs; the father or sage urging the son or disciple to be wise
and so bring happiness. The second half, however, includes
a new thought. The term "critic" or "someone who treats me
with contempt" is used also in Psalms 69:9 and 119:42, the
lesson being the son whose wisdom brings joy to a father's
heart also gives him such a lift that he can answer anyone,
even someone that criticizes him.

27:12   Verse 12 is almost identical to 22:3; with its lesson that
prudent men are cautious and pull back from danger while
foolish men who are oblivious to risk keep going. They will
eventually suffer for their carelessness.

27:13   The proverb in verse 13 is the same as 20:16; be sure you
get collateral (such as a coat) from a man who co-signs a loan
with a risky partner such as a "wayward woman."

27:14   People who rise early in the morning should be sensitive
to others who may be still sleeping says verse 14. There is a
proper time for everything (Eccles. 3:1–8), even blessing and
praise. Loud singing or exuberant "praise the Lords," no matter how sincere, should never infringe upon the rights of others. Even knowing when to praise requires wisdom.

27:15–16   The "quarrelsome wife" of verses 15 and 16 is the same
one that is mentioned in 19:13b, but here more is said about
her. Here she is likened to the monotonous "dripping on a
rainy day." No one is able to stop her from complaining. Re-
straining her is as futile as "stopping the wind" or "trying to
hold oil in your hand." The only way to deal with her is to
remove oneself from her until she cools down (cf. 21:9, 19).

27:17   The "sharpening" of iron against iron and man against
man in verse 17 is a verb which appears only six other times
in the Bible (Hab. 1:8; Ezek. 21:9, 10, 11). The image here
is striking; as knives are sharpened by other tools of steel, so
scholars, artists or athletes can "sharpen" each other by com-
petition, the exchange of ideas, and constructive criticism.

27:18   Verse 18 talks about rewards; the man who takes care of
his fig tree gets to eat figs while the servant who cares for his
master will win praise. The lesson here is literal as well as
symbolic; anything we prune, cultivate, and work hard at will
yield benefits as well as win praise. Even our heavenly master
honors those who honor him.

Mirrors, like reflections in a pool of water, don't lie, says **27:19** verse 19. Neither does a man's heart or mind reveal something different from what he is. In Hebrew it is a cryptic proverb with no verbs and two pairs of repeated words ("Face to face and man to man"), but the correct sense seems to be that which we have in our standard modern English translations. Our actions tell others what goes on inside us.

The "Death" and "Destruction" (or *sh^e'ol* and *Abaddon*) of **27:20** verse 20 are never satisfied; these places of the dead always want more. So too human desires (literally "eyes") are "never satisfied." People who have still want more. The comparison of restless eyes to the grave is probably intentionally sinister here; cemeteries are full of people who died still thinking wealth could bring them happiness.

The first half of verse 21 is identical to 17:3 but the second **27:21** part seems a bit uncertain. As silver is tested by the crucible and gold by a furnace, a man is tested by "praise." But is this the praise he receives or people and things he praises? If the second meaning is correct we might well ask ourselves what excites and thrills us enough to elicit praise. What do we pay money for and spend time to see? "Your heart will be where your treasure is," Jesus said (Luke 12:34).

Some English translations omit the middle line of verse 22 **27:22** about grinding grain in a pestle while others paraphrase the entire proverb. Regardless of which translation is used, the teaching of the verse is clear; fools are so stubborn that even if they are ground in a mortar (like grain) they still won't give up their foolishness. "Drunkards sober up," says an old Jewish proverb, "but fools remain fools."

Verses 23–27 form a beautiful little unit which teaches a **27:23–27** lesson drawn from rural life. The passage is rich with farm language including five different terms for animals (vv. 23, 26, 27), and three for hay (v. 25).

An investment in livestock is probably less risky than other commodities, say verses 23 and 24. The view reflects the obvious agricultural bias of ancient Israel while stressing the transcient nature of wealth (see also 10:2; 13:11a; 18:11; 20:21; 21:6; 28:20, 22).

Just as the livestock must be cared for so the fields too must be put to best use, staggering plantings so that crops may be harvested at different times, and rotating crops to get the best yield possible.

The crop of hay, if properly timed, will feed lambs and goats, which, in turn, will provide wool (v. 26), milk (v. 27), and money (v. 26) which can be used to purchase more land.

The major lesson of this passage is that we must exercise wisdom in planning so that we can take proper care of our assets and make them work for us. Healthy animals, productive fields, timely harvesting, and judicious use of its yield all require wisdom.

28:1 Why does the wicked man of verse 1 (chapter 28) run even though no one is chasing him? Probably because he has a bad conscience. God said that if his people disobeyed him they too would run even though there was no enemy (Lev. 26:17). Deuteronomy said too that guilty men would run from their enemies even though they were few (28:25; 32:30). Righteous men, on the other hand, are "bold as a lion," ready to take on the forces of the wicked. Their courage comes from God who is on their side. Their cause is just; even a few of them can defeat the enemy (Lev. 26:7 – 8).

28:2 What was true of ancient Israel is true today; instability and economic hardship produce the kind of unrest in a country that makes governments and regimes topple, while wise and informed leaders (such as Solomon) "maintain order." Verse 2 is vivid commentary on the history of Israel itself; when kings were good they usually reigned long and the country prospered. Bad kings, on the other hand, were quickly dethroned and the country forced to suffer at the hands of outside oppressors or internal droughts and famine.

28:3 Verse 3 uses one word that is unclear; is it a "ruler," "poor man" or "evil man" that oppresses the poor? Regardless of which word is chosen, the point is this man "like a driving rain that leaves no crops" destroys the only improvable assets he has. He is cruel, foolish, and despicable.

28:4 The dominant theme in chapter 28 is respect for the law and government. The antithetic parallel of verse 4 contrasts the lawbreaker with the lawkeeper. Laws were made to protect good men from the wicked, so men who side with the wicked thus oppose the law. Those who uphold the law, on the other hand, are against evil men. Incidentally the word for law here is *torah*, perhaps referring to all the teachings of the Bible rather than just to civil law.

The lesson of verse 5 is much like that of the preceding verse; evil men don't "understand" or align themselves with justice, while those who "seek the LORD" or obey his laws understand justice well. The term "justice" here is more than just a legal term; it suggests moral and religious standards as well.

Verse 6 is typical of the kind of generalizations Proverbs makes; of all the combinations possible in life, here we see only two. It's better to be poor and honest, says the sage, than rich and dishonest. Surely we would all rather choose to be rich and honest — like Solomon himself. But then he would probably ask, "what's more important, riches or honesty?"

Verse 7 includes a rather new description; a son is advised to keep the law and not become a "companion of gluttons" (elsewhere "profligates," JB, or "good-for-nothings," TEV). Gluttons as companions represent a poor choice, equated with drunkards, sluggards, and fools who become poor through laziness coupled with expensive tastes (23:20, 21). The son who hangs around people like that soon becomes like them, thus "disgracing his father" and his teaching.

Verse 8 is the only reference to usury in Proverbs. Mosaic law actually prohibited usury (Exod. 22:25; Lev. 25:36, 37; Deut. 23:19), but this proverb does not forbid it as much as tell what happens to people who charge exorbitant interest. The punishment is neatly appropriate; "the money he amassed will be redistributed to the poor." Will someone take him to court and convict him of usury? Will he die without heirs? Or will God simply see to it that his fortune is suddenly lost? How it happens doesn't really matter; the point is these men reap what they sow.

The "deaf ear" of verse 9 becomes more significant if we realize Hebrew does not have separate words for "hear" and "obey." To do one is to do the other. This proverb simply says that if we don't listen to or obey God he won't listen to us when we pray.

Verse 10 is three lines long in some translations and four lines long in others because some translators thought it looked incomplete with three. Regardless of its length, the lesson here is clear; men who seek to trap good men into evil will fall into those traps themselves (see also 26:27). Doing evil is bad enough, but tricking others into doing it too is so odious that it reaps swift punishment. "Blameless men," on the other hand, will not be punished like wicked men but will instead inherit good.

28:11   The rich man who is "wise in his own eyes" in verse 11 is a proud know-it-all, but poor men "with discernment" are supposedly able to "see through" him. How well do we see "through" the facades of people who are rich and famous? How often we equate wisdom or expertise with the ability to make money, score a touchdown, or thrill an audience? Do we really "see through" that facade?

"It makes no difference if you're right or wrong; When you're rich they think you really know," says a line from "Fiddler on the Roof." We should know better. Do we?

28:12   Verse 12 sounds like other verses yet is significantly different from all of them. It speaks about the elation that accompanies the triumph of the righteous in contrast to the fear that is produced by the wicked man's rise to power. A strong, stable government ruled by honest leaders is a wonderful blessing; far too many people in this world labor under the tyranny of unjust rulers. Perhaps those who "go into hiding" when wicked men reign are doing the wisest thing. They hope that the seeds of the regime's undoing which it carries within itself will soon germinate, sprout, and effect its overthrow.

28:13   Some people think sinners who break the rules always win while good people who keep them always lose. Verse 13 says just the opposite; if you want to succeed in the game of life you must keep the rules.

The proverb is an antithetic parallel which neatly contrasts the man who "conceals his sin" and "does not prosper" with the man who "confesses and renounces his sin" and "finds mercy." John might have been thinking of this proverb when he wrote:

> If we say that we have no sin, we deceive ourselves, and there is no truth in us. But if we confess our sins to God, he will keep his promise and do what is right: he will forgive us our sins and purify us from all our wrongdoing. (1 John 1:8–9, TEV)

28:14   Some translations add "the LORD" to verse 14, thus providing a subject for an otherwise passive verb. It then reads

"Blessed is the man who always fears the LORD" (NIV) instead of "Happy is the man that feareth always" (KJV). In contrast to this happy man, the one who "hardens his heart falls into trouble."

Verse 15 as well as many others in this chapter speak about oppressive governments. According to verse 12 people hide when bad men rule as well they should; here bad rulers "rule over helpless people like a roaring lion or charging bear." These ferocious animals were common enough in Palestine to be used as vivid examples of cruel rulers (cf. 19:12 and 20:2).

Verse 16 also speaks about government, here faulting the "tyrannical ruler who lacks judgment" while commending one who "hates ill-gotten gain." One is short on sense and long on cruelty while the other who has good sense will live long.

Literally verse 17 reads, "A man oppressed by the blood of a soul will flee toward a pit; don't support (or grab) him." The man here is a murderer so tormented by his guilty conscience that he tries to kill himself ("pit" meaning grave or death). Does the last part of this verse really advise not helping the poor man? Perhaps; aiding or abetting a criminal is, in itself, a crime. The verse might also be suggesting we shouldn't interfere with a man's self-induced punishment; no one tried to stop Judas from hanging himself after he betrayed Jesus.

A few samples of how this verse reads in different translations should illustrate how varied its interpretations are:

A murderer's conscience will drive him into hell. Don't stop
    him! (LB)

A man charged with bloodshed
will jump into a well to escape arrest. (NEB)

A man guilty of murder is digging his own grave as fast as
    he can.
Don't try to stop him. (TEV)

A man guilty of murder will take refuge in a pit,
but nobody should help him. (Beck)

The Hebrew of verse 18 which says literally "the man who is devious in two ways and will therefore fall in one" may be suggesting a meaning that is obscured in traditional translations. Modern versions speak about a man whose ways are so perverse that "he will suddenly fall" (NIV); but the original suggests a more colorful illustration. The man who is devious "in two ways" is like a two-faced, forked-tongued, Dr. Jekyl-and-Mr. Hyde-personality; sooner or later his double life will catch up with him.

28:19   Both halves of verse 19 use the same verb. The one who works hard will be "filled" with food, while the one who vainly chases after other things will be "filled" with poverty. The verse is the same as 12:11 except for the last two words.

28:20   Proverbs often speaks against money that is too quickly acquired (cf. 10:2; 13:11; 20:21; 21:6; 28:22), thus teaching the sense of hard work and long-range planning within the boundaries of socio-economic traditions. Wealth acquired too quickly can have disastrous results; those who are "eager to get rich," says verse 20, "will not go unpunished." Learning how to handle money is an art learned through long, slow experience. Those who have not learned it may find wealth is more of a burden than they ever expected.

28:21   Some people say every person has a price, meaning that for a big enough purse people will steal, murder, prostitute themselves, or pervert justice. The man in verse 21 is so eager to pervert justice that he will "do wrong for a piece of bread." Perhaps the very contrast here between "perverting justice" and its puny reward points up the need for values. How important is integrity, morality, honesty, or fidelity in everyday life? Are we willing to compromise it for a "piece of bread"?

28:22   Verse 22 is another warning against wealth from a king who had it all; if Solomon had been a little less wealthy might he have served the Lord more faithfully? Meanness of soul does not go away just because a man gets rich; he is just as miserable with it as he was without it. Eventually his poverty of soul becomes actual poverty when death robs him of all he has.

28:23   Daring to rebuke another person may cause temporary alienation says verse 23, but if that person is truly wise he will later return to thank you. Flattering someone who ought to be rebuked is like encouraging a fool; the wise man sees the difference and is grateful for correction.

28:24   Stealing from parents is unthinkably sinful, says verse 24, but the child who blatantly says "It's not wrong" places himself in another league altogether. He is just like a destroyer, says the proverb, suggesting perhaps he is an ally of the devil himself.

Verse 25 speaks about greed as a source of trouble, thus repeating a theme from earlier proverbs about how impatience (15:18; 29:22), gossip (16:28), and irritability (26:21) cause trouble. The opposite attitude is one of trust in the Lord. An eternal perspective gives us the ability to deal more effectively with the shortcomings of others.   28:25

An earlier proverb (3:5) told us "Trust in the LORD with all your heart and lean not on your own understanding." Verse 26 repeats that thought with "He who trusts in himself is a fool." The wise man knows better than to trust in himself, knowing his vision is limited by his fallibility and sin. Only the Lord and his way of wisdom are fully trustworthy.   28:26

In the days before life and health insurance, government welfare, and social security benefits, people in financial trouble depended on the charity of others to get them through hard times. Today because of all our elaborate systems of financial aid those who have rarely come in contact with those who have not, and even if they do they aren't aware of the extent of need. Without the awareness, of course, it is difficult to show compassion. In Bible times the poor were not hidden so well. Their needs, in fact, were so obvious that a man had literally to "close his eyes" to avoid seeing them. Such self-induced blindness and hard-heartedness deservedly reaped curses from the poor.   28:27

The first half of verse 28 sounds much like verse 12, but the second part is different. When the oppressive rule of wicked men ends righteous people come out from hiding and take control, furthermore, they "increase" (RSV) or "thrive" (NIV) in good times.   28:28

We can do two things with advice; take it or leave it. If we ignore it, says verse 1 of chapter 29, we may become insensitive or "stiff-necked," immune to the help of others. Eventually this might become a kind of "chip on the shoulder" and this pride might someday keep us from listening to a "remedy" that could prevent our own destruction.   29:1

Verse 2 (along with 11:10, 28:12, and 28) says good government makes people happy while bad government makes them miserable. The moral of the story is work hard for good government, and if you won't, then don't complain when it's bad.   29:2

29:3   Verse 3 reminds us of earlier chapters in Proverbs that advised a son to follow his father's teaching instead of lusting after prostitutes. Here the writer compares two sons: one who "loves wisdom" and thus adds to his father's joy, and the other who loves the company of prostitutes and thus subtracts from his father's wealth.

29:4   Verse 4 almost sounds like Solomon's commentary on his son, Rehoboam. Rehoboam who "rejected the advice of the elders" to make the "yoke" of taxation even heavier for his people (2 Chron. 10:13–16), was so greedy for "bribes" or gifts of money that he "tore down" his country. Solomon, on the other hand, was known for his wisdom and justice; consider, for example, how he settled the case of two women who fought over one live baby. Such "justice" gave the nation stability; Israel enjoyed a golden age that was unparalleled in splendor.

29:5   One who flatters, says verse 5, "is spreading a net for his feet," but does this net then trap the flatterer or the person he flatters? One translation (TEV) suggests the flatterer himself gets trapped; consider the Don Juan who tells too many girls they are each the most beautiful only to have them compare notes later on. The trap quickly springs shut on this smooth talker.

Most translations, however, say the one who is flattered is harmed the most; false words may only encourage foolishness and prevent someone from truly becoming wise.

29:6   Verse 6 speaks about a different kind of trap; here a "snare" instead of "net" traps an evil man. This is another proverb that teaches man reaps what he sows; wicked men are "snared by their own sin" while good ones can sing and be happy.

29:7   Verse 7 is another antithetic parallel (like about half the verses in this chapter) which simply says good men care about "justice for the poor" while evil men do not. Compassion for the needs of others flows out of a heart that is right with God while wicked men are insensitive to the poor because they are blinded by sin.

29:8   The Hebrew for "mockers" or "scoffers" in verse 8 is used only one other time in Proverbs (1:22); this kind of troublemaker being particularly destructive. He is so powerful his mockery can "stir up a city." Does he perhaps stir up anger against the government or rulers and incite protests against their policies?

A wise man, on the other hand, is an agent for peace. He may not agree with a government's policies either, but uses wisdom to decide whether to openly "rebuke" an administration or "go into hiding." In either case he does not respond out of anger nor does he stir it up in others.

The fool doesn't take anything seriously, not even a lawsuit, says verse 9. He cannot appreciate or distinguish the good or the bad, the ugly or the beautiful, the safe from the dangerous. He treats all people, regardless of the honor they deserve, in the same stupid way. Elsewhere the proverbs counsel corporal punishment as the only kind that makes an impression and then only very slowly (10:13; 18:6; 19:29; 26:3). 29:9

The very presence of an honest man among the wicked is a silent rebuke to them, says verse 10. They hate him so much that they want to see him dead; better to kill him than to face his silent testimony against their sin. 29:10

The word for "anger" in verse 11 is the Hebrew word for "wind," "spirit," or "mind," implying the fool gives "full vent" or shoots off his mouth about things that make him mad. The wise man, on the other hand, refrains from talking too much, thereby giving himself time to think through something that bothers him before he speaks (see also 12:16). 29:11

"If a ruler listens to lies," says verse 12, "all his officials become wicked." A king sets his own policy, but he must depend on information from advisers to help him formulate that policy. If he only listens to lies from advisers (like King Ahab who rejected the prophecy of Micaiah in 1 Kings 22), then all the men who surround him will cater to his depravity and become wicked. 29:12

Verse 2 of chapter 22 says the LORD made both the rich and the poor; verse 13 now says he gave eyes to both the poor and those that oppress them. Does that mean that in one area, at least, both are equal? Or does it suggest that both are fully aware of the sin that is being committed and that God himself has his eye on both of them, the eye of judgment on the oppressor and the eye of mercy on the poor? 29:13

Verse 14 seems to enlarge on what verse 13 said; the king who has his eyes open to the poor and "judges them with fairness" will be blessed with happy people and a stable government. 29:14

29:15   Verse 15 is a kind of intrusion on the teachings of government and justice toward the poor; this proverb brings us back to the subject of raising children. Children who grow up with an occasional spanking will become wise, while those who are "left to themselves" will be undisciplined and "an embarrassment to their mothers."

29:16   Verse 16 brings us back to the theme of government. Here wicked rulers condone evil while good men wait patiently for evil to destroy itself. The verse promises that right will triumph but doesn't say how long it will take.

29:17   Verse 17 is another insert about child-rearing which again urges parents to discipline their children. The son who is disciplined, says the sage, "will give you peace and bring delight to your soul."

29:18   Verse 18 has been misinterpreted for many years, probably because of the way it reads in the KJV; "Where there is no vision the people perish." "Vision" here does *not* refer to one's ability to formulate goals and work toward them, nor does it mean eyesight or the ability to understand. "Vision" instead is a synonym for what a prophet does. Thus its real meaning is God's "guidance" (TEV), "revelation" (NIV), "authority" (NEB) or even "prophecy" (NAB).

The second word which has been misunderstood in this verse is the word "perish." It does *not* refer to the unevangelized heathen who will die in sin, but rather to people who cast off restraint when they abandon the word of God. Such action might result in destruction, but what the verse really says is the nation that ignores God's Word can expect spiritual and political anarchy. On the other hand, "happy" is the man, church, or nation that keeps God's law.

29:19   Verse 19 says servants who "understand" but do not "respond" cannot be corrected by mere words. Is the author suggesting here that all foolish servants that cannot be reasoned with can only be corrected by corporal punishment? Note the unusual distinction here between understanding and unresponsive; servants who seem to hear and don't obey really hear nothing at all.

29:20   In all the verses of Proverbs only two kinds of men rank lower than the fool; the man who is "wise in his own eyes" (26:12), and now "the man who speaks in haste" in verse 20. "Talk is cheap" goes the saying. It may also be insensitive, malicious, foolish, destructive, wasteful, and indiscreet. The man who blurts out anything may cause great harm to others as well as to himself. "There is more hope for a fool," says the proverb.

Verse 21 includes some problems. We are fairly sure the Hebrew verb in the first half means "pamper," but the meaning of the verb in the second half is very uncertain. One translation says the master who "pampers" a servant from childhood will "in the end find him his heir" (RSV), while another says the pampered servant in the end "will bring grief" (NIV). Regardless of its meaning, however, the lesson is clear. Servants are to be disciplined just as children are or they will become worthless liabilities.

29:21

The first half of verse 22 is the same as 15:18 except for the word "anger," but this verse is a synonymous parallel while 15:18 is an antithetic parallel. Verse 22 says an "angry man stirs up dissension" just like a "hot-tempered one commits many sins." The proverb is a clear warning against losing control of one's emotions.

29:22

Verse 23 contains an interesting word play on "downfall" and "humble" which are from the same Hebrew root. The NIV preserves this device with the use of "low" and "lowly"; pride brings a man "low," while the "lowly" man receives honor. The man who demands respect will be humiliated by receiving none while the man who claims nothing will be honored. God delights in reversing the ways of men (cf. Matt. 23:12 and Prov. 3:34).

29:23

A literal translation of the second half of verse 24, although almost unintelligible, would be: "an oath he hears but does not talk." What this probably means is that the accomplice of a thief takes an oath in court yet cannot honor it because he is afraid. Thus he perjures himself and compounds his guilt. Leviticus 5:1 is an even stronger indictment; the person who does not "speak up" or "testify" is actually held responsible for the crime he has witnessed.

29:24

In verse 29 the sage speaks about the universal human malady of pleasing men rather than God. Most of the rewards we seek in this life do come from men so it follows that we would exert most of our efforts to please them. Yet how permanent are those rewards and how lasting is that approval? Isn't this drive to please men really a "snare" that locks us

29:25

into transient, imperfect goals? How much better to "trust in the Lord" and place one's confidence in eternal values. This proverb is in the category with other "impossible" commands such as "be perfect because God is" or taking every thought captive and making it obey Christ (2 Cor. 10:5).

The proverb's teaching is clear; wean yourself away from what other people expect and do what God expects.

29:26   Verse 26 is an illustration of verse 25. Here men seek rewards or approval from a ruler instead of God. The picture becomes clearer when we think of how people "honor" government more than the Lord today. How many pay income tax without hesitation yet balk at tithing to give God his due? Who do we trust more to protect our rights, the courts or God? Do we run first to a lawyer or judge, or the Lord? Verse 26 says many seek justice from rulers but it is from the Lord that we get justice.

29:27   The poetic symmetry of verse 27 in Hebrew is nicely preserved in English. Righteous men "detest the dishonest" while wicked ones detest honest ones. The proverb is an interesting conclusion to a long section of miscellaneous proverbs (chaps. 10–29). It includes the fundamental teaching that God and those that serve him hate Satan and his followers, while Satan and his followers hate God and his people. The universe lines up on one side or another; the choices we make in life are clear evidence of which side we have chosen.

PART FIVE

The Words of Agur

Proverbs 30

The first verse of chapter 30 is probably the most difficult verse in the entire Book of Proverbs. There is hardly a word but what there are several opinions on it.

The first problem is Agur, and the second is his father Jakeh. Who are they? Since no one knows of any such people, some translators have suggested the Hebrew *Agr* and *Jkh* do not represent names but rather something like "gather." Thus these sayings come from the "collector" of proverbs.

The next problem is the word *Massa*. Is it a place or the common noun which means "oracle"? No one knows if a place like *Massa* even existed. The word is used again in 31:1.

Another uncertainty is how many verses should be included in the collection. Is it six or thirty-three? If we include only six as Agur's words, then who wrote verses 7–33?

A comparison of different translations of verse 1 quickly reveals these problems. The phrase which reads "The man says to Ithiel, to Ithiel and Ucal" in the RSV sounds a lot different in the TEV where *Ithiel* is translated as "God is not with me," and "I am not God" in the NAB. It fits with what follows. *Ucal* could mean "I am helpless," (TEV) or "I am weary" (Smith-Goodspeed).

Another problem is the mood of the whole passage which seems more reminiscent of Ecclesiastes than of any other section of Proverbs. The words here are dark ones born of sorrow and defeat, forming questions rather than answers. We should be cautious in seeking to understand this section on the basis of our tentative translations from the Hebrew. Perhaps our copies of the original are not fully reliable.

30:2   In verse 2 the speaker decries his stupidity or ignorance, saying his understanding is subhuman. The words are hyperbole, of course; a man devoid of intelligence could never have written these words. The point is, the author is desperately unhappy with himself because God is not with him.

30:3   Verse 3 offers clear evidence that this man who has been abandoned by God at least recognizes his own problem; "I have not learned wisdom." It's a big step in the right direction. If we can get people to see their hopelessness then there is hope.

30:4   Verse 4 asks five questions, each a poetic device to prompt the reader to answer "God." The section reminds us of the questions asked in Isaiah 40:12–21 or Job 38–39.

The God who "goes up to heaven and comes down" in this verse sounds a lot like the Son of Man who "came from heaven" and then went back into heaven in New Testament passages such as John 3:13, Acts 2:34, Romans 10:6 and Ephesians 4:9. The words "his son" though not always referring to Christ in the Old Testament (cf. Ps. 2:7, 12), may have been the basis for the New Testament's allusions to this verse.

30:5   Verse 5 is a bit more upbeat from the previous verses. Here the sage actually gives us a positive statement about God. His word is totally inerrant, he says (like gold purified in a fire), and God himself is a shield to those who trust him.

30:6   Verses 5 and 6 clearly go together (linked by God's "words"), yet verse 6 is difficult to explain or even to accept, especially by people who write commentaries. "Don't add to his words," the sage warns, "or he will rebuke you and prove you a liar" (NIV). See also Deut. 4:2 and Rev. 22:18.

30:7–9 Verses 7 through 33 include several clusters of verses which are introduced by numbers such as "two" (7–9 and 15a) and "four" (15b–16, 18–19, 21–23, 24–28 and 29–31).

The sage begins verse 7 by speaking in the first person singular. He asks for two things before he dies, protection against falsehood and lies, and fulfillment of daily needs in a position somewhere between the extremes of poverty and wealth.

The writer says specifically in this second request, "Give me only my daily bread," thereby implying a distinction between wants and needs.

Verse 9 explains why we must ask only for our needs to

be satisfied; too much can make us so independent that we "disown" the Lord as our provider. If we have too much, we might trust in riches to provide us with everything we need.

On the other hand, too little is not good either. Poverty which might bring one man to God might also cause another to become so frustrated or envious that he might be tempted to steal. This, of course, would result only in dishonoring the name of God. Moderation is the key here (see also Eccles. 7:15–18).

Verse 10 is uniquely different from other verses in this passage, yet its teaching fits nicely with other advice regarding control of the tongue. Although it isn't clear who curses whom in the verse, a strong possibility is the servant who curses the one who "slanders" him. The lesson here is that anyone who doesn't mind his own business will pay for it in the end. **30:10**

Verses 11–14 all begin with "those," a word which literally means "generation." The verses are specific warnings against the dangerous behavior of such people as well as against the tendency to become like them. **30:11–14**

Verse 11 warns against "those" who do not honor their parents. Note the inclusion of both mother and father here; not honoring them is a direct violation of the fifth commandment.

Verse 12 speaks against "those" who are "wise" or "pure" in their own eyes. Such self-deception or egomania blinds people to their own faults and prevents them from responding to rebukes or criticism from others which might serve to rid them of their faults.

Verse 13 also speaks about "those" who deceive themselves. The idioms here vividly illustrate the arrogance and conceit of people who in the long run turn down God's offer of redemption. For to take his offer is to renounce self-righteousness and claim his blood and righteousness.

Verse 14 is a vivid portrait of "those" who mistreat the poor. Figuratively speaking, their mouths are fitted out with swords and knives. With these weapons they "devour the poor from the earth." The image of the cruel eating the powerless is also in Psalm 14:4.

Verse 15 uses a Hebrew word that is widely translated "leech," although since it appears only here in the Bible its **30:15–16** meaning is very uncertain. Still, its basic thrust is clear; a bloodsucking greedy man sires daughters who are also unsatisfied. "Give! Give!" they cry. The verse shifts to introduce three things that are "never satisfied" and four that "never say 'Enough!' " Like the leech and his daughters these things demand more than anyone can give. Verse 16 names them: the grave which always has room for more bodies (cf. 27:20); a barren woman who will only be satisfied with a child; dry ground (such as the parched soil of Palestine) which never has enough rain; and fire which literally consumes whatever is put into it. None of these things has the willpower to say it is full or has had enough.

The lesson here is obvious; greed merely feeds upon itself resulting in unsatisfied cravings. What is it we seek in life? Are we yawning graves, empty wombs, parched soil, or consuming fires because we look for satisfaction in places, people, and things that can never fill us up?

30:17   Verse 17 is much like verse 11; both speak of children who will be punished one day for refusing to honor their parents. Here the results of such behavior are unusually severe; first blinding and then death and dishonor by means of ravens and vultures.

30:18-19   There is a widespread idea that what the four things in verses 18 and 19 have in common is tracelessness. None of the four items leaves behind any evidence of its having been there. Verse 18, however, says it is the mysteriousness — how an eagle flies, and so on. I maintain that because of the unusual word for woman ("virgin" in some versions), the similarity lies in the fact that none of the four is going over old territory. Rather, an eagle, a snake, or a ship all can go where there are no paths. Likewise in the last of the four, the man now is moving into untracked "virgin" territory as he and his lover pursue their affection for one another.

30:20   The adulteress of verse 20 is a harsh contrast to the "mysterious" virgin of verse 19. While a young couple falling in love is a beautiful thing, an unfaithful wife makes a mockery of her vows and commits adultery as easily as she eats a meal (for such is the Hebrew euphemism). The verse then harks back to a major theme of the book, anti-adultery.

30:21-23   Verses 21-23 list four things which are intolerable because of the gross inappropriateness. The first one is like 19:10; it simply is not right that a slave should rule. Similarly, a well-fed fool could be intolerably arrogant. A marriage not based on love is likewise most unfortunate, and one described here involves either a hateful or hated woman. The last category is like the first — an inferior usurps his superior.

The thrust of the proverb here is that the natural order of things is best left alone. Disturbing that by giving power to the incompetent or rewards to undeserving is to ask for social upheaval. Harmony in society results when each member of the family or the community knows who he is and what is expected of him. Chaos comes when inferior or inexperienced people try to rule over those who have been placed in authority over them.

All this sounds rather opposed to freedom, equality of opportunity and other noble tenents of our country. But we must remember that this was written three millenia ago to a people whose government was much different. We would say it was quite unfair that only descendants of David should be king or only the Levites should go into the ministry. While we don't live under those strictures it is a sound principle to know yourself, your capability, and your worth, and to find satisfaction in doing what you are able and required to do.

Verses 24–28 introduce us to four things on earth which 30:24–28 are small but smart. First there is the ant which has "little strength" but exhibits remarkable foresight in storing up food for winter. The lesson for us is obvious. Compare 6:6–8.

The second animal is the rock-badger. Its claim to fame is the ability to make a home in the most impossible of places — among the rocks. Perhaps the lesson here is that we must improvise even under adverse or difficult circumstances.

Locusts "who have no king" are the third "small thing" that is commended. Even without a king they mobilize, march, and conquer. The illustration suggests the unity and harmony that result when each member of a group or society works for the good of all rather than at odds with them or for himself.

The fourth animal is the lizard who "can be caught with the hand" yet easily finds a way into the palaces of kings. The animal, without bribes or trickery, enters chambers we might not, even with a lifetime of effort ever reach. Perhaps the sage stresses here that humility and honesty reap their own rewards while status-seeking, social-climbing efforts often fail. The lizard's job incidentally is a humble one but of inestimable service to us humans: they eat insects.

30:29–31   Verses 29–31 speak of four things that are "stately in their stride," three of which are animals and one a king. Of these four only the first is easily translated; certainly anyone would agree the lion, "mighty among beasts," moves with an impressive gait. Problems arise, however, with the "strutting rooster" (from the Greek) which is translated "grayhound" in the KJV (because the Hebrew looks like a word that means "girded of loins" and a grayhound has narrow hips). "He-goat" is fairly straightforward, but the king who is *surrounded* by his army is really a guess at a preposition that is undecipherable.

Still, the point of the passage is that we should recognize superiority as well as inferiority in the world of animals and man. Just as the lion rules the beasts, so kings rule people. All of this is part of God's harmonious order. We must not try to resist that order or change it for that would surely result in disaster.

30:32–33   Verses 32 and 33 conclude this chapter with a teaching against anger. Quarrels often begin when fools hold greedy or stupid positions. The problem could end quickly if they would just "clap their hands over their mouths" but the more tenaciously they hold on, the more belligerent they become. It begins when they fall in love with themselves and their ideas and it ends in a bloody battle in which righteousness rarely triumphs.

The tripartite structure of verse 33 is clear even in English. What is not obvious is that it is the same Hebrew verb in each part although translated "churn," "twist," and "stir." It's a down-home sort of analogy with an additional play on words because in Hebrew "nose" and "anger" are the same word and "blood" can also mean "bloodshed/murder."

It sometimes requires great restraint not to pursue an argument or insist on the last word in a discussion, but we must remember that Scripture has called us to peace (Rom. 14:19; 1 Cor. 7:15).

PART SIX

The Words of Lemuel

Proverbs 31:1–9

Unfortunately we don't know who Lemuel is in verse 1   31:1
of chapter 31 anymore than we knew who Agur was in 30:1.
The rabbis thought Agur was another name for Solomon so
that Proverbs ends with a lecture from Bathsheba as it began
with a reference to David (4:3–4). Still, efforts to pinpoint
him as Solomon or the king of Massa have been futile.

Verse 2 is the introduction by the mother of Lemuel to her   31:2
speech. In style this verse is an interesting example of stair-
case parallelism where each phrase repeats something from
the prior phrase yet adds something new. A literal rendering
of verse 2 would look something like this:

> What, son of mine?
> What, son of my womb?
> What, son of my vows?

The mother warns her son about two vices, sex and alco-   31:3
hol. Verse 3 talks specifically against spending your strength
or losing your vigor on women. Overindulgence in sex was
surely Solomon's great weakness (consider his 700 wives and
300 concubines), and one which eventually turned him away
from God and effected his downfall (Neh. 13:26).

More is said in verses 4–7 against the dangers of alcohol,   31:4–7
although this problem is not documented in the life of Solomon. Still, alcohol did contribute to the downfall of the Israelite king Elah (1 Kings 16:9) and Syrian king Ben-hadad
(1 Kings 20:16), so the advice is well-intended.

The warning was vital not only to Lemuel but to all kings,

215

princes, or people in authority. Think of how alcohol is abused by our leaders today. How can we expect legislation against drunk driving and drinking-related accidents if our leaders themselves are addicted to it? None of them should drink, says the proverb, lest they forget the law and ignore or abuse the poor. Ironically, verses 6 and 7 prescribe beer and wine to people who are "perishing" or "in anguish," as if to say their lives are hopeless anyway so why not drink to forget it all. We wouldn't hold those people responsible as we would a governor, congressman, an airplane pilot, or the driver of a car.

31:8 – 9   Verses 8 and 9 are positive words for Lemuel which urge him to speak up in behalf of the poor and the powerless. It isn't enough for rulers to abstain from vices. They must also exert themselves in a positive sense over those they rule. They must "speak up for those who cannot defend themselves" and deal justly with those who cannot afford legal aid.

PART SEVEN

The Noble Woman

Proverbs 31:10–31

Several things are worth noting about the unusual conclusion to Proverbs titled "Epilogue: The Wife of Noble Character." First, the section is an alphabetic acrostic, meaning each of its twenty-two verses begins with a consecutive letter of the Hebrew alphabet. English translations are totally unable to reproduce this poetic device, although some translations (JPS, Smith-Goodspeed, Beck, and JB) include the Hebrew letters. This acrostic device is also used in a number of Psalms such as 119, and in the first four chapters of Lamentations.

In light of its extended warnings against unfaithful wives or prostitutes in early chapters (2, 5, 6, 7, 9), it is remarkable that Proverbs ends with an essay on a "wife of noble character." It is also remarkable considering the numerous references that were made about nagging wives (12:4b; 19:13; 21:9; 25:24; 27:15–16) in contrast to few that spoke of virtuous wives (12:4a; 18:22; 19:14). Chapter 31 is a nice redress of that imbalance.

The chapter may at first seem to be out of step with the rest of the book, still nothing in it is out of line with other parts of Scripture which extol women as examples of bravery, wisdom, and devotion. Consider Deborah (Judg. 4–5), the woman who killed Abimelech (Judg. 9:53), the wise woman of Tekoa (2 Sam. 14:1–20), the woman of Abel Beth Maacah who surrendered up Sheba the rebel (2 Sam. 20:16–22), the Huldah the prophetess (2 Kings 22:14ff.).

One noteworthy thing about the woman in Proverbs is the leadership she exhibits in her home. Although she is married to an honorable man we get the distinct impression that she runs the house and makes the important decisions. Ancient Israel may have been like many other cultures where the man was the designated leader while the real "power behind the throne" was the woman.

This epilogue is probably not a part of the advice from Lemuel's mother, but a separate pericope.

31:10   Verse 10 says this noble wife is more valuable than rubies. The Hebrew word behind "noble perfection" (JB), suggests excellence (NASB), worth, (NAB), and ability (NEB). This verse underscores the scarcity or rarity of such women. Like Lady Wisdom she is comparable to jewels (cf. 8:11).

31:11   Trust is an essential ingredient in any marriage and this woman inspires "full confidence" from her husband, says verse 11. Furthermore, she is a good money manager. Her husband lacks nothing because she knows what he needs and makes sure he has it.

31:12   This woman is dedicated to her husband. All she says and does is meant to support, build up, encourage, and affirm him. Life is difficult enough for a man who makes his way in this world without adding to that burden a wife who does not understand or support him.

31:13   Verse 13 begins the actual catalog of her activities, the detailed account of what fills the hours of her day and the days of her week. Judging from this, and verses 21, 22, and 24 she spends a good part of her time in buying raw materials, spinning, weaving, and sewing.

31:14   Shopping too is a daily duty just as it is in many places today where refrigeration is unavailable. She is compared to a ship that sails into distant markets with goods to sell and returns home with things she has bought.

31:15   She is the first one up in the morning, says verse 15. She rises with the dawn to make breakfast and give instructions to her servants. We get the impression here that this is a wealthy and honorable family with riches earned not by graft or corruption but by hard work and shrewd investing.

31:16   Verse 16 says this woman not only works hard at home; she also invests in real estate. There is no way we can interpret this to say less than what is obvious. This woman apparently does buy and sell land. The money earned from other enterprises she re-invests in a vineyard. This capable woman will multiply and compound her assets through the wise manipulations of her holdings.

31:17   Verse 17 says this woman does all her work with vigor and strength. She is no weakling who is backed into her role but an energetic, enthusiastic participant in life.

A Russian proverb says "There are two fools in the market. One asks too much and one asks too little." This woman knows the value of her merchandise and demands the right price for her goods. What she produces is quality merchandise which others must pay for. Long into the night she works on other profit-making projects. 31:18

Verse 19 refers to her "distaff" and "spindle," tools of her trade in cloth-making. Imagine how long it took to spin a thread, then weave a piece of cloth! Consider how much time every woman had to spend spinning and weaving in ancient days. Yet this woman does it all without complaint. 31:19

This noble woman is not so busy with her own household, however, that she forgets the needs of others. She is not wealthy because she is selfish or stingy but because God blesses her generosity. She is the walking example of Proverbs 11:25 which says: "Be generous, and you will prosper. Help others, and you will be helped." 31:20

Verse 21 says she wonderfully provides for the needs of her family, "clothing them in scarlet" when it snows. The word for "scarlet" can also be read as "twice" or "double," and this is in fact how some translations take it. In winter does this mother clothe her family in red or in "two cloaks" (NEB)? Snow may be rare in Palestine, yet even the rarest of emergencies do not throw this lady. She is always prepared. 31:21

Skill, industry, and wise investments pay off; verse 22 says this woman has managed to do everything so well that she is even able to make "coverings for her bed." She herself is clothed in "fine linen and purple"; evidences of wealth since purple dye was extracted in minute quantities from certain shellfish, making it costly and rare. Note that her use of fine things is not condemned but commended as rewards for her hard work. 31:22

Verse 23 finally tells us something about this woman's husband. He is an honored citizen. Sitting at the gate does not mean he loiters the days away. More likely it means he is a judge or an esteemed and respected member of a judicial body that meets daily to determine questions of law. That he made a living off it is doubtful, but such a position does carry with 31:23

it prestige, honor, public trust, and grave responsibilities. You can see such a court in action in Ruth 4:1–12.

31:24 This woman not only makes clothes for her own family, she also makes some to sell. Verse 24 says she does anything she can to generate income.

31:25 Verse 25 says this woman is "clothed with strength and dignity" and thus is able to "laugh at the days to come." This doesn't mean she trusts only in her wealth and investments to meet future problems, but instead demonstrates a self-confidence born of right living. She isn't worried about to-morrow because, like the ant, she has "stored up food for the winter."

31:26 Verse 26 tells us about the "gold and silver" qualities of this remarkable woman. She not only spins, weaves, buys and sells fields, helps the poor, and provides for her family; but her talk is always wise and instructive. Her strength comes from the Lord who enables her to do everything that she does.

31:27 Verse 27 says the woman "watches over the affairs of her household." She has no time to be idle because there is always so much to do.

31:28 Verse 28 says such a woman receives the highest reward from her children who "call her blessed" and a husband who "praises her." Is there any better commentary on her work and worth than these sincere words of tribute?

31:29 The words in verse 29 are likely those spoken by the woman's husband even though the word "he says" are not in the Hebrew text.

31:30 Verse 30 is the capstone of this woman's noble character. She may be charming as well as beautiful, but her real beauty rests in her total commitment to God. Praise befits such a woman "who fears the LORD."

31:31 The last letter of the Hebrew alphabet begins the last verse in Proverbs concerning this outstanding woman. "Give her the reward she has earned," the sage writes, "and let her works bring her praise at the city gate." What she does, not what others say about her, makes her the most noble woman of all, but husbands and children may unite in praising the noble wife and mother.